A Vulcan Odyssey

*To Stephanie & Paul,
Congratulations on your nuptials.
"Live long & prosper."
Fondly, Patricia &
Lawrence Doutaigne
27 June 2009*

Copyright © 2006 Lawrence Montaigne
All rights reserved.
ISBN: 1-4196-5798-4

To order additional copies, please contact us.
BookSurge Publishing
www.booksurge.com
1-866-308-6235
orders@booksurge.com

LAWRENCE MONTAIGNE

A VULCAN ODYSSEY

A Vulcan Odyssey

TABLE OF CONTENTS

PREFACE		xv
PROLOGUE		xix
CHAPTER ONE	In the Beginning	1
CHAPTER TWO	A Career is Born	11
CHAPTER THREE	Welcome to La-la Land	17
CHAPTER FOUR	New York, New York	31
CHAPTER FIVE	Return to Rome	41
CHAPTER SIX	The Holy Land	49
CHAPTER SEVEN	A Star is Born	97
CHAPTER EIGHT	And the Show Goes On	113
CHAPTER NINE	Deutschland Uber Alles	139
CHAPTER TEN	Fifteen Minutes of Fame	173
CHAPTER ELEVEN	Georgia on my Mind	205
CHAPTER TWELVE	What Goes Up Usually Comes Down… With a Bump	209

CHAPTER THIRTEEN Closing the Circle   225

CHAPTER FOURTEEN Star Trek Revisited   253

CHAPTER FIFTEEN   What Goes Around   287

POWER OF STAR TREK   295

The worst day of my life was when I realized that the world did not revolve around me. I believe I was six at the time.

ACKNOWLEDGEMENT

Without the encouragement of the members of the Anthem Authors Club in Sun City Anthem, Henderson, Nevada, this book would never have come to fruition. The members with whom I came in contact were supportive of my efforts from the day I joined and I was eager to prove to them that I could complete this undertaking.

I wish to thank Marianne Donath for her patience in reading my work and making suggestions and corrections of my European references.

I also want to thank Bobbye Sansing who meticulously red-penciled my grammatical mistakes and made suggestions when I overlooked errors in the timeline of the text. And thank you for encouraging me "to keep my voice."

The pastel likeness on the cover is reproduced with permission of the artist, Deborah Downey. 2001. Other work by this talented artist can be seen on the Internet. (DeborahLyonsPortraits.com)

Thanks to Great Bird 0f the Galaxy Production, Inc. for permission to use the photos from their film, *Of Gods and Men*.

http://lawrencemontaigne.net

To
Robby And Katherine
Nathan Ignatius And Stella
Bryna And George

PREFACE

This is a novel. It began as an autobiography but in trying to recount events of my passed life, I find that my memory, in many instances, fails me.

Was it 1950 or 1951 that I hitchhiked from New York to Los Angeles, California? How did I end up carrying a rifle for a surveying team in the Negev Desert? Was I still married to my first wife when I married my second wife? Exactly how long was I married to each of my four wives? And why didn't any of my marriages last?

These questions, and many more, baffle me to this very day. Trying to write an autobiography is like trying to do a humongous puzzle with some of the pieces missing. When memory fails, imagination prevails. I have tried to be as honest as my subjective perspective allows but I cannot speak for the other people involved. We see relationships and events through our own eyes and we respond, each of us, in our own way. Those who actually shared those events with me may not share what I remember. Fortunately, many of the people with whom I came in contact over the years and about whom I have written, have pre-deceased me so there are very few left that can question my veracity. In many instances, trying to keep track of times and events is like trying to retrieve an egg from an omelet.

It is not my intention to denigrate or cast aspersions on anyone's character. "I calls 'em like I sees 'em." How I felt about a particular person or how I reacted during a certain event are my own personal recollections. The adage, "One man's meat is another man's poison," is apropos in this instance. I have tried to be as true to the past events as the passage of time allows. In looking back, I sometimes question many of the events as I recount them. Did they ever really happen? I wonder if some of the strange and interesting characters I met along the way ever really existed. Were many of the events and the people merely figments of my imagination? Possibly.

To wane philosophic, I sometimes wonder if all our lives aren't, to one degree or another, merely a work of fiction. A hundred years from now, will we be spoken of or remembered? As an educator, I once wrote, "I walk the halls of learning like a ghost, neither casting a shadow nor leaving footprints in the sands of time." My legacy is only that which I pass on to my students and what they pass on to others, until slowly my teachings diminish and they are no longer mine but are diluted by new generations.

Finally, my life has been a blast! I have been fortunate to live in the most exciting time since the Creation. I have lived through wars, I have traveled throughout the world, I have taken advantage of education. I have developed a respect for the arts, music, literature, theatre, and the great masters. I have learned to appreciate the great gift of sharing this planet with animals. In short, I have been gifted with a passion for life.

PROLOGUE

About thirty years ago, when I was a working actor going from one television role to another, I got a call from a guy telling me that he wanted to invite me to be a guest at a convention being held at a hotel down by the airport. I was skeptical and graciously declined his invitation. But a few weeks later, he called again, and again I declined. Then, a young lady called and since I have always been a sucker for young ladies, I agreed to attend. It was a *Star Trek* convention and one of the first of its kind and since I had appeared in two episodes of the original series, among *Star Trek* enthusiasts, she explained, I was something of a celebrity. So on the Saturday morning in question I drove down to the hotel having no clue what to expect. At the hotel I paid ten dollars for parking which ticked me off since "guests" should not have to pay, I thought. And as I entered the hotel I immediately realized that I was way out of my element. There were acres of people dressed in costumes replicating many of the characters from the series. It was eerie seeing grown people running around like kids on Halloween. My first impression was to get the hell out of there and fast. But a promise is a promise and I found my way to the registration desk where I had been told to check in.

"That will be twenty-five dollars," said the Vulcan decked out with his pointy ears.

"I think there's a mistake," I said. "I was invited to come here as a guest. My name should be on your list."

"Let's see. There's Leonard Nimoy and Bill Shatner and..." He read down a list of names. "I don't see any Lawrence Montaigne. That will be twenty-five dollars."

With no small amount of disappointment I shelled out the twenty-five bucks with the hopes of getting my money back when I found my contact. But when I entered the great hall there appeared to be thousands of aliens milling around in mass confusion. I got the attention of someone wearing a nametag and explained that I was an invited guest and that

I was looking for so-and-so. Mr. Nametag had no idea who that person might be. For fifteen or twenty minutes I went from one nametag to another trying to get some attention to my quest but without success. Finally, in frustration, I left the great hall, retrieved my car from the parking lot and drove home in anger.

I had been had. I never heard from anyone asking why I didn't make an appearance as promised and for the many years after, I remained in a state of pissed about that *Star Trek* convention incident.

* * *

I had been on a roll, one acting job after another for the past four years since my return from abroad where I had lived for six years. I was riding the crest of a wave and true to my background, I walked around with a pit in my stomach the size of a taxi waiting for the other shoe to drop and I'd be out of work. Typical actor. I was just finishing up a film over at Universal when my agent, Paul Wilkins, called to say that I had an interview for a guest shot in a new television series called "Star Trek" over at Paramount. When I asked what it was about, he vocally shrugged. Star Trek. How does one dress or prepare for a show called "Star Trek?" I asked myself. So that afternoon, dressed in a pair of jeans and a sport shirt, I went over to Paramount to meet Gene Roddenberry, the producer. He was a big man, quite impressive and over-bearing. He spoke with authority, handed me a script titled "Balance of Terror", and gave me a few minutes to look it over. Then, I read with the casting director. I had no idea what I was reading. "Commander of a Romulan vessel..." What the hell was that? The casting director said that "the character was the Commander of an intergalactic space ship that was about to engage the Enterprise in battle." Yeah, sure. So I read, thanked everyone, and split. When I arrived home I called Paul.

"This is all very hush-hush," he told me. "It's a new project that Paramount has on the books and if you get the part, it could be a good way to get onto the Paramount lot."

I had not been able to crack Paramount. I was getting most of my work from Fox, MGM, Columbia and some of the smaller studios. Hey, Paramount would be good.

A few days later I got a call from Paul. "I've got good news and I've got bad news," he said. "Which do you want?"

"Bad news," I said. "Always lead with the bad news."

"Okay. You didn't get the role of the Commander in the Star Trek series..."

"Shit!" I replied. Sure I didn't get the role. I had no idea what the role was all about. "Okay, let's have the good news and make it good," I said.

"I'm running out of sympathy for you. There goes your commission."

"They want you to play the role of the First Officer, Decius."

"What the hell is a Decius?" I asked.

"Well, from what I could get from casting, he's a Romulan officer who instigates the battle between the Romulans and the Vulcans..."

Well, that really cleared things up. "What happened to the role of the Commander?" I asked.

"Another actor by the name of Mark Lenard got it. I don't know his work."

I knew his work. He was a damn fine actor with whom I had worked on a show called "Here Come the Brides," a short-lived thing that lasted some thirteen episodes and then vanished into television oblivion. Mark and I had worked together and I hated to admit it, but he was a lot better choice for a Romulan Commander than I would have been. I hated it when other people were right.

"Have we got anything else in the works?" I asked. "Maybe a one-liner on the Flying Nun?" I was being facetious. I had recently done a guest shot on the Flying Nun playing her Spanish agent who was obsessed with getting her into show business. It had been a blast, working with Sally Fields.

"No Flying Nuns," he assured me. "Star Trek is the only thing currently on the books," he said. "I think you oughta do it," he offered.

Since I was just coming off a film, there was a lull in my career. There is an old adage that an actor is only as good as his current job and being out of work did not attract a whole lot of attention in the industry. But if the agent calls up a producer or casting director and says that his client is working on such-and-such a show, it's like the key to the kingdom.

"Okay," I said. "You set the deal."

The following week I reported to Paramount Studio in Hollywood. I was given a car pass at the gate and then directed to the wardrobe department where I met with Gene Roddenberry and Vincent McEveety, the director. I had worked with Vince before so it was comfortable talking to him about the relationship he wanted to create between the Commander and his first officer, Decius. Roddenberry didn't say much but just stood there, quietly observing the conversation. I was intimidated by his presence. He was neither friendly nor adversarial. I knew he had been a cop before he sold Paramount on doing Star Trek and here he was observing the scene of a crime and I was a suspect. Actors have great imaginations. So I got fitted for my costume, and was given a shooting schedule by the casting director, and that was that. A few days later I reported to the studio to begin shooting. Mark Lenard and I worked quite well together.

The shoot only lasted for three days but in the final analysis, Paul had been right. I followed Star Trek with two episodes of *"Mission, Impossible"* and shortly thereafter, I flew down to Nashville to work on *"Framed"* with Joe Don Baker. Decius had been a good role for me and little did I know at the time, but he would eventually become a part of Star Trek history.

At the beginning of the second season of Star Trek, I got a call from Paul. "Leonard Nimoy is leaving Star Trek," he informed me. "I just got a call from Paramount casting. Gene Roddenberry wants you as Nimoy's replacement."

I guess I should have gotten excited about the prospect but in truth, aside from the episode that I appeared in, "Balance of Terror", I was not a Star Trek fan. I never watched the show and from what I read in the trades, Star Trek was not very popular in its first season and stood to be cancelled. And during that year, I had gone from one role to another with barely a break. But Paul said that Roddenberry was prepared to make a very attractive offer and that I should reserve judgment. Over the next few weeks Paul negotiated while I continued to work. With each contact, Paul revealed to me that he and Roddenberry were about to close the deal. Then the shit hit the fan. I am not privy to all the details of what transpired between Nimoy and Roddenberry, but the bottom line is that Nimoy recanted on his plans to leave the show and re-signed for another season. Nimoy in. Montaigne out!

In the second season, I was called on to play the role of Stonn in the episode, *Amok Time*. When I got the script I went ballistic. The character had all of five lines and spent the entire episode glaring at other actors. I informed Paul that I didn't want to play the role and to thank Gene but perhaps when something more substantial came along he would call me. I had been fortunate during those years to have gone from series to series playing all sorts of interesting characters and I had made the transition from bit player to supporting player in a very short period of time. Playing a five-line bit part would have been a giant step backwards for me and would have done nothing to propel my career forward. I explained all this to Paul and although he did not agree with me ("Work is work," he philosophized) he passed my sentiments on to Gene. The following day I got a call from Mr. Roddenberry.

"I'd really like you to do this part, Larry," he said. (I hate being called "Larry," even in those days.) There was a tone in his voice that was not a request; it was more of a command.

"I'm sorry, Mr. Roddenberry, but I don't think it's much of a role for me..." I was being put in a very compromising situation because actors were not supposed to be talking to producers about doing roles. Only the agent was supposed to set deals and act as intermediary. Here was the producer calling me directly and I was very uncomfortable about it.

"This is a very important role," said Gene. "We had you in mind when the writer was writing it."

Bull shit, I thought. They wanted me for the role because of my facial resemblance to Leonard Nimoy. That was why they considered me for Leonard's replacement when he threatened to leave the show. And now, since we were both playing Vulcans, I was a natural for the part. It wasn't an acting role; it was more like something they would offer an extra. I had absolutely nothing to do but stand there and look menacing. I wasn't sold. And then he said something I shall never forget and that really got my attention. "You do like working at Paramount, don't you?"

Now, I don't know how you read it, but when I read between the lines, what he was really saying was, "If you don't play Stonn, you won't work at Paramount again."

"Well, you work out the details with my agent and thank you for the call, Mr. Roddenberry." End of conversation. I immediately called Paul and told him what had transpired. I also reaffirmed my position that I did not want to play the role of Stonn. Paul gave it some thought and said that he would set demands he knew Roddenberry would not accept. "We'll ask for co-star billing. The part doesn't warrant it. Then I'll ask for some outrageous figure that I know he'll never pay. Don't worry," he assured me, "you won't have to play Stonn."

The following day, Paul called to tell me that Gene had accepted our terms. I was to play Stonn.

The first disaster occurred when I reported to wardrobe for my fitting. They had decided on a jazzy little dickey type costume that revealed the upper part of my chest. "You'll have to shave your chest," said Joe Pevney, the director.

"No way," I emphatically said.

"Well, Vulcans don't have chest hair," he said.

"This Vulcan has chest hair. I'm only a Vulcan for five days and then I'm an itchy actor for the next three months while the hair grows back," I informed him.

Words went back and forth and the next thing I know, here comes Gene Roddenberry into the Wardrobe Department. "What's the problem?" he asked, as if he were still a patrol officer about to issue a citation.

"Montaigne won't shave his chest," said Pevney.

"You've got to shave," said Roddenberry.

"Call my agent," I said.

I swear, they must have been in conference for hours until the situation was finally resolved. They got me a turtleneck sweater, cut off the sleeves, and I wore it under the dickey to hide my chest. It looked fine but the damage had been done. By the time we began shooting, no one was talking to me, including my agent who felt that I was being unreasonable in my demands. He may have been correct but the bottom line is that I didn't want to play the role of Stonn in the first place.

So here's the punch line: I worked as an actor for over forty years and made a comfortable living. I did more than twenty-five films; in some of them I played the lead. I did over two hundred-guest shots on episodic television. But the only things I am remembered for by the fans are the two roles I played on Star Trek! Ain't life a bitch?

CHAPTER ONE
IN THE BEGINNING...

I was six months old when my parents packed up and moved from Brooklyn, New York, to Rome, Italy. The year was 1931. As I grew to adulthood, I often questioned my parents and other members of the family as to the details leading up to that move. Confusion reigned; I never got the same answer from any two relatives. But as close as I could determine, it all had to do with my father's job with Emanuel & Emanuel, a brokerage house on Wall Street in lower Manhattan. The United States was just coming out of the Great Depression and fortunately, my father was gainfully employed with a well-paying job as a specialized auditor during those lean years. He was responsible for keeping track of all the customer accounts, posting all the transactions, and reconciling the company books after the close of the stock market each day. It was an important job and pre-dated the computer so all the postings had to be done by hand, a most tedious and exacting job for which he was well paid.

By 1931, there began the rumblings of unrest throughout Europe and the world. Barely ten years before, the world leaders had met in Geneva to declare the end of "the war to end all wars." No sooner had the ink dried on the Versailles Treaty than there was unrest in the Far East with China and Japan rattling the chains of war, and Europe was once again watching with jaundiced eyes as Germany was politically threatening the short-lived tranquility of peace. In Rome, his Minister of Finance was advising Pope Pius XI that the church had to look to diversify its foreign holdings as protection against another conflagration in the not too distant future.

Emanuel & Emanuel was one of the leading brokerage houses with accounts throughout the world. One of those accounts was the Vatican in Rome. My father, along with a team of financial experts from the company, was dispatched to Italy in order to expedite the movement of funds and holdings from various European countries into American and Swiss trusts. The job, that was initially supposed to take a year, got bogged down in international monetary law and it was seven years before we were invited by the Mussolini government to get out of Italy.

I don't remember much about Rome in those early years. I remember we had an apartment not far from Vatican City where my father worked. We lived in the area called Trastevere on the southwest side of the city within two blocks of the Tiber River. I could walk to school from our apartment and I remember the music, always the music that wafted through the air day and night. Sometimes it was opera and other times it was popular Italian music sung by men lamenting the loss of a love. But the music was a way of life on our street.

I guess I was seven when things began to change in Italy. *Il Duce* was making overtures to join forces with the new German government and he was recruiting an army of brown shirts that was terrorizing Rome and other major cities. But Rome was the worst. I had no understanding of what was transpiring but my parents grew nervous by the day and when I learned that the local synagogue, just a few blocks from where we lived, had been attacked by young men in brown shirts, had beaten some of the parishioners and painted strange crosses on the side of the building, the tension mounted. Shortly after that incident of the swastika paintings on the temple, I came home from school with a note from the principal informing my mother that I could no longer attend classes. All Jewish children were being expelled from the public school system in Rome. That night we began packing and the next morning we were on a train to Livorno. We caught a ship heading for England and then on to the United States. It would be many years before I returned to Rome.

* * *

Shortly after our return to the United States, my parents decided to divorce. Even at that young age, I could tell that all was not well in Paradise. My mother was a very beautiful but tempestuous woman who expressed herself by yelling whenever she was frustrated or not able to get her way. I learned low profiling whenever she was in one of her moods and more often than not, I was the recipient of a blow to the side of the head or a good old-fashioned leather strap whipping. In later years I attributed her volatile behavior to her Hungarian blood that seemed to be at a constant boiling point. She was spoiled rotten as a kid, the apple of her Hungarian father's eye. What Katherine wanted, Katherine got. The one thing she did <u>not</u> want was to be sent away to private Catholic school in Milwaukee where the family resided at that time. The nuns at Marymount School were strict disciplinarians and my mother defied authority on a daily basis. Katherine was the daughter of Jewish parents, which placed her outside the strict Catholic rituals expected of Marymount students. But a Catholic school education in those days was the finest that money could buy and for twelve long years, Katherine remained defiant in spite of daily disciplining by the strict nuns of the school. She was rebellious right up until the time of her graduation. She was barely eighteen when she met my father and in an act of defiance, married him to prove a point; she didn't need anyone to tell her what she could or could not do. Shortly thereafter, I was the product of that union.

My father, Robby, on the other hand, was a docile, hardworking, gentle person, who lived to get out of the office early in order to take the train down to Brighton Beach where he would meet up with his friends and play handball. He had a passion for playing handball. When the weather was inclement, he would run uptown to the West Side YMCA and play. He was a handball addict. He was also very family oriented and I remember that each Friday night my dad would drag me out to Edgemere, Long Island, to have dinner with grandmother Bryna and the clan of brothers and sisters. It was a ritual that lasted right up until the time of her death.

After the divorce, I was knocked about from pillar to post. My mother took a job in Washington, D.C. working for Senator Al Wald while my father donned the uniform of the United States Navy and went off to fight in the war. I was enrolled in the Barnard McFadden School in Ossining, New York (also the home of Sing Sing Prison) where I stayed for two years. Then I was sent down to Miami, Florida, to live with my mother's mother, Stella. I was just entering my teens and that didn't work out too well because she was afflicted with rheumatoid arthritis so badly that she could barely boil a pot of water. I took to hanging out with a number of Army recruits that were based at the various hotels along Collins Avenue and they adopted me as a mascot. I was thirteen when I was introduced to the evils of tobacco and liquor. My grandmother couldn't handle me and it was decided by my parents that I should be enrolled in military school. I was sent up to Virginia where I was enrolled in Massannutten Military Academy in the beautiful Shenandoah Valley, situated between the Blue Ridge and the Shenandoah Mountains. I was my mother's son and did not take too well to authority. I was constantly in trouble spending most of my free time marching around in a circle with a rifle at port arms in order to work off my demerits. It was at Massannutten that I became involved in sports, mainly track and boxing. I took a lot of beatings in those early years. Being considered a Northerner in a Southern school was like having a large target painted on my backside. Every rebel infused with the Klan mentality wanted to take a shot at the Yankee Jew-boy. Not a day went by when someone wasn't kicking the crap out of me, either in the gym or out back behind the garage. But I lasted three years before I took a swing at the headmaster of the school, Major Benchoff, and I was immediately invited to pack my gear and get out.

Those early years, right up until my mid-teens seemed to establish a certain gypsy mentality in me that I later lived by. I was inflicted at an early age with the travel lust and could not stay in one place for very long; I had to move. In Yiddish it's call *shpilkus*. I returned to New York to live with my father who laid down the law. "You will finish high school," he demanded. I could not get my records from Virginia because there was an outstanding bill that my parents refused to pay because I did not finish my junior year before being expelled. The only school that would take me without transcripts was Commerce High in Hell's Kitchen on the West Side of mid-Manhattan. It was the perfect school for a miscreant teenager looking for trouble around every corner. I ran with an Italian gang that fought with the "spicks and niggers" on a daily basis. Hell's Kitchen was aptly named.

One day I attended an assembly meeting of the student body where a couple of representatives from the Marine Corps were trying to sell us on the virtues of being a Marine. They were attired in dress blues and being an impressionable sixteen years old, I got my father to lie about my age and I became a reserve Marine, attending meetings once a week on the S.S. Prairie State permanently moored at 125th Street and the Hudson River. I was hot stuff in that Marine uniform and I soon gave up the gang mentality for Marine discipline.

A Vulcan Odyssey

The high point of my year at Commerce High came in the person of Eli Brand, a freckle-faced, redhead, who befriended me. I guess she saw something in me behind that bravado that was worth cultivating. We hung out together and it was Eli who introduced me to what would become my goal in life. Together we attended matinees of Broadway shows on Saturdays and Wednesdays when we could buy cheap tickets. I was getting the bug. Eli came from a very erudite family of artists. Her father was a screenwriter who wrote *The Snake Pit*, starring Olivia DeHaviland, an Academy Award film at that time. Her mother, although deaf, was a successful writer of magazine stories and articles. Eli and her mother lived a few blocks from Commerce High and after school, we'd go to her forth floor, walkup, coldwater flat to study. Eli helped out her mother by making a few dollars babysitting for a couple of young actors that lived on the floor above. After the kid was put to sleep, Eli and I could study. Jocelyn, the kid's mother, was appearing on Broadway in *Mister Roberts* and her husband, Don Hanmer, was appearing in *The Man* with Lillian Gish. Since I knew very little about the theatre I wasn't all that impressed with their credentials. Jocelyn's brother would sometimes come to the flat to play with his nephew, Mighty Mouse (as he was called). The brother wasn't very talkative but Eli tried to impress me with the fact that the brother, Marlon, had played the lead in a short-lived Broadway show called *Birth of a Nation*, and was about to open in a new show called *A Streetcar Named Desire*. Marlon Brando was not very friendly and I was not very impressed with him but when I later decided to enter the theatre, Brando had already achieved super-stardom and I was sorry that I did not have the foresight to pick his brains about the craft.

One evening, as we were studying, Eli had a bright idea. Since we were only a month away from graduation and since I had no idea what I was going to do with my life, she suggested that we apply to a stock company to work as apprentices for the summer. She had bought a copy of Leo Shull's *Show Business* that had a page devoted to stock companies looking for actors and apprentices. She had circled one that was located in Belgrade Lakes, Maine. I could spend the summer with Eli, learn about the theatre and be with actors. It would be fun. We sat down and composed letters to the Belgrade Lakes Playhouse and excitedly sent them off. In a few days, what with exams upon us and my weekly meetings on the Prairie State, I had all but forgotten about our impulsive idea to go away to summer stock. But just before graduation, I got a letter from Ruth Bender, co-owner of the theatre. Yes, they would like to have me join the company as an apprentice for the summer. No pay but lots of experience. I immediately called Eli. She, too, had been accepted. For the next couple of weeks we were engrossed in making plans. She would take a bus up to Maine but I decided to save money and hitchhike. (In those days hitchhiking was a common mode of getting from one place to another without fear of losing one's life.) Shortly after graduation and receiving permission from my commanding officer on the Prairie State to be absent for the summer, I hit the road to Maine. My father advanced me fifty dollars to tide me over and I had no idea how long that would last but I'd cross that bridge when I came to it.

Eli never showed. And I never heard from her again...

* * *

I arrived at the Belgrade Lakes Playhouse amidst confusion and pandemonium. It was Wednesday and the first play of the season was to open the following evening. The theatre was a converted barn that stood right on the edge of a lake. It was a most beautiful setting. I finally found the Benders, the owners of the theatre, and they immediately put me to work with a young man by the name of Tony Primavera who was in charge of building the sets. Without formal introduction, we worked through the night, all the following day and right through the opening night's performance. No one knew I was there. The cast and management were housed in a modest wood-frame structure directly across the highway from the theatre. When the curtain came down on the last act of the opening night performance, everyone connected with the show took off to celebrate in theatre style at one of the estates in the lakeside community. Since no one asked me, I curled up on a heap of muslin rags at the rear of the theatre and went to sleep.

Beside the Benders, the other actors in residence included Janet Ward, Janice Mars and a character actor, Peter Harlow. The two ladies went on to have very successful careers on the Broadway stage and I remember seeing Janet in a number of fine films over the years. By and large, everyone was pre-occupied with his work and I was soon to learn that acting was very serious business. Ruth Bender found me a place to stay beneath the stage in back of the theatre since there was no room for me in the main house with the actors. I didn't mind the isolation at all.

My little room faced the lake and sometimes, early in the morning, I'd sit outside and watch the sun come up and the fish jumping after bugs and shadows. Was it any wonder that I fell in love with the theatre? I was soon convinced that my whole life was going to be just like this. Wrong again, Jocko!

It wasn't long before my fifty dollars was gone. I couldn't write to my dad for more money and I couldn't take a job on the side because the Benders had me working almost eighteen hours a day when we were preparing for a new show, which was weekly. I guess I was so excited in my new environment that the thought of food wasn't my primary concern. But after going for three days without anything to eat, one morning I found that I couldn't get out of bed. I lay there all day thinking that if I had to die, Belgrade Lakes was as nice a place as any to check out. It was late in the afternoon when I heard footsteps outside my door. There was a gentle knocking and as I managed to muster up strength to sit up, the company character actor, Peter Harlow, had come down to my room to see why I hadn't reported for work that day. When I explained that I had not had anything to eat for the past few days and that I was not being paid by the company, Peter stormed out of my room. It wasn't fifteen minutes later when he returned with a fist full of money, which he handed to me. He must have had no small amount of influence with the Benders because from that moment on, I was on the payroll; twenty-five dollars a week and free room. I was the luckiest person on the planet!

We were five weeks into the ten-week season when Tony had a motorcycle accident and ended up in the hospital. I was surprised how much I had learned in the last five weeks because the responsibility of building the sets and the theatre maintenance was now on my shoulders. My pay was increased to fifty dollars a week, I was cast in three plays as an actor. They were walk-on parts in three comedies and if you ever want to get hooked on theatre, play a comedy, get a few laughs and realize the power you have to milk an audience. Damn, this was cool! The summer flew by and before I knew it, it was time to say goodbye.

* * *

I returned to New York but I kept in touch with some of the members of the company. Janet Ward was soon married to a very fine actor, Arthur O'Connell, who garnered an Academy Award for his role in the film, *Picnic*. Arthur and I became good friends but when the marriage went bust, he thought I took sides with Janet and never spoke to me again. Meanwhile, I stayed in touch with the Benders and shortly after that summer stock season, Jim passed away. It really affected me. These people had played a very important part in my life. They had introduced me to what would eventually be my goal in life, the theatre.

The greatest influence from that period in Maine was the character actor, Peter Harlow. Years after, when we had become good friends, he confessed to me that when he came down to my room at the theatre, he had planned to put the make on me. I had no idea that he was gay; I didn't even know what it meant to be gay. Peter was a beautiful man who taught me that if I wanted to do anything serious in the theatre, it was not enough to wish for it. I would have to work my ass off for it. Over a period of time he gave me speech and diction lessons. I still had a slight Italian accent dating back to my early childhood in Italy and he referred to my speech as a product of "lazy mouth." I pronounced all my "t's" like "d's" and I spoke with a New York accent that would have put John Travolta to shame.

Shortly after my return to New York, I got word that my reserve unit was being called up. The Communists in China had begun to march south into Shanghai Province and a number of Marine battalions were being called up for active duty. The men of the Prairie State were being mobilized for duty!

I sat down with my dad and we discussed my dilemma. I did not want to go to China; I did not want to get stuck on active duty for an indefinite period of time; I did want to go to school and study acting. But Uncle Sam had priority and we had to figure out what I was going to do.

"If it were me..." my dad began, "I would transfer out of the reserves and into the regulars. At least you'll know how long you'll have to serve. In reserve, they can keep you indefinitely."

Unfortunately, he was not always right! Two weeks after I transferred out of the reserves my outfit was back on the Prairie State, having been de-activated. Three months later, after boot camp, I ended up in Tsing Tao, China. I was only there for two weeks while we evacuated American and English consulate workers with the intent of returning them to their points of origin. I was reassigned for duty on Guam.

Let me be quite candid. I respect all those brave men who served in the Corps. I grieve for the many who gave their lives fighting while in the Corps. Today, I know a number of ex-Marines who talk about their time in the Corps as if it was some great religious experience. I hated the Corps; every minute of it. I could take the discipline, I could take the beatings from anti-Semitic assholes from the swamps of Louisiana who were wearing shoes for the first time in their lives, I could take the typhoons that hit the island regularly and wreaked untold damage that we had to clean up. What I couldn't take was the demeaning job to which I was assigned for eleven months. When I went on active duty, I was given a test to see what I might be qualified for in the way of a job. I had a 126 I.Q. and three years of R.O.T.C. from when I was in military school. Was I considered for a tech job? OCS? Hell, no. Each morning I would go to the equipment shed and check out a machete. Then I would walk to the edge of the jungle, get down on my hands and knees, and begin to hack away at the resilient growth. In a way, this job had merit because in eleven months, I don't think I moved from outside an area the size of a Mack truck. No matter how much I cut, the following day it had all grown back and I had to begin all over again. So when I was discharged almost three years after my enlistment, I swore I had had it. Three months after my discharge in 1950, war broke out in Korea. I was contacted by the Marine Corps to see if I would like to re-enlist, but I graciously declined without a second thought. Unfortunately, many of the men with whom I served were shipped right to the front and died in that war. I guess it just wasn't my time.

CHAPTER TWO
A CAREER IS BORN

After my discharge from the Corps, I immediately headed for the Dramatic Workshop on 48th Street in New York City. Before entering the Corps, my initial plans were to take acting lessons and try my hand at acting. The Dramatic Workshop was the perfect place to begin. I believe it was Janet Ward, with whom I worked in Maine, who suggested that I look into it. Some of the finest actors in the theatre were alumni of the Workshop: Marlon Brando, Shelly Winters, Harry Belefonte, Harry Guardino, Albert Salmi, Tony Franciosa. The director of the workshop was a German by the name of Erwin Piscator and once one got over his politics, it was obvious that the man had a genius for the stage. My teacher, the person with whom I was to come in contact on a day to day basis, was a funny-looking little Russian man with a shock of black, unruly hair that went in every which direction. His name was Raikin ben-Ari and he had studied with the great Stanislavski and worked with the Habima Theatre in Russia before immigrating to the States. He had a practical understanding of "the method", a technique of acting that became very popular in the theatre in the late thirties and forties. One of the great things about the Workshop was that it gave me a vocabulary with which to work and communicate with other actors. Up to that time, I felt as if I was functioning in a vacuum. I didn't know how to express myself in theatre jargon and I didn't know how to arrive at a character in a play. Ben-Ari gave me the basic tools with which to work and they were tools that I used throughout my career.

The Workshop turned out to be more than a place for actors to work on scenes. It was a total entity with two theatres, The President Theatre on 48th Street and the Second Avenue Theatre located in a seedy but colorful part of lower Manhattan. Aside from scene study, each student was required to take Voice and Diction with a very fine teacher, Elaine Eldridge. Movement Class was also a requirement since moving on stage is not at all like moving in real life, the actor having to be constantly aware of his audience and be careful not to upstage himself or other actors. Fencing was a requirement. We also took Theatre Management, Theatre History and Shakespeare. Classes were scheduled every day and between classes, the students got together and rehearsed scenes. In the evenings, we congregated at a little bar across from the President Theatre, and shared information on what was happening along the Great White Way (Broadway) and who was casting what and where. We were all a part of "The Theatre" and we lived and breathed it every day of our lives.

One rule that Erwin Piscator would not bend was that first year students were not allowed to appear in productions. We could work on crews backstage and we could work in scene study classes, but we could not appear in a production at either the President or Second Avenue Theatres. I believe the only exception to that rule was with the casting of Ben Gazarra in a play called *The Circle of Chalk*. At almost the same time, I was cast in a minor role in a play about Abe Lincoln, starring Tony Franciosa in the title role. When Piscator heard that I had been cast, he confronted the director, Brett Warren, and had me dropped from the cast. Brett tried to stand by his guns, but in the final analysis, Piscator had the last word. I was crushed. I had attended all my classes religiously and felt that "the no-first-year- student" rule was unfair and discriminating. I spent many long hours crying in my beer in the bar across the street from school until one of the students told me about a play that was being done at the Cherry Lane Theatre in the Village. Everyone knew about the wonderful tradition of the Cherry Lane Theatre. It had turned out many an actor who went on to Broadway and the cinema. It was a converted stable set on a quaint street in a very fashionable part of lower Manhattan. I called, made an appointment to audition and showed up at the allotted time. I gave a substantial reading for my first time out, and much to my surprise, I was cast in a fairly good role in the English drawing room comedy by Frederick Lonsdale, *Aren't We All*.

An actor needs only one such disaster in his career. Neither my fellow actors nor I were very well equipped to pull off an English drawing room comedy complete with accents and timing. The *coup de grace* came when the producer disappeared one night, never to be heard from again. We were all very young and enthusiastic so we decided to chip in and put on the play with our own money. The Village Voice, a local rag, buried us and the second night, there were more people on stage than were in the audience. We held out for a miserable week and finally, one dreary night, we up and vacated the theatre. I had gotten a taste of my first real audition and the exhilaration of knowing I got a part over all others. I would know this feeling many more times in my life and it never failed to lift my spirits just as drugs must affect an addict. The failure of our venture at the Cherry Lane was unimportant. I was now an "actor."

As a bona fide actor, I learned that I had to do what other actors did; I had to make the rounds. I took a job at Schraaft's serving ice cream and waiting on tables. I believe that every potential actor I knew in those days had at one time or another worked at Schraaft's. When I saved up enough money, I invested in a photo session and put together a composite. Then, with copies of my photos in my brief case I went from office to office inquiring about casting and dropping off pictures. It was a long and tedious process and only the strong of will and conviction survived. I continued my studies at the Workshop until the end of the first year. Then, my Hungarian blood began to boil and I longed for the open road and new places. I told my teacher, Raikin ben-Ari, that I would not be returning for the next semester. We were standing at the rear of the theatre when I broke the news to him. His eyes filled with tears as he wished me well.

"I wish I could tell you something sage that will carry you on your journey," he said in his thick Russian accent. "Perhaps my best advice to you is, forget everything that you have learned here. If it is not a part of you by now, don't let it hold you back. Out there, you are either an actor or you're not an actor." It was very sound advice.

* * *

The year was 1951 and what better way for a young man to travel across the country than by thumb? I stopped in Allentown, Pennsylvania, where my dad was now working, and put the touch on him for a few dollars. He was a prince; he never turned me down. Then, he drove me to the edge of town and wished me the best of luck. I had already hit up my grandfather for a small loan so I had a couple hundred dollars to tide me over.

Hitchhiking across the United States in the dead of winter is akin to stripping down to the buff and jumping into an ice covered lake. Every ride was a process of thawing out and I dreaded when that ride would come to an end. I would have to stand in the freezing wind or rain or sleet to wait for my next benefactor. I immediately headed south in quest of the sun. But the clouds followed me all the way to Texarkana, on the border between Texas and Arkansas. I was standing by the side of the road in the middle of the night wondering if saving a few dollars by not taking the bus was a smart move, when up pulled a huge Nash Rambler, the kind where the front seat folded back into a bed. The driver was a middle-aged Army sergeant being transferred from the east to the west coast. His name was Woodrow Wilson Hargrove and he was happy to have someone to talk to in order to keep awake on his long trip. He was not at all like the Marine sergeants I had know in the Corps. He was easygoing and fun to talk to. Some two hours out of Texarkana, we stopped for breakfast and he insisted on picking up the tab. After refreshing ourselves at the rest stop, we climbed back in the car and proceeded on our way.

With a good breakfast under my belt and the warmth of the car, I could feel sleep overcome me. I tilted back the seat and drifted off. I was dreaming of Hollywood and acting and women, especially women, when I suddenly bolted upright. I could hear the sound of gravel against the underside of the car and I pitched from my side over to the driver's side and back again to my side. The car was out of control. It careened from one side of the road to the other with Sergeant Hargrove asleep at the wheel. The old Nash was a heavy car and with the sergeant being transferred, the rear of the car was loaded with books and cartons of papers and personal effects. I tried to reach over and grab the wheel to get us back on the road but my efforts were too late. The car shot off the highway at about seventy, jumping a wide ditch and careening through a barbed wire fence. We were suddenly in an orchard and the car was rolling over and over, three, four, five times, before it came to a stop, resting on its roof. I was certain that I was dead because I had momentarily lost consciousness. Now, everything was dead silent. I was gently pinned down to the seat by the steering wheel and the sergeant was nowhere in sight. I extricated myself from the wreckage, taking time to notice that my side of the car had been completely demolished. Had I not been thrown over into the driver's side, I could imagine the outcome. My leg was in terrible pain and as I climbed out of the open window on the driver's side, I noticed a small trickle of blood. It was coming from my face but the pain in my leg was so severe that I could not determine from where I was bleeding. I pulled myself to my feet and stood looking back at the path the vehicle had taken through the apple grove. Trees were randomly felled and debris from the car was scattered all over the field. Sergeant Hargrove was nowhere in sight. Daylight was just beginning to break and I could see that I was about fifty yards from the highway. As I started to limp towards the road, I could see the headlights of an oncoming car. I put two fingers in my mouth like my father taught me when I was a kid, and I whistled for all I was worth. The car pulled over to the side of the road and a man got out. The sound of his voice cut through the clear, cold Texas morning air.

"Who's out there?" he called.

"I need help," I returned. "Can you get an ambulance? I think my friend is hurt!"

"Stay right there. I'll get someone." And in a flash, he was gone. It seemed like an eternity until help arrived, sirens blaring, lights flashing. Perhaps a dozen men converged on the scene led by a short, stocky man wearing a Western hat and boots. He was the Sheriff and as they followed the path the car had taken on its crazy charge through the orchard, I could feel myself getting sick. Halfway between the road and where I was standing, the group stopped. The Sheriff called out to me, "You alone, boy?"

"No, sir, " I called back. "I'm with another man, a sergeant in the Army..."

"This him?"

I limped over to where the men were standing in a group. There on the ground was Sergeant Woodrow Wilson Hargrove. "Oh, my god..." And before I could say another word, the Sheriff stuck the toe of his boot under the sergeant's back and kicked him over. The sergeant breathed one last breath, like a big sigh, and then he died. His back had been broken in the crash. There was a trickle of spinal fluid on his lip coming from his nose. The Sheriff knelt down and took the sergeant's wrist in his hand. As he stood up, he turned to the other men and began shouting orders. "All right, let's get this mess cleaned up. You orderlies, get a stretcher down here. You other men, see if you kin find some boxes and save all these papers. If this guy's Army, they'll want everything we can salvage." He turned to his Deputy. "Get this kid up to the hospital and see how bad he's hurt." He turned to me. I was still staring down at the body of Hargrove who, just a short time ago, had been a living, laughing person. Now he was dead. It was such a waste.

"Where you hurt, boy?"

"I guess it's my leg."

"That blood all over yer front ain't from yer leg, boy." He turned to his deputy. "Get him over to the hospital but don't let no one talk to him, ya understand?"

The Deputy understood. He took me by one arm and helped me walk the distance to the car. I took one last look back over that peaceful scene in the middle of nowhere in Texas.

At the hospital they found that there was an inch-long gash under my chin where I had obviously made contact with something sharp. A doctor sewed me up, a nurse sponged down my jacket, and they did a probing examination of my leg. It was only a matter of a few minutes and I was out the door with the deputy who drove me to the station. The sign on the station door told me that I was in Albany, Texas.

The Sheriff asked me a number of questions and when he discovered that I was a hitchhiker, he became very cold. "We don't like hitchhikers in our county. Now, the Deputy here is gonna drive ya to the edge of town where you kin get a lift. I don't wanna see your face round here agin, ya understand, boy?"

"Yes, sir."

And before you could yell "murder," I was standing on the road heading West to California. It was a grizzly experience and to this day, I wonder if there was ever an inquiry into the death of Sergeant Hargrove because I swear, that Sheriff killed him!

CHAPTER THREE
WELCOME TO LA-LA LAND

I arrived in California with my face swathed in blood-soaked bandages and the front of my dark blue suit caked with highway dirt and drippings from my chin. What a sight! I checked into the downtown YMCA until I could get my bearings. The lobby of the Y was teaming with the weirdest group of questionable males I had ever encountered. Even in my unsavory condition, I got whistles and loud propositions amidst roars of laughter. I had to get some fresh air so I raised the collar of my suit jacket and stepped out into the street. I hadn't gone a block when a blue and white pulled over to the curb, an officer jumped out and ordered me to put my hands against the building. His partner came up from behind and ran his hands over my body. They called in my description as I was made to stand in that position until they got word that I was not public enemy number one. A number of late night curiosity seekers and some winos gathered to gape at the "kid" who was being worked over by the cops. After some deliberation, I was informed that I was free to go. I decided that the Y looked pretty good compared to the street. As I headed back to my room, there were tears of anger streaming down my face. I could only think, "Welcome to L.A."

I lost no time in getting out of the downtown area and into Hollywood. My address book was filled with a collection of numbers I was instructed to call from friends and relatives. Connie was the son of a woman who my Uncle Richard knew in his childhood, etc, etc. Connie invited me to share his small utility apartment for as long as I pleased. He was rarely home and made his living at the racetrack. It wasn't long after he taught me how to handicap the horses that what remained of my two hundred dollars was almost gone. It didn't take me long to learn that "lady luck" and I were not compatible.

The next name on my list of those to contact was Don Torpin at Twentieth Century Fox. He and my dad had done most of their military service together, having served on the same ship and later at the same land station. Don greeted me warmly and invited me out to the studio for lunch. At that time he was an assistant director, which to me meant that all he had to do was speak to the powers that be and I would be on my way to stardom. Yeah, sure. What Don was able to do was to place a call to the Twentieth employment office and get me an interview. The following week I began work in the mailroom. Not quite stardom but what the hell, I was on the lot. I think what took most of the air out of my sails was speaking to some of the other mailroom employees that had been working at the same job for two or more years. In most cases, the mailroom was a dead end. But I was sure that I would figure out a way to make it pay off.

The Studio Club, which was for employees, was putting on their annual gala show. That included dinner, a play and dancing into the wee hours of the morning. I read for the play and got the part of a smartass kid from the streets of New York. Since most of the cast was recruited from office workers and not the Twentieth talent pool, the show came off like a lead balloon. But the audiences were appreciative and I got to meet a lot of secretaries and blue-collar workers; but not one thing to enhance my quest to be an actor.

Michelle King was a lovely looking lady some five years my senior. She was playing the role of a hooker in the play and each of us thought that the other was duly typecast. We did not hit it off. Michelle was a reader, someone who read books and magazine stories and analyzed them for their potential as motion picture properties. It was near the end of February. We had just finished our Friday evening performance and most of the cast had already left the theatre. I offered to walk Michelle to her car. I finally got up the nerve to ask her to join me for a drink.

"Tomorrow is my birthday and I don't know anyone in town and I don't feel like going home just yet..."

"I'd love to," was all she said and we were off to The Seven Seas on Hollywood Boulevard where, at midnight, the management turned on a special effect that sounded like rain on a tin roof. With the lights lowered, the atmosphere was terribly romantic and Michelle was getting more beautiful by the moment. At the stroke of midnight, she leaned across the table and gently kissed me on the lips.

"Happy Birthday," she purred.

I was twenty-one years old and this was my first true love. Within a month we were talking marriage. Michelle was living on Franklin Avenue near Western with her five year old daughter so we both had to use the utmost discretion. I took a small room in a boarding house just up the street and we were together every chance we could steal. Once we decided to marry, I knew that I would have to leave Twentieth. I think my salary was a big twenty-six dollars a week, hardly enough money to take on the responsibility of a family. I got a job at Lockheed Aircraft over in Burbank working the graveyard shift from twelve at night till six-thirty in the morning. Michelle went off to work at eight in the morning. On most mornings we could grab a cup of coffee together before she had to run off to the studio. Then I would retire to my room, which overlooked Franklin Avenue, and try to get some sleep amidst the noisy traffic below. Most evenings, Michelle's little girl stayed with a sitter. Normally, that would have given us some quality time together but Michelle had this compulsion to be a dancer, and each evening, after work, she would rush off to The American School of Dance on Hollywood Boulevard where she would stretch and grunt and sweat five evenings a week. I took to sitting in the waiting room of the studio, patiently watching until class was over so we could run off together for a quick snack before I had to head out to Burbank and the assembly line. It was by no means an ideal situation. Some evenings I would fall asleep right there in the studio waiting room while Michelle was taking class. Something was not working and I grasped at straws trying to hold our relationship together. One evening she offered up a solution.

"Instead of sitting here every night, why don't you take class?"

"You mean, do all that...stuff?"

"That stuff is good for your body, not to mention your mind. Try it."

And try it I did. Here was this hulk in black tights and little ballet slippers trying to master the refined movements of ballet. *Turning out* was anathema to my physical being; my body did not take to change without rebelling. My muscles and joints were in constant pain. But if that was what I had to do to keep our relationship in tact, so be it. I mixed ballet classes with Modern and Tap, which I found more to my liking. So there we were, Michelle and I, each evening skipping and jumping and stretching and sweating our evenings away. But nothing seemed to help our decaying relationship. One evening, some three months after I began taking classes simply to appease Michelle, she dropped the bomb.

"We have to call it off! You're too negative for me. You're creating negative vibrations in my life which are depressing me."

That's the way she spoke: negative vibrations, karma, her soul. It was a crushing blow and with very little sleep, I felt as if I was standing with one foot on the edge. I got into my 1929 Ford coupe that I had bought for almost nothing from an ad in the newspaper, and drove out to Lockheed.

That night, while using a riveting gun, I began to drift off and rammed the machine through the skin of the side of the plane creating a hole that I could have climbed through. My tenure with Lockheed came to an abrupt end. I got into my car and started back to town at three in the morning. Along the way I had to jam on the breaks to avoid a collision and as the car skidded to a halt, two of my tires blew out. I felt as if my world was unraveling. I abandoned the car and walked the rest of the way back to the boarding house. I thought it would be about that time when Michelle would be getting her little girl ready for school. The pain was almost too much to endure. I sat on the edge of the bed wondering where I could turn. Calmly, I got up, went into the bathroom where I soaked three towels with water. Then I forced the damp towels around the windows and filled in the space under the door. My mind was numb. On the floor a few feet from my bed was a gas heater. I calmly turned on the jet and without lighting it, I returned to the bed and lay down. I needed sleep. My mind returned to Michelle. My whole life had been wrapped up in her and now that she was gone, there was a terrible, aching void. What could I do? Soon I would be able to sleep. I could hear the sound of the early morning traffic as it began to congest in the street below. My hearing became acute. I realized that I could hear the gas escaping from the jet clear across the room. The sound of the escaping gas was keeping me awake. By now the room was filled with gas fumes and as I got up from the bed, it was all I could do to make my way across the room to the heater and turn off the jet. I removed the towels and raised the windows to let in fresh air. I sat on the edge of the bed for what seemed like hours trying to decide where I would go from here. I realized that suicide was not my bag but it was a good dramatic touch. First off, I had to get Michelle out of my mind. I had to do something that would fill the void created by her absence, preferably something physical that would vent my hostility. I changed clothes and headed up to the American School of Dance. Eugene Loring, the director of the school, was behind the desk.

"I'd like to sign up for a full schedule of day classes." I told him. I began to take six hours of ballet, modern and tap every day. I could be out of the studio by the time Michelle arrived for her evening class. I found employment working nights in a Laundromat around the corner from the school and on weekends I washed dishes at Snow White's Restaurant on the corner of Hollywood and Highland. When I had enough money saved, I moved from Western Avenue to a rooming house on Orange Grove, which was closer to the school. The rooming house was a large wooden structure with a swing on the porch and two rooms in the attic that were rented out to tenants. I took one of the rooms and directly across the hall from me resided two sisters from Florida that had come to Hollywood to make it in the movies. Their names were Kilo and Mega Watts! I swear! They were both ice skaters that decided there was little future on the ice and possibly more of a future as ballet dancers. The three of us took to "hanging out" like the Three Musketeers. Together we attended dance classes and movies and plays and dance recitals.

One evening, when I wasn't working, Mega knocked on my door to see if I would like to go with her to a dance recital that was being held just around the corner at the Perry Studio on Highland Avenue. It was free.

The young man who was giving the recital, Henry Hirsh, was a fabulous technician. He never missed a move and he seemed to float forever each time he left the floor; his elevation was awesome. His one flaw was that he should have been wearing a tutu and toe shoes because he was so effete that it was almost impossible not to think that he was a woman. And as I sat there watching him, I realized that I would never be a dancer, never a true dancer with flawless technique like Henry Hirsh. But studying the dance had a momentary place in my life and I was determined to continue with classes until I could figure out my next move that would get me back into acting. I had a feeling that if I just stuck with the dancing, something would transpire that would get me back on track.

After the recital, Mega and I went back to congratulate Henry on his performance.

"Are you a dancer?" he asked. He was eying me up and down as if I was on a menu.

"Not really. I study."

"He's being modest, Henry," interjected Mega. "He's becoming a fine dancer. All he needs is a little more technique…"

I needed a hell-of-a lot more than technique. I still walked like a truck driver but there was no way in the world I would swap places with Henry and the way he walked.

"Well, I just wanted you to know how wonderful we both thought you were," I said, being sure to emphasize "we both."

"Say your name again for me, " he asked. I repeated it. "I like that. It's French, isn't it? I'm sure we'll meet again," he said and then floated away to be with his other guests.

* * *

My routine of working two jobs, taking classes six hours a day, and socializing with the Watts sisters, went on for three months. One Friday afternoon between the Laundromat and Snow White's, I was in my room when I heard the landlady calling up from the landing below.

"Telephone."

I could hear Mega open her door and call down. "Who is it?"

"Woman says her name is Lotte Goslar."

"Oh, my god," yelled Mega. "That's the choreographer from the Hollywood Bowl. Tell her I'll be right down."

"Not for you," came the reply. "It's for him."

There was a sudden knock on my door and Mega entered without waiting for an invitation. "Do you know who's on the phone?"

"Jesus?"

"I didn't know you auditioned for the Bowl."

"I didn't."

"Well, don't keep her waiting…"

I didn't mean to show Mega my ignorance but I had never heard of a Lotte Goslar. As I got to the phone, Mega was hanging on my shoulder. The woman on the other end of the line spoke with a distinct German accent. She was very friendly. "This may sound strange to you but we have just had our annual auditions for the Hollywood Bowl Ballet Company. I've auditioned over two hundred dancers and I'm exhausted.

I need one more dancer and you come highly recommended. Would you be interested in a job?"

Needless to say, I was dumbfounded. "Yes, ma'am, I sure would."

"Tomorrow is Saturday but the office will be open. You can come up after ten and sign the contract. We begin rehearsals Monday morning at nine. I'll see you then." And she was gone.

Now, I've always loved a good joke from time to time and I would have bet dollars to donuts that Mega and Kilo were up to some fun at my expense. I walked back up the stairs with Mega close at my heels. I closed the door and Mega barged in with her sister.

"What happened?" Mega demanded.

"Come off it you two. The joke is over. I fell for it."

"What are you talking about?" asked Kilo with a quizzical expression on her face.

"Oh, that's good, Kilo. That should be worth an Academy Award nomination."

"Will you tell us what Lotte wanted or do we have to beat it out of you?" threatened Mega.

"Okay, you want to play this game right to the end…." I proceeded to tell the girls what had transpired over the phone. I admitted that it was a good joke but I was emphatic when I told them "a team of wild horses couldn't get me to go up to the Bowl on Saturday morning and make a total ass of myself." The girls swore up and down that they had nothing to do with this and threatened that if they had to physically drag me, I was going to be at the Bowl the following morning.

Kilo took my place at the Laundromat as Mega drove me in her car up to the Bowl. She literally had to take me by the hand and lead me up to the office. When the secretary finally shoved a Chorus Equity contract under my nose with my name typed in the space that said "performer," I realized that this was for real. I was going to be a dancer…maybe.

My first impression of the Hollywood Bowl was like a worshipper's upon entering St. Peter's Basilica. It was awesome. I had not slept all weekend. I was nervous; my hands were shaking, my stomach was tied in knots, and big blotches of sweat were forming under my arms. I was a mess. This was an honest to God Ballet Company and someone was going to expect me to do ballet, and me with only six months of training.

The whole thing was crazy. Should I stay? Should I leave? What to do? Trying to be as inconspicuous as possible, I sat down on the edge of a group of some forty dancers waiting for the choreographer. The musical orchestration was playing over the loudspeaker system, very waltzy, very Strauss. The first show of the season would be *Die Fledermaus*, with Yvonne DeCarlo in the leading role of Prince Orlovsky. Who knew she had a trained operatic voice? The entire opera was one waltz after another and for some reason, I couldn't count up to three! Lotte finally arrived and began to team up the dancers. I was teamed with the tallest, largest girl in the company, Eugenia Popoff. I prayed that I would not have to lift her but much to my surprise, she was as light on her feet as any of the shorter girls in the corps de ballet. In fact, she was the most beautiful and talented of all the dancers. As the music for the first number began to play, Eugenia lead me around the stage as I held on for dear life. I was supposed to be leading the girl but I had no idea what I was doing so Eugenia saved my butt. But it was obvious to the trained eye that I was out of my element. I stumbled through the first week, stepping on Eugenia's toes, tripping over invisible objects on the stage, and all in all, displaying my ineptitude as a ballet dancer. That Friday afternoon, when rehearsal was drawing to an end, Lotte called me aside.

"Do you go to church on Sunday mornings?" she asked.

"No, ma'am."

"Why don't you plan on meeting me here at seven on Sunday morning and we can go over some of the steps…"

And that Sunday morning, before she and her husband went off to church, Lotte taught me how to waltz on the stage of the Hollywood Bowl.

I hate to keep dropping sad endings to my stories but one cannot change the truth…entirely. Die Fledermaus was responsible for closing the Hollywood Bowl for the first time in thirty-one years! After five weeks of performances, the Bowl Association ran out of money and we were all given our notices of closing.

Oh, yes, one other thing; how I got the job. It was Henry Hirsh who had recommended me. He was Lotte's assistant and all the time we were at the Bowl he never once made reference to our meeting at his recital. I'll bet he never again recommended another dancer without first seeing his work.

* * *

A Vulcan Odyssey

My timing was perfect. We no sooner got notice that the show was closing than Equity sent out word to all its members that the Screen Extras Guild would be taking applications for dancers. The studios were producing so many musicals that there was actually a shortage. As a technician I was less than competent, but I was six feet tall and quite strong from working out regularly at the gym. A strong back and a firm grip were definitely prerequisites for adagio (working with a partner.) The Screen Extras Guild had jurisdiction over all dancers and all calls for auditions came through Central Casting. I don't know what the ruling is today, but in those days the Extras Union was a closed shop. Even when the Taft-Hartley law outlawed closed shops, Central Casting kept the membership to an exclusive group. It worked this way: if you could get work they could not keep you out of the Union. But the studios did not deal with the Union. They called for extras and dancers through Central Casting that was a clearinghouse. Even if one had a Screen Extras Guild card and he was not registered with Central Casting, he could not get work. It was a Catch-22 situation.

I did not particularly want to join SEG. I had heard that working as an extra in films was the kiss of death for actors. "Once an extra, always an extra." There were a few who were able to overcome the stigma and go on to careers as actors, but they were in the minority. On the other hand, if I wanted to continue to work as a dancer, I had to join SEG and register with Central Casting. And Central demanded that the dancers do extra work. If a dancer refused to do extra work he would not get calls for dance jobs. It was like being between a rock and a hard place. But it would be crazy to try to fight the system at this stage of the game so I went along with the flow, paid my way into SEG and did as little extra work as possible in order to qualify for dance auditions.

My first audition was at MGM for *Lovely to Look At*, a musical film starring Kathryn Grayson, Howard Keel, Red Skelton and Zsa Zsa Gabor. The choreographer was Hermes Pan. The audition consisted of a simple ballet phrase and as many of the dancers were eliminated, I found myself in a group of some twenty dancers that were selected to work on the film. We were to be paid one hundred and twenty-five dollars a week! That was a whole lot of money in the early fifties. Six months before I was working in the mail room at Fox for twenty-six dollars a week. I was on my way!

I took the weekend to relax before I began work at MGM. I had quit the Laundromat and Snow White's when I went to work at the Bowl. I had also moved out of my room on Orange Grove, said a fond farewell to the Watts sisters, and taken a one room apartment (I believe they call it an efficiency) up in the hills behind the church on Franklin Avenue. It was very charming with a Dutch door that split in the middle so I could open just the top half and look out on a cobblestone patio with trees and smell the jasmine. The single room was furnished with knotty pine walls and all my cooking was done on a hot plate. One would be surprised at the gourmet meals one could conjure up on a two-burner electric grill. It was late Friday and I was just lying around wallowing in my good-fortune when the phone rang.

"This is Walton…Walton Walker. Remember me? I'm the assistant choreographer to Hermes Pan."

I could tell by his voice that my success as a dancer was about to be short-lived.

"I was just going over the list of dancers and realized that you live on the hill just behind me. What a coincidence. So I was thinking, how would you like to come over for a party?"

"But Mr. Walker…"

"Walton."

"Yes, Walton…it's awfully late, isn't it? Who did you say was coming over?"

"Well, when you get here, there'll be you and me."

I was dead! "I'm sorry, Mr. Walker, but I've got company," I lied. "Perhaps another time." The party on the other end of the line hung up.

Monday morning was no less than I had expected. When we arrived at the studio, I was called over to the desk of the assistant director, Howard Koch.

"Looks like we won't be needing you for a while," he informed me. He was looking over the production schedule. "I'd say in about ten weeks. So you go on home and come in every Thursday and pick up your check. I'll give you a call when we're ready to use you." He looked up at me and gave me the biggest wink possible. He knew. And for the next ten weeks, I was paid right along with the all the other dancers that were required to report for work every day. (Howard Koch went on to become the head of Paramount Studios and a fine independent producer in his own right.

Some years later at a social function I tried to remind him of the incident but he didn't remember me from Adam.)

It was during this period when I had free time on my hands and money in my pocket, that I decided to return to an old love that was introduced to me at the Dramatic Workshop...fencing. I was quite good for the little time I had been exposed to it and I fashioned myself to be another Errol Flynn or Douglas Fairbanks. I found my way to Faulkner Studio where I enrolled in fencing classes with an emphasis on foil and saber. I continued with my dance studies moving from the American School of Dance to a studio above the Greyhound Terminal where I took classes with Michael Panaiff. But with all this activity, it appeared that I was not getting any closer to my acting goal. I would have to rethink my plan, but not now. I was on a roll.

Coincidence seemed to be the mother of invention where I was concerned. Good things just continued to happen to me.

It was a Saturday morning and I got a rush call from Central Casting for an audition at Fox Western (which is now a supermarket.) When I arrived at the studio, there must have been some two hundred male dancers waiting to audition. They ran us through in groups of ten as the assistant choreographer put us through one of the routines. It was a modern hillbilly number with the dancers backing up Mitzi Gaynor. After each group had auditioned, the choreographer, Bob Sidney, picked out the dancers he wanted and dismissed the others. The group kept getting smaller and I kept being sent over to the side with the ones who were told to stay. As we got down to ten dancers, we were lined up according to height. I was getting really nervous. What if they only wanted a small group and I had to actually dance? I was comfortable in a large ensemble where I could get lost and blend into the background (as I was able to do at MGM when I worked for Gene Kelly on *Singing in the Rain* where there were over a hundred dancers) but a specialty number would be way over my head. As the choreographer matched us for height, he counted off four from the left and sent the rest on their way. Now I was in for it, I told myself. Nowhere to hide with only four dancers; I had to think of a way out. We were informed that we would be doing a specialty number with Mitzi and we would have to join the Screen <u>Actors</u> Guild. The pay would be two hundred and fifty dollars a week! I knew I had to bail out before I got in way over my head. As we were given our call to report for work on Monday morning, I held back until the other dancers left the hall. Then, I approached Mr. Sidney who was talking to his shapely, female assistant and interrupted.

"Mr. Sidney?"

He turned to me and eyed me up and down. He was every gay person I had ever met all rolled up into one. "Yes?" he inquired.

"Mr. Sidney, I'm afraid I can't take the job."

"And why not?"

"I don't think I can dance well enough to do a specialty number."

"Is this some kind of a joke?"

"Oh, no, sir. Honest. I just don't think I can cut it."

"But I auditioned you myself and you passed the audition..."

"That was just an audition. I don't have the experience to do this big a job." I thought I was being quite honest.

"Well, tell me, young man, what are you doing here?"

"To be honest, I'm an actor who picks up a dance job now and again."

He took me by the arm steering me towards the door. "Are you a good actor?"

We arrived at the door and he opened it. "Yes, sir. I think so."

"Fine. Then show up Monday morning at nine o'clock and act like a dancer." And with that, he gave me a gentle push out the door and closed it behind me.

Bob Sidney turned out to be a first class s.o.b. Every impossible dance task was thrown onto me. The film was called *Bloodhounds of Broadway*, a loose adaptation of a Damon Runyon story about New York gangsters. When the going got tough all I had to do was think of the two- hundred and fifty dollars a week I was being paid and I worked that much harder. And when Mr. Sidney told me to jump from a platform four feet above the stage floor and land on my knees, I did it. We had to work barefoot and the surface of the floor was not smooth to do pirouettes. At the end of a working day, there were little splotches of blood where the skin had been torn away from the dancers' feet. A gypsy's not to reason why; his is but to do or die. I had so abused my knees on this film that my dancing days were going to be numbered.

I finished the job and moved on. Some years later I ran into Bob Sidney in a small shop on Melrose Avenue. He looked at me for a moment with a glint of recognition. After all, it had been over twenty years.

"Are you still dancing?" he inquired.
"No." I said.
"Thank God!"

I managed to pick up one dance job after another, enough work to cover my overhead and pay for my classes. The fencing classes at Faulkner's were consuming more and more of my time. I really loved the swordplay. One evening, while I was competing with another fencer, two stunt gaffers from MGM entered the studio. Mr. Faulkner introduced one of the men as Paul Stader. He told the group of fencers that he was working at the studio on a film called *Scaramouche* and was looking for two or three good fencers to work as stunt men. After introductions, he began to put us through our paces; attack, parry, thrust, etc. Stader came over to me where I was taking a breather.

"Want to work at MGM?" he asked.

I didn't mention that I had worked at MGM as a dancer. I thought it might be stigmatic so I just kept my mouth shut. He'd find out sooner or later. So a few days later, I got a call to report to the studio where I worked for three months on *Scaramouche*. From there I went on to *Julius Caesar*, with Marlon Brando. One day on the Julius Caesar set I casually mentioned to Marlon that we had met when I was baby-sitting his nephew in New York but he just grunted and went about his business. Boy, did I make an impression!

We finished Julius Caesar on a Friday and on Saturday I got a call from Paul Stader. He was gaffing a job at Columbia for Sam Katzman and he was looking for fencers. I joined up with Paul the following week where we began work on a series of ten films, all low budgets with no more than ten-day shooting schedules. The work was grueling but the pay was great and I was getting to feel comfortable in front of the camera. Sometimes Paul would call on me to do a fall or some little extra business for which I got paid extra. It was a great gig! I was able to stash away a few bucks in the bank for a rainy day.

I slowly worked my way back into acting when I auditioned at the Player's Ring Theatre on St. Monica Blvd. in West Hollywood. In those days, all the agents and casting directors worth their salt went to the small theatres scattered around the city. There was a plethora of young acting talent in those theatres and many of the studios hired actors from the plays. I did three plays at the Player's Ring but did not light a spark. I worked at the studios by day, either as a dancer or a stunt person, and I worked at the theatre at night, without pay, of course. But I knew that sooner or later I would get into acting if I just stayed the course.

CHAPTER FOUR
NEW YORK, NEW YORK

It had been nearly three years since I first arrived in Hollywood and I was beginning to miss New York and my family. It was late summer and production was slow at the studios. It was a good time to take a vacation and head back East. I returned to New York late that summer. My mother and I had not been on speaking terms for most of the time I had been in Los Angeles so this was a good time for me to mend fences. I also missed Gramps and I longed to see my dad. But in the back of my mind, I was thinking that if I really wanted to act, New York was where I should be. I immediately enrolled in classes with J. Edward Bromberg, a really fine character actor who was having a tough time since he was indicted by the McCarthy Hearings for un-American activities. In those days, half the actors I knew who were politically active were either Socialists or Communists. None of them advocated the overthrow of the U.S. government, as charged; they just wanted more federal funding for theatre and the arts. That's another story.

I enrolled in ballet classes at Carnegie Hall, fencing classes with Santoni, and Afro-Cuban-Primitive dancing with Archie Savage who had once been the dance partner of the great Kathryn Dunham. I was a young man in a hurry and I could feel the time slipping away.

A group of California gypsies that had come east to appear at the Mark Hellinger Theatre in the musical, *Hazel Flagg*, with Helen Gallagher and Thomas Mitchell, was in the process of adding some new numbers to the show when I entered the theatre by the stage door. I stood in the wings watching the dancers go through one of their routines. The assistant choreographer was a very funny lady by the name of Helen Silver, and when she saw me, she came bounding across the stage like a bunny. In a moment, I was surrounded by a group of friends from the West Coast all wanting bits of news from home. They had been in New York some six months, the show having opened in the early spring to rather cool reviews by the press. The producers had decided to close the show down for the summer, make some changes and open again in the fall. When the kids were called back to the stage, Helen took me by the arm and led me off into the wings.

"How would you like to dance in a Broadway show?" she asked.

"Who do I have to kill?"

"We just got word that Johnny Brascia is leaving the show. That means that one of the kids in the chorus will move up into his slot to do his specialty numbers and I'll need someone to cover in the chorus…"

Here we go again, I thought. Please don't call Bob Sidney for a recommendation. "I don't know, Helen. I was watching some of that ballet number and I don't think I can handle those double tours."

"Can you do a single? So you won't do a double, you'll do a single. Trust me. Of course, I don't want to talk you into anything…"

"I'd like to try it."

"Good. C'mon, I'll introduce you to the musical director. He'll wanna hear you sing."

"Helen, the person hasn't been born yet who would wanna hear me sing!"

I sang God Bless America and Buster Davis, the musical director, said I could have the job if I promised I would not sing while onstage. I promised.

I had ten days to learn eight numbers. Helen was an angel, working with me from morning till night until I was comfortable with the routines. The closer we came to opening night, the more I was sure that I would be responsible for screwing up the show. True, each member of the chorus is like a cog in a wheel, but unlike the wheel, if one of the members is a weak link it doesn't mean that the show closes down and the world comes to an end. But no one could tell me that as the minutes ticked down till opening night.

No one can ever explain to another person the myriad of emotions a performer experiences on an opening night. I'm not just referring to the few actors fortunate enough to have the leads because I've worked both the chorus and the roles with top billing. Believe me, the nuclear reactions one experiences in the pit of the stomach has nothing to do with the billing. I have rarely met a performer that did not go through the opening night jitters.

As I stood in the wings waiting for my cue to go on, I knew I was going to be sick. With controlled panic, I walked over to the broom closet, leaned over the sink and barfed up my dinner. I quickly popped a mint into my mouth, walked out on stage and as the lights came up I produced a flawless double pirouette where the previous dancer doing the same role had done a double air tour. I wish I could say that the evening passed without incident. My partner for the ballet number was a nymphet of sixteen years, a sweet little thing by the name of Sherry. We both wore tights, she in her Betsy Ross tutu and I in my George Washington frilly-laced shirt and wig. There were four couples identically dressed and at one point in the number the men were required to throw their partners straight up in the air and as they came down, we were to catch them about the thighs, gently letting them slide down our chests and when they landed on solid ground, the four girls would run forward to the center of the stage, touch hand in an arch and as the lights came up, Helen Gallagher would make her entrance. What could be simpler?

Everything went off according to schedule right up to the part where I threw Sherry up in the air. But as I started to let her down I could feel a tugging at my neck and the weight of Sherry sliding down my chest was pulling me over. As Sherry touched the floor, she started forward to meet the other girls center stage but she was dragging me across stage with my face attached to her rear end! Try looking nonchalant in that position. As the girls formed their arch I knew I had to get away from center stage, so with a sudden effort I stood upright. All the ruffles of my shirt pulled away and stuck to what was left of the seat of Sherry's tights. I could immediately tell what had happened. One of the fancy buttons on the ruffles of my shirt had found a tiny hole in the seat of Sherry's tights and they mated, a one in a million shot. I stood center stage looking like Marlon Brando in Streetcar Named Desire where Stella rips his shirt and he stands there bare-chested. As I sheepishly backed out of the lights the audience was delighted at the comedy but Sherry had turned scarlet and Helen Gallagher wasn't too happy trying to follow that act!

The revised version of Hazel Flagg lasted ten weeks. A show that fails is akin to a death in the family. On Saturday night the curtain came down for the last time, the cast and crew shared a last glass of champagne together, someone turned out the lights and it was all over.

I spent the weeks and months that followed making the rounds. I auditioned for everything listed in the actor's bible, a rather pulpy weekly called Leo Schull's *Showbusiness*. I attended classes religiously. I joined other actors in deep philosophical discussions until the wee small hours of the morning at Downey's or the Footlight Bar. The building where I rented a sixth floor walkup flat on Sixty-first Street (now part of Lincoln Center) was a beehive of talented young people who dotted the Broadway scene. Yuki Shimoda was a ballet teacher who was currently appearing on Broadway as the Japanese houseboy in *Auntie Mame* with Rosalind Russell. Alan Case was playing the male lead in *Damn Yankees* and his roommate, Jimmy Thompson, was in the chorus. Jimmy had been the lead dancer with the Hollywood Bowl Ballet Company and was under contract to MGM when I was on the payroll for *Lovely to Look At*. Julie Mosser was in the chorus of *West Side Story*. And there were actors doing off-Broadway and appearing in plays in cellars and churches and tenement centers and wherever they could hang a curtain and set up a few lights. And to me, they were all stars! They were all talented young people who could dance or sing or act with the best of them, if and when someone gave them that one big chance. I remember Marlon Brando once said, "The greatest talent on Broadway is walking the streets undiscovered." Amen, Marlon.

After a few months, my savings were gone and I took any kind of job to stay alive and pay the rent. On weekends I worked in a printing plant melting down lead type and pouring the molten lead into iron molds to make pigs to be used to make lead type that was later melted down, etc. etc. I did some "life" modeling at the Art Student's League on Fifty-seventh Street and I made collections from nightclub concessions after closing for a big shot "business man" by the name of Abe Ellis. When work was scarce we learned how to live on air but we paid cash for our lessons and we rehearsed and we learned.

After waiting for a number of months, I got a call to audition for Liam Dunn who was the casting director for CBS. Each actor had to come prepared with a scene and a partner. I forget what scene I did or who my partner was but in those days I probably had no less than twenty scenes in my repertoire, from Shakespeare to Miller. I could do soliloquies from most of Shakespeare's plays and numerous contemporary plays. I was a walking memory bank. I would recite monologues aloud walking down Broadway going from one office to another. And I was not alone. Sometimes I would be walking along and come to the end of a monologue and someone behind me would pick up the cue and throw me the next line. The city was alive with actors fired up and looking for that one big chance.

A week after my audition at CBS I got a call to come in for a reading. No, it was more than a call; it was...a callback! A callback is a thing between an audition and the job. It separates one actor from all the other actors and narrows the field down to a selected few. And from that few will be chosen that one person who is to get the part. What a magnificent process, almost like...like...pulling a number out of a hat! At CBS I was to read for the lead heavy, Kleeto, the electric man, on the Saturday morning live children's show, *Rod Brown of the Rocket Rangers*. I didn't care that it was a piece of network crap; to me it was Hamlet. It was my big chance to show the whole world what I could do...just so long as the whole world's mentality was between the ages of six and ten and was awake and watching Rod Brown on Saturday morning at eight o'clock. Needless to say, I got the role.

It is a very exciting experience to work for a big company like CBS or any of the majors where they can afford to pay for you to come into the wardrobe department and they design a costume just for you. God, the importance of it all. They built a silver-cloth outfit for me that could have been made of cardboard because the show was transmitted in black and white, so who knew from silver anything? My boots were silver and my helmet was silver. I was a vision of silver loveliness that got his power from huge electric eels that were kept in a large tank in my laboratory. I had to be careful to hit my mark because they superimposed a tank of eels over a blank space on the wall. If I was just off by a few inches...my head would be photographed inside the tank with all those disgusting eels. I never did find out who moved that tape mark on the floor. As I glanced past the camera, I could see arms madly waving at me to move to one side of the tank or the other. Another minor disaster in my career. Unfortunately, I didn't get a second chance on Rod Brown of the Rocket Rangers.

It's hard to believe that Cliff Robertson got his start as Rod Brown. There is hope for us all.

* * *

I don't know exactly when I became aware of it or what precipitated it, but in my twenty-fifth year I had a compulsion to return to school to get an education. I had attended Los Angeles City College for a few months while on the Coast, but I soon dropped out when work got too demanding. I made application and was accepted into NYU at the Washington Square Campus in Greenwich Village. This was like a precious jewel set in a bed of rocks. Washington Square was a student's delight. Between classes, one could sit on a park bench to study amidst the sounds of children playing in a sand pit a few yards away, and nannies pushing their wards through the tranquil setting. I enrolled as a full time student in the English Department with the goal of receiving a teaching credential. I figured it would be a good backup for my acting career. I found it difficult to turn down that first call for an interview because it might interfere with one of my classes but I managed to do it. I felt as if I was being tested. Sometimes, late at night, when I was studying, I longed for the life of the gypsy, those endless interviews, and the anxiety that comes after an audition when one awaits the outcome. I guess I was addicted.

I soon learned that I could use my fencing skills by trying out for the fencing team. Hugo Costello was the coach and I learned much from his expertise. But as fate would have it, also on that fencing team was a beautiful, exotic "princess" by the name of Phyllis. She and I became romantically involved, much to the disdain of her father who looked upon me as a loser, a person without a future, definitely unfit for the likes of his daughter. "An actor? You call that a job? He's a bum." He did everything in his power to discourage Phyllis from getting involved with me, but we were young and in love. Not even parental intervention could keep us apart. Phyllis had been brought up in a household immersed in culture; music, dance, fine art. She would bring records of David Oistrach to my small uptown apartment, where we would make love to the sweet sounds of his violin caressing the notes of some complex composition set down by one of the great masters; Beethoven, Bach, Brahms. I was infused with an appreciation of classical music, of which I had heretofore been impervious. I became a classical music snob.

I was a good student. I had discipline when it came to studying for long hours. Whenever possible, Phyllis and I would enroll in the same classes so we could study together. And between long hours of study, we would take time to make passionate and tender love.

Through the Human Resources Department at the University, I found a job at the New York Times, working in the morgue. It was here that every day, every article that appeared in the paper had to be cut out and filed in cabinet folders to be used as background material for current topics being worked on by the news writing team. There were acres of filing cabinets and each article had to be meticulously cut out of the paper, stapled together and filed, most often under more than one heading. It was tedious work from eight at night until three in the morning. But if I managed to finish early, I could use the time to study. Some nights, Phyllis would come to the office and we would study together late into the night. My grades in school were exceptional; mostly A's with very few B's.

Phyllis and I had managed to maintain our loving relationship over a period of two years bonded by our common interests. And through this entire period, I was never invited into her home to meet her parents. Daddy was a manufacturer of a very fine line of women's dresses and business must have been good because it was during this period that he moved the family from a flat in the upper Bronx to a luxurious apartment at Number Two Fifth Avenue, right on the corner of Washington Square. But there appears to come a time in every young girl's life when romance must take a backseat to reality. Phyllis had to make a choice between continuing our romantic relationship or spending the coming summer in Europe, all expenses paid by Daddy. When the devil rears his head, he do wear much finery!

I guess one could say that I am pretty consistent. When Phyllis departed, my heart was broken. My grades in school plummeted, I was dropped from the fencing team and I received several warnings at work that my performance was less than adequate. Thankfully, suicide was not an option since I had unsuccessfully given that a try back in Hollywood. I was once again plummeted into the lower depths of my life.

Inadvertently, it was my mother who came to my rescue. We had patched up our differences upon my return to New York and we visited weekly. On a yearly basis, usually in the spring, Katherine would weed out clothing and furniture that she would advertise for sale in the papers. This year it was time to get rid of a very beautiful and very old Steinway piano that had been given to her by her father some years before. She had ceased playing and the mammoth piano took up too much room in her cozy Brooklyn apartment. A gentleman by the name of Peter Lawrence responded to my mother's ad and asked if he could come by to see the piano. At first sight, he had to have it and made an offer that Katherine accepted. In the course of conversation, my mother learned that Peter Lawrence was a Broadway producer who had recently closed his successful run of *Peter Pan*, starring Mary Martin. He was in the process of preparing a new musical with Eartha Kitt and Eddie Bracken, entitled *Shinbone Alley*. It was based on the writings of Don Marquis, about the love affair between a cockroach and an alley cat. Peter didn't have a chance. My mother jumped on the occasion, expounding the virtues of her son and all his talents. A meeting was planned.

When I met Peter, I explained that I would like to work in production and that I was willing to work full time on the show. I could not very well expect to audition as a dancer since it had been two years since I had taken any classes. Peter decided to take me on as an assistant stage manager. We went into production in the fall of 1956. My job was basically to coordinate rehearsals and auditions, run for coffee and take notes for the director when his assistant was busy doing something else. It was a job that required twenty-four hours a day and I was prepared to give it my all. I dropped out of school and said farewell to my co-workers at the Times.

Rehearsals for the show were clouded with one disaster after another. We were scheduled to open on Broadway after a ten-week rehearsal period and without an out-of-town tryout. After the first four weeks, we lost our director who walked out one day in a rage and left a full company of actors, dancers and singers hanging by the seat of our collective pants. A new director, Norman Lloyd, was hired to take over the directorial duties. Somewhere in all this confusion, I was assigned the task as company understudy with an increase in pay, but it proved to be a false blessing. One evening, in a crisis, I had been required to work right through the night and be to the rehearsal studio in the morning to open up and check in the cast. When everything was running smoothly, I found two chairs, put them together and laid down for a much-needed nap. I don't know who reported to Peter that I was sleeping on the job, but I was immediately terminated. It wasn't until some days later that I was able to make my case to Peter who admitted that he acted rashly, but for whatever reason he could not re-hire me as assistant stage manager. But

A Vulcan Odyssey

he did say that I could stay on as company understudy. Some two days prior to opening, one of the singer/actors took ill and had to be rushed to the hospital. I was informed that I would be going on opening night. The role consisted of three whole lines which in no way taxed my talent, but I do remember that during dress rehearsal the musical director stopped the orchestra, looked directly at me and asked if I had been singing. I smiled and confidently assured him that I had indeed been singing with the twenty-five-piece chorus.

"Don't sing!" he ordered and went on with the rehearsal.

So there I was, waiting for my big moment to emote my three lines. I felt like an ass. But I didn't have to feel that way for too long. On opening night, there was a newspaper strike in New York City. We had had no feedback because we hadn't opened out of town where we could have plugged up any loose ends if the show wasn't cooking. We opened on Broadway, cold turkey! One review came out at midnight in a paper that was not affected by the strike. It was glowing! We were all on cloud nine and the champagne flowed like wine. But at two in the morning, all three-television stations reviewed the show...and buried us. The success of the show had only lasted for two hours.

After ten weeks, Peter called the company together to inform us that he was pulling the plug. Another nail in the coffin that was my career. I do believe that I was coming to the reality that show business was not a very stable occupation. Unfortunately, I didn't have time to mourn the passing of Shinbone Alley.

Shortly after the show closed, Gramps became deathly ill and was taken to the hospital. During his later years he had suffered no less than ten heart attacks, he had been operated on more times than I could count, but he was always able to beat the grim reaper. So why should this time be any different than the others? As I sat by his bed in the Polyclinic Hospital, he would motion for me to remove the tubes that were causing him pain and discomfort. He was suffering from uremia, a poisoning of the blood caused when the kidneys fail and urine seeps into the bloodstream. In later years, this disease would be rare what with the advent of kidney transplants.

I had no idea how very sick the old man actually was and like the boy who cried wolf, I was sure that in a matter of days he would get up from his bed and laughingly walk out of the hospital. One evening I had stayed by his bedside until late when his day nurse, who was just about to go off duty, came by for a last minute check. We got into a conversation and I offered to buy her a cup of coffee. She accepted. She was a lovely, tall, blond Scandinavian type who took me home to her bed and gave me comfort during my ordeal. One could say that she went far beyond her sacred duty as a nurse.

Early the following morning I returned to the hospital. Gramps was not in his bed! I was absolutely convinced that he had gotten up under his own power and gone back to his room at the Seville Hotel. Even as I made my way uptown to the Westside Funeral Parlor I was sure that there was some terrible mistake that would soon be rectified.

As the few friends and relatives left the graveside, I lingered to look down at the coffin in the ground. A woman mourner, whom I had never seen before, came over and gently placed her hand on my arm. "It's bad luck," she said, trying to console me.

I looked her in the eye. "Piss off!" I said.

I went back to my apartment and sat for hours pondering the life I had known with Gramps. Who was there now to save my ass? My last thought was that I never did get the name of that nurse.

CHAPTER FIVE
RETURN TO ROME

New York without Gramps would never be the same. Throughout my life I have often been accused of being impetuous, of acting without considering the consequences of my actions. I've always chalked it up to my Hungarian blood, but in truth, it just might be that I am playing the game of life with only half a deck. Case in point:

In his will Gramps had bequeathed me three thousand dollars. I booked passage to Naples on the S.S. Italia departing New York the first week in February 1958. I felt that something was drawing me back to Italy. I sold off my furniture and transferred the lease to the apartment back to the owners. It wasn't easy to give up a fifty-dollar a month apartment in midtown Manhattan; quite a bargain even in those days. I stored some personal effects with my mother in Brooklyn and the rest of my stuff I dumped on my dad. I was planning on traveling light; as light as one could travel with a six months old German Shepard puppy that my mother had bought for me.

The killer dog SHAH as we were ready to embark for Europe 1958

I was to learn much from traveling with my dog, Shah. I discovered that sometimes we humans fail to examine our motives when we expose our pets to our follies. Dragging that puppy with me half way around the world was probably the cruelest thing I could have ever done. It cost a small fortune for transportation and puppy food was not readily available in any of the countries in which we traveled. Whatever food I was able to find for him was lacking in nutrients needed by a growing dog. But my ego dictated that Shah was mine and that I loved him and there was no way I could think of leaving him behind. Bad, bad, bad.

We weren't a day out of New York when I was stricken with terminal seasickness. I shared a cabin with three other men in the bowels of the ship while Shah was berthed in first class, the only class that had a kennel. For two days I tried to hold back the bile in my stomach that was threatening my throat. I finally succumbed and after throwing up the lining of my stomach, I felt great. It was late into the second day at sea when I joined most of the passengers in the main salon for dancing and entertainment. I was almost immediately smitten at the sight of this gorgeous, voluptuous blond girl standing off to the side of the salon. I finally mustered up the courage to ask her for a dance and for the next hour, I talked incessantly about everything under the sun giving her time to only respond with a timid "yes" or "no." And when I finally slowed down to take a breath, the grave reality finally hit my brain; the lady in my arms did not understand a word of English! But we talked into the wee hours of the morning without being hampered by language. What a beautiful experience!

One of the men who shared my cabin was an Italian who spoke both English and French. Mario was to become my personal translator for the duration of the voyage. The young lady, whose name was Lydia, had been spending the previous year with her brother and his family in Quebec, Canada. She was an artist, a sculptor and a violinist who had performed as a soloist with the Toronto Symphony Orchestra. She was returning to her home in Geneva, Switzerland.

I took Lydia up to first class to meet Shah and it was love at first sight for both of them. Shah could not contain himself as he tried to climb all over her, licking her face and rolling over on his back in ecstasy while whining like a spoiled infant. We spent most of our days up in first class where we were given permission to visit Shah. I purchased a dictionary at the ship's store and took a crash course in French and she used the converse side of the dictionary to learn English. We brutalized each other's native languages and spent most of the time laughing at our ineptitude. And finally, when words failed us, we kissed...and touched. Sometimes Mario played Cupid by keeping the other two occupants of our room busy while Lydia and I made love with the chain on the cabin door. I was falling head over heels in love with this magnificent woman and one day out of Naples, we approached the Captain and had him marry us at sea. It was beautiful. Mario served as best man and as the Captain performed the service in Italian, Mario translated in both English and French. Lydia and I had no idea what we were doing or where we were going with this critical act in our young lives but we were young and very much in lust.

The ship arrived late at night in Naples. There was a light mist over the city as Lydia, Shah and I stood curbside waiting for a taxi. I had not made hotel reservations so our first priority was to find a room. The taxi driver was most helpful driving us though the city and he soon dropped us off in front of a small pension after charging me the equivalent of some thirty dollars. We later learned that the *pensione* was a mere three blocks from the pier. There was no heat in our room and what with the marble floors there was no way that Shah was not going to share our bed. After Lydia and I had settled snuggly under the covers, Shah took a flying leap onto the bed, which collapsed with the weight of the three of us, and in a fit of laughter, we finally fell asleep.

The following morning we were on a mission. In going through Lydia's possessions I found a small cloth bag filled with Canadian and United States coins. Had Lydia changed them in New York she would have probably gotten the equivalent of one hundred dollars. But from a moneychanger in Naples, we finally had to accept ten dollars. I was livid and she was crestfallen but as the day wore on we managed to laugh over the coin incident. Our second task was to find a kennel for Shah until we could figure out what we were going to do.

My original plan was to spend a week in Rome and then get in touch with a man I had met at the Cherry Lawn School in Darien, Connecticut, where my half-sister, Ada Joan, had been enrolled. Larry Frisch claimed to be a film producer who was preparing a film to be shot in Israel. "If you're ever in the neighborhood," he joked, "give me a call. I'm sure I can find a role for you." I was so naïve. But what the hell; it was worth the price of a phone call from Italy to Israel. So once we got Shah settled in what appeared to be a very clean kennel, we proceeded to take a train on to Rome.

The trip from Naples through the Italian countryside was a trip back in time. Our eyes were bombarded with the glory and history of ancient Italy. We were like children, running from one side of the train to the other to see, first some ancient artifact and then some remnant of the recent war. The two hour trip to Rome was over before it began.

We managed to find the street on which I had lived as a child but it held no memories for me. I didn't recognize any landmarks and it was as if I had never been there. Halfway up the street was a sign, Pensione Roman Holiday, so we rang the bell and entered a charming courtyard, only to be greeted by an English-speaking proprietor. He showed us to a rather large room with a view of the street and at a very reasonable price. It was actually a lover's dream. It was early March and the rains were constant but Lydia and I were determined to see every bit of Rome before we moved on to our next destination. We walked in the rain for hours at a time discovering small, picturesque side streets emptying into piazzas that held the most beautiful works of sculptured art that spoke of the history of Rome. On one occasion, we found ourselves in front of The American Bar. It was a landmark for tourists from the States and as we entered, the English language could be heard. It was like coming home. Well, it was for me, not for Lydia. As we ordered our drinks, one of the patrons sitting next to us leaned over our way.

"You Americans?" he asked.

"I am. My wife here is from Geneva," I replied.

"Tourists?"

I laughed. "I'm not sure. We're on our honeymoon and then who knows? If we stay in Rome I'm going to have to find some kind of work."

He held out his hand. "Mike Billingsly," he said with a great smile. "I've been living here for six years and I love every minute of it. Have you found a place to stay?" he inquired.

I mentioned the Roman Holiday and he assured me that it was a good choice.

"What kind of work do you do?"

"I was an actor and stunt person in Los Angeles for a few years and I worked as a dancer on Broadway, but I'd consider any kind of work if we could stay on here for a while."

"Have you ever done any dubbing?" he asked.

I had heard of it but I'd never done it. It's a process where actors fit their voices to match the actors on the screen, thereby transforming the original language into the target language. If the film was shot, say in Italian, and it was to be released in an English-speaking country, the dubbing company would hire actors to lip-synchronize the English over the Italian. It was a technical process that was prevalent in most European countries but rarely done in the U.S.

"I work for a company called CDC and they're always looking for people with acting skills to dub down films into English." He handed me his card. Again Lady Luck had intervened. "Give me a call and I'll set up an appointment for you to meet the woman in charge. She's an Italian lady and as volatile a woman as you'll ever meet, but you'll love her..."

A couple of days later, after Lydia and I had walked our feet down to the bones, I decided to give Mike a call. He made an appointment for me to meet him at CDC over by the Piazza del Popolo. Lydia came with me and we met up with Mike who introduced me to Annalena Limentani, the head of production. She was a fiery redheaded lady who could scream equally in Italian and English. But she was very patient with me as I tried to synchronize the line on the page with what I was seeing on the screen. It took quite a few takes before I caught on but once I got the knack of it, I was a natural. During that first session I managed to pick up a hundred dollars and was invited back to work the following three days. Good fortune was with me because I was aware that my funds were fast diminishing and I dreaded having to write to my dad again for help. If this dubbing thing was viable, it would be hard for me to drag myself away from Rome. With my newfound wealth, I took Lydia on a shopping spree to the Mercato Nero, a huge outdoor marketplace, where it seemed that everyone in Rome shopped on Sunday mornings. The Americans we met at the dubbing sessions were *molto simpatico* and invited us into their homes to dine with them in Italian fashion.

The following week Mike Billingsly called me to see if I would like to work on the new Hercules film. When I arrived at the studio I learned that Annalena had been taken to the hospital the previous day with a serious illness. I had only met her the few times I had worked for her but I felt very upset at her misfortune.

We worked for a week on the Hercules film. The evening I finished work, Lydia informed me that she had spoken to her parents in Geneva and it was time for her to return home for a visit. I didn't want to let her go. Everything was perfect and I dreaded the thought that it might change. The idea of me staying in Rome while she ventured to Switzerland was unsettling to me; what guarantee did I have that I would ever see her again? I grew sullen as the time for her departure drew near. I took her to the train station, kissed her tenderly goodbye and as her train pulled away from the platform, I fought back the tears. Men don't cry, I reminded myself. As I walked back to the Roman Holiday, the brusque winter weather no longer held its charm for me. I was cold to the bone and the dampness of the drizzle was suddenly uncomfortable and unfriendly. In less than an hour after her departure, I was lonely and missed her terribly.

As I passed by the American Express office in the *Piazza di Spagna*, I decided to place a call to Larry Frisch in Tel Aviv. Fortunately, it was dinnertime and I caught him at home. He was very excited to hear from me. He explained that his plans to make his film were fast materializing and that if I was interested, there was a leading role in the film that was just perfect for me. But as usual, with every positive development, there appeared to me a negative one to go with it. He could not afford to pay my way to Israel; the passage would have to come out of my own pocket. But in a matter of moments I was agreeing to his terms and I assured him that somehow I would get to Israel in plenty of time to begin filming in four weeks. I wrote down all the information I needed and we had a deal. While at the American Express I inquired about passage to Haifa and then and there, I booked my passage aboard the S.S. Israel three weeks ahead. I still would have three weeks in Rome and there was so much to see that I couldn't scratch the surface. True, it would have been much more fun to have explored Rome with Lydia but that would have to wait for another time.

The following day I worked at CDC. At the end of the session I inquired about the state of Annalena's health. I asked for the address of the hospital and decided that I would make a small gesture of thanks for her kindness by taking some flowers to her bedside. After all, I had time to spare. There was no work the following day so I made my way to the hospital where she was deeply medicated from her operation. A nun showed me to Annalena's room when I assured her that I was family and as I entered, the mood was very somber. Annalena was on a respirator and it seemed that there were tubes coming out of her nose and mouth and other places I could not see. An elderly woman dressed all in black sat by her bedside and I assumed this was Annalena's mother so I handed the flowers to her. I tried a few words in Italian but thankfully, a gentleman of middle age touched me on the arm and said that he spoke English. I was taken aback by his presence because he was wearing a *yarmulke*, a small cap worn by Jews, usually when they are at prayer. He seemed out of place because over Annalena's bed was a large cross with the likeness of Jesus looking protectively down on her.

The gentleman was her Uncle Bernardo and he and the other members of the family, some eight in all, had been keeping vigil since her operation for cancer three days before. I was surprised that the hospital let me visit without carefully checking that I was truly family but this was Italy and the year was 1958. I stayed for an hour, talking quietly with Bernardo so as not to disturb the other members of the family. I explained to him that Annalena had shown me a kindness and I was there to pay my respects. And Bernardo must have been aware that I kept staring at his *yarmulke*. He finally explained to me that the Limentani family were Italian Jews that migrated from Russia almost a century before. They had all taken refuge in the church during the war and as thanks for their safety, many of the Limentani family converted to Catholicism. Those present in the room were mostly Jews that had chosen to retain their original faith. So Annalena was Jewish. What a surprise. In my mind, no one exemplified a fiery Italian woman more than Annalena. I had to smile. In a way, we were related.

When I wasn't working for Mike over at CDC, I would go by the hospital, almost on a daily basis, to sit vigil for Annalena. One afternoon, when the family had departed, Annalena opened her eyes. She looked at me wondering who I was and what I was doing there. I touched her hand but there was no response. I called the nurse. Annalena was out of the woods. When I returned the following day, there was a return of color to her face and her hair had been attended to. I could tell that she was trying to place me but her mind was still clouded from her medication and she made no sign that she really recognized me. But on the forth day after her awakening, when I entered her room I could tell that she knew who I was. I spoke to her in a whisper. I told her that I was leaving the following day to do a film in Israel and her eyes lit up. She smiled as I bid her goodbye. I bent down and gently kissed her forehead. Who knew if I would ever see Annalena Limentani again?

* * *

This time I did not hold back the tears. I cried like a baby as Shah tried to climb all over me. Had it been almost a month since I had abandoned him? And he looked terrible. He was all bloated from a diet of pasta and his fur was rough and unkempt. The owner of the kennel presented me with a bill that could have choked a horse and although I was angry as hell, I chalked it up to just another screwing in Naples. I would get Shah back to health starting the minute we got aboard the ship to Israel.

CHAPTER SIX
THE HOLY LAND

The voyage from Naples to Haifa was uneventful but as soon as I boarded the ship, I did notice a definite hostility towards me from both the passengers and the crew. Admittedly, my personality has sometimes been alluded to as being abrasive but that usually comes only after knowing me. Here I was, a total stranger with one foot in Naples and the other on board the ship and I was suddenly overwhelmed with rudeness. I soon learned that it had to do with Shah.

Many Jews had last seen the likes of Shah staring out from behind barbed wire in the concentration camps. He was barely seven months old but I noticed grown people cringing from him when he pulled on his leash in their direction. Who was the great philosopher who said, "Vee are too late shmart und too zoon dead!" I was very late smart!

If ever one plans to travel to Israel I strongly recommend that they do so by ship and arrive in Haifa. It is a memorable experience. While still beyond sight of land, I stood at the rail and I could see a golden light above the water. As the ship drew closer to shore I could discern that the golden light was coming from the dome of the beautiful Bahai Temple situated high up on Mount Carmel. It was late afternoon, the sun was bright and the air was cool and clear. This was my first glimpse of the Holy Land.

After clearing customs, Shah and I caught a late train to Tel Aviv. I damn near had to sit on Shah to keep him from trying to make friends with every hostile traveler in the car. And then, to really make friends, he squatted and dumped about four pounds of pasta on the floor of the new railroad car. That went over real big! I got the distinct impression that Israel was not ready for me or my act.

Immediately upon arriving at the Tel Aviv station, I called Larry Frisch. From the tone of his voice I could tell that he was not very happy to hear from me. He informed me that the film had been pushed back a month and that if I would get in touch with him then...

So there I was, your average run-of-the-mill tourist, alone in Tel Aviv with a ferocious beast that had suddenly acquired a screaming case of diarrhea. It was too late to catch the last train back to Haifa so we caught a *sheroot* (a communal taxi, for which I had to pay full fare for Shah) and we headed north for Kibbutz Hazoraya, located just south of Haifa. Sometime back, when overcome with a moment of lucidity, I had contacted the Jewish Agency and informed them that I might make a trip to Israel and if I did, where could I put up for a while if I were willing to work to pay my way? In defense of the Agency, I forgot to mention that I would be traveling with the killer beast so when I showed up at the Kibbutz office, occupants began to scatter as if the S.S. had just entered. And poor Shah was totally confused; all he wanted to do was make friends and play.

I was immediately informed that we were not welcome at Hazoraya. How was I to know that it was a German community, most of whose inhabitants had been repatriated from Auschwitz and Buchenwald. But fortunately, there was one rational human being that came to our rescue. He appeared to have some voice of authority, apologized for the unfriendly reception, and showed us to a hut where we could bed down. He later came by with a bowl of milk and some leftover bread for Shah. We could stay until I was able to make other plans. I was too emotionally upset and tired to think about what our next move would be; tomorrow would have to take care of itself.

Our reprieve lasted through the week. The only food I could find for Shah was cheese, which I smuggled from the dining room. I had never heard of cheese being a popular diet for dogs but I was sure that it was a damn site better than pasta. I had to get to a phone. I had an address book full of numbers, any one of which could get me out of my predicament. But the work schedule on the farm was from sunup to sundown, six days a week. And on the seventh day, they rested. It was on the day of rest that I learned there would be a gala show in the dining room later that evening. Their idea of a gala show was two singers from Tel Aviv with a flute. But I soon learned that these were not just any singers; they were Ilka and Aviva, part of Israel's modern heritage. Ilka played a reed flute that he had carved by hand and when he sang, his voice was deep and resonant. He was tall and lean, with red hair and a red beard. He walked with a crutch, having lost one leg in the Forty-eight War. Aviva was dark skinned and quite exotic-looking. She had a lovely, piercing voice that complimented Ilka's basso. Aviva was of Yemanite background and he was Russian. Their music was quite unique and the audience was more than appreciative demanding encore after encore. It was quite late when they were finally able to get off the makeshift stage and as they headed for their car amidst the group of well-wishers, I managed to intercept them. I introduced myself and explained that I needed to get a message to someone in Tel Aviv and if they were going there, would they be so kind as to make a call for me. Upon hearing me speak English, Aviva firmly took me by the arm and led me to their chauffeur driven car. Once inside, we were free to talk without interruption. They both had a beautiful command of the English language.

"What are you doing here?" asked Ilka.

I explained about Larry Frisch, my wife Lydia and my dog Shah, all without taking a breath. I had to get it all in before they drove away without a promise to help. But my anxiety was unfounded. They were planning to stay the night in a nearby village and the following evening they would again sing at Hazoraya, after which they would be appearing in a settlement in Nazereth. Although the hour was late, they invited me to join them for a drink at a nearby café with a promise to return me to the Kibbutz. We drove about half an hour to the artist community of Ein Hod where the one café stayed open half the night. Most of the residents of this community were artists that were receiving stipends from the government to perpetuate their work. Most were painters but there were sculptors and writers as well. And in the dim light of the small café, Ilka, Aviva and I shared stories of our backgrounds and we bonded. They took me to their bosoms as if I were a long lost friend and promised that they would help me out of my dilemma. They were both witty and bright and it was easy to understand why they commanded so much attention both in Israel and abroad. They had appeared on numerous occasions in the States and had great success in the folk singer genre that was quite popular in those days.

The following evening, after their performance, Aviva took one of the Kibbutz elders to one side and a few minutes later, she returned with permission to take me along with them to Nazareth. She also arranged for someone to look after Shah while I was gone.

We arrived in Nazareth late at night. The streets were deserted and we were stopped at a roadblock. One of the policemen immediately recognized the celebrities and explained that there had been rioting in the streets all that day by Arab insurgents and the military had declared a curfew. The date was May 14th, 1958, the eve of the tenth anniversary of Israel's War of Independence.

Even in those days, Nazareth had been a thorn in the side of Israel. At that time, Israel's Arab population in and around Nazareth numbered over two hundred thousand. It was an internal hotbed of political unrest among the young militants while the surrounding Arab countries constantly reminded those Arabs who continued to live under Israeli rule that they were traitors to Islam. This was years before anyone outside Israel had ever heard of the PLO or Hezbollah.

What I had observed in Nazareth was quite different from what the Arab population was being fed by their leaders. The city was clean and there was almost no unemployment. Education for Arab children, both boys and girls, was mandatory and social services, such as medical care, were free. On the other side of the coin was the communist contention that the Arab population had no voice or representation in the government. This was true but it was a most unique situation. The Arab population of Nazareth represented more than ten percent of Israel's total population. It was a small country in which ten percent of its people were potential fifth columnists sworn to the violent overthrow of the government by force. The problem had never been equitably resolved which finally led to the rise of Yassir Arafat and the PLO. I do not mean to minimize the plight of the Israeli Arabs but to get a true picture, one must also be a pragmatist. Those in the U.S. who have been the most severe critics of Israel fail to look back at our own history. From the very beginning, we isolated the Native Americans and relegated them to reservations. During the Second World War we isolated over one hundred thousand Japanese and interned them in detention camps "for national security." Today, we look back with shame on the travesties that had been committed. Perhaps history will judge Israel as being too harsh in their handling of the Arab question within her borders. My strong allegiance to Israel and my deepest sympathies with the displaced Arabs during those early years have been emotions that have troubled me for many years. Unfortunately, the situation in Israel has multiplied tenfold and I see very little hope on the horizon for a lasting peace in the Middle East.

A Vulcan Odyssey

Back to the travels of Marco Polo Montaigne...

When we arrived at our hotel, we were greeted by a cordon of reporters eager to fill us in on the day's activities. There had been shootings and stone throwing and the soldiers had made a number of arrests. And there was a consensus of opinion that the following day was going to see a blood bath. One of the reporters was a very close friend of Ilka and Aviva. His name was Francis Omir Offner and he was a reporter for The Christian Science Monitor. As we sat having a drink and listening as Francis reported on some of the events of the day, he kept eyeing the camera that was dangling from around my neck.

"Do you know how to use that thing?" he asked.

"My camera? Sure, I know how to use it." It was a very impressive looking instrument. It was the first model of the Mamayaflex with interchangeable lenses, Japan's answer to the German Rolleiflex. It was a large and bulky camera to be used for anything other than fieldwork but I could anticipate Francis' next question.

"My cameraman couldn't get clearance to get to Nazareth and I need pictures. Do you think you could help me out?"

He didn't have to ask me twice. Ilka and Aviva assured me that they wouldn't leave without me and that they too would like to stay. It was settled. I would meet Francis the following morning at Mary's Well at six and we would go from there. I got very little sleep that night.

I was up and dressed before anyone else in the hotel had stirred. Sometime in the sleepless night I realized that I had only one roll of film! At five thirty in the morning, I managed to find an Arab merchant who owned a camera shop beneath his living quarters. I purchased ten rolls of film which was all he carried in that size. One disadvantage of my camera was that I would have to reload after every twelve shots. I would figure it out, I thought.

The day began with a parade to commemorate the Day of Independence. School children from nearby Kibbutzim marched to the music of a military band. There were marching policemen carrying batons and shields that reminded me of pictures I had seen of Roman gladiators. Then there came the tanks and half-tracks pulling large guns, a show of Israeli military might. The streets were lined with spectators and Francis and I weaved our way in and out of the crowd trying to anticipate any activity that might prove newsworthy. We did not have to wait long.

By ten o'clock the May sun was blinding. Francis and I chose to stay alongside a company of marching policemen. If trouble was to break out it would surely come in the form of reprisal against the hated Moroccan Jews whose number dominated the Israeli police. The company of marching police emerged from the cover of the buildings lining the street and out onto the open highway with no protection on either side. A sloping hill, devoid of any cover, was on the opposite side of the road where we were keeping abreast of the parade. We could see spectators lining the rooftops of the buildings situated on top of the hill. Suddenly, there was a fusillade of rifle fire followed by a hail of rocks and stones raining down on us. The policemen used their shields as protection against the flying missiles but they were as vulnerable as we were to the raining bullets. Francis and I both hit the ground as the police disbursed in every which direction. Francis began yelling orders to me.

"Get a shot of that policeman, the one who's bleeding! Get a shot of that woman who's covering her little boy with her body! Get a shot of those policemen running!" I was suddenly on my feet and running with the advancing police. We ran up an embankment and started up the hill that was devoid of cover. Halfway up the hill it was time to reload. I knelt down and shielding the film from the direct rays of sunlight with the shadow of my body, I reloaded the camera. And as I was performing this necessary task, a barrage of flying rocks forced the police to retreat back down the hill. When I looked up, I was out in front of the police by at least a hundred yards and about the same distance from the Arab position on top of the hill. I was in no-man's land!

A police officer finally realized my dilemma and blew his whistle so his men would not fire. On top of the hill, the Arabs could see that I was only a photographer as I raised the camera and held it high above my head. There was a sudden cessation of hostility. As I looked down the hill, the police officer was frantically waving for me to come back down. I looked up the hill and the Arabs were waving for me to come up to their position. The choice was clear; I ran up the hill as fast I could to join the Arabs. No sooner had I taken cover than the bullets and rocks resumed. A young Arab, not more than twenty years old, came running over to me. He seemed to be the leader of the rock-throwers who were mostly children of school age. He spoke to me in Arabic. Then he tried Hebrew. I shook my head.

"English," I said.

"Ah, you are Englishman." He was most pleased.

"No, American." That was the key. He produced a great smile and yelled to his friends that I was an American.

"You come with me, please."

I followed him up into the Arab Quarter, through a maze of streets and out into a small plaza. I was surprised to see that not all the populace was involved in the hostilities below. Here, people were relaxing in the shade of a café, enjoying their morning coffee. We came upon a small group of men who appeared to be engrossed in a very serious discussion. As we arrived, the young man called out to the group explaining what had happened and how I happened to be on the hill.

One of the men stood up. "I am Habib," he said. We shook hands. He was short and dark with a two-day growth of beard. "Who are you and what do you want?"

I explained my situation and as soon as I mentioned the name of Francis Offner, a big smile came over his face.

"How is my good friend Francis?" he asked. For the next two hours I sat in that café and listened to the grievances of the Arabs against the Israelis. I asked questions of the communist leader and he answered quite intelligently without the fanatical yelling I had observed on the hill. Then, Habib and his friends posed for me while I burned up film getting as many pictures as I could. In all the time I spent with that group, no one bothered to ask me what were my political convictions or if I was a Jew. They were only concerned with telling their story to someone on the outside that would tell the world of their plight. When we finally said our goodbyes it was early afternoon. The young man guided me back down the hill. There was no sign that only two hours before the Arabs and Jews were embroiled in a skirmish. I found my way back to the hotel. The greeting was anything but cordial. I explained to the group that there was really no way I could make contact. But Aviva was downright angry and Ilka was his usual philosophical self. The three of them had checked the police station and the hospital fearing that I had been hurt in the fracas. But when I told them where I had been and that Habib sent his regards to Francis, all was forgiven. I turned over all the exposed film to Francis and he took copious notes and asked questions as I tried to recreate the text of my conversation with the communist leader.

The following day, the story and some of the photographs appeared in the Monitor and there was a special caption; "Photos by..." with my name. I was hoping that Francis would ask me to work with him again but after receiving a check for my work and a short note of thanks, I never heard from him again.

Aviva had decided that I was to return with them to their home in Natanya, a beautiful seaside community just north of Tel Aviv. Shah was a bit of a problem because they had two small children, one still a toddler, and even to two world travelers like them, Shah was as large a dog as they had seen in all of Israel. I promised that I would keep him outside the house and away from the children. We drove back to Hazoraya, collected Shah and my meager belongings, and headed for Natanya. During the drive, Ilka, in his most practical Russian manner, informed me that Larry Frisch had a reputation for more talk than action and suggested that I not raise my hopes too high. I had held off writing to Lydia until I had a firm commitment to do the film. If it didn't materialize I was determined to return to Italy where I was sure I could find work with Mike Billingsly and Annalena. I wondered how she was getting on and if she had fully recovered from her ordeal.

Ilka and Aviva had a modest home (by American standards but quite comfortable by Israeli) and they treated me like a most honored guest. I spent many evenings listening to the two performers working on new songs and making preparations to travel abroad. When they went on the road for two or three days to perform for the troops at some remote outpost or to some Kibbutz at the other end of the country, I remained their guest without question. They had a Yemenite housekeeper, Yona, whose job it was to look after the children and do light housekeeping. She was very pretty and sometimes, late at night, when everyone was down for the night, she would come to me where I was sleeping on the couch, and she would rub my back. No sex. Just a lot of serious back rubbing. She had the greatest hands in the whole world.

A letter from my dad arrived at the American Express office. It appeared that I had a relative living in Tel Aviv. His name was David ben-David and he was my father's first cousin. During the Diaspora prior to the Second World War, he was the only relative that survived the Holocaust. The rest of the family had perished in the camps. The family in the States expressed a desire that I should make contact with this distant branch of the family and see if they were in need and if there was anything the family in America could do to help.

This request from the family both excited me and depressed me at the same time. It was exciting to know that there was indeed a member of the family that survived the war and had found his way to Israel. On the other hand, it was depressing to think that I would have to listen to lots of stories about a lot of people that I had never known and their ultimate demise at the hands of the Germans. It was not a meeting I looked forward to with great anticipation. On the other hand, Aviva was a great romantic and she immediately took charge. The ben-David family was not listed in the phone directory, which meant that we would just barge in without letting them know that I was coming. Barging in was an Israeli custom since most of the population could not afford phones so people got into the habit of just "visiting."

Aviva and I drove to the ben-David apartment on Rehov bin-Nunn in the North of the city. I had no idea what to expect or how to act. I was truly out of my element as an ambassador of the family from the United States. But Aviva charged right ahead. She was beaming as she dragged me up the three flights of stairs and knocked on the door.

A woman with very thick glasses and wearing a simple housedress came to the door. Since the stairwell was enclosed, one pushed a button on the ground floor to turn on the lights and a few moments later, the lights went out leaving the visitor in the dark. Therefore, it was perfectly natural for the person living in the apartment to invite a caller in or he would be left standing in the dark. The flat was very simple and we were invited into the living room that was decorated with the barest of furnishings. A simple table with four chairs stood near the doorway leading to the kitchen. Against one wall was a sideboard upon which stood a menorah and two photographs, one of a young man and the other of a teenage girl. Across the room was a door that led out onto a patio and against the other wall was a couch that spelled double bed by night.

Aviva handled the introduction with the utmost tact. They spoke in Hebrew and I could only surmise what was being said. But as I watched the woman's face I could tell that Aviva was getting close to the punch line. Suddenly, the woman put down her glass of tea, sprang to her feet and was kissing the top of my head and squeezing me to her bosom as I sat at the table. She began to cry and Aviva began to cry and I began to cry. It was a very happy event. Her name was Tsipora (which translates to "bird" in English") and she was a stocky woman with a face that was lined with hardship and a tough way of life. Through Aviva she was able to relate to me the story of her escape from Europe with ben-David, one step ahead of the Nazis, and their clandestine entry into what was then Palestine. She mentioned, only in passing, that she and ben-David were the only known survivors of the entire family. I was quite relieved that she did not go into great detail about the demise of each and every member of the family that perished. I know this may sound callous but from the time I sailed from Europe and through the weeks I had been in Israel, I had been inundated with stories of atrocities during the war years. There was nothing I could hear that would shed new light on the subject and I could not offer any solace to the survivors.

It was almost time to leave when the young girl from the photo on the sideboard entered the apartment. She was eleven and immediately recognized Aviva but she was apparently confused to see such a celebrity in her home. When I was introduced as her cousin, she threw herself onto my lap and covered me with kisses. More tears. Her name was Bracha and in broken, schoolroom English she expressed how happy she was that I had come to visit. And finally, when Aviva announced that we had to leave, Tsipora protested by saying that we had to wait for ben-David to get home from work. She and Bracha were most convincing and extracted from Aviva a promise that we would return the following day.

On the way home to Natanya, Aviva could sense my discomfort. "You didn't care for them?" she asked. "We don't have to go back tomorrow. They will understand."

"Of course I like them. What's not to like? I just have this overwhelming sense of guilt for being alive."

Aviva took a moment to digest this. "But that is what Israel is composed of...guilt. We, the survivors, feel guilty because we did not perish. And we feel guilty that we have to ask other countries for help in order to survive. And we feel guilty because we cannot reach our neighbors and that many of our sons will die in wars not yet fought. Guilt is a common emotion among Jews. You will learn to deal with it...or you will not."

The following day we returned to the flat on bin-Nunn to meet the family patriarch. There was no doubt for a moment that he was a

Montaigne. His face was gaunt and his eyes were hazel and wide and he had cheekbones that pressed against the skin and his cheeks were hallowed. He could have been my father's brother, so strong was the resemblance. David ben-David greeted me with a kiss on both cheeks and Tsipora poured tea and opened a tin of homemade cakes and cookies. A few moments after our arrival, Dov, the twenty-year-old son of David and Tsipora, bounded up the stairs to meet his cousin from America. He was a clean-cut looking *sabra* (native born Israeli) who had chosen a life in the Kibbutz rather than follow his parent's choice of life in the city. I admired his dedication.

Life was not only hard in the Holy Land but also very expensive. Pay was way below the level to afford the most basic conveniences of life. Ben-David held down two jobs in order that his wife could remain at home and raise the children. By day, ben-David worked as a white collars worker for some government agency while at night he labored over a sewing machine as an independent contractor at home. Their rent was next to nil because as an immigrant to Israel he was entitled, under the law, to a modest dwelling for himself and his family. He would someday own this flat on Rehov bin-Nunn. David was not a healthy looking man; his skin had a pallor of a man who had never known exercise or practiced healthful habits. He was a worker. Dov, on the other hand, had the ruddy complexion of one who worked out in the open and enjoyed being close to the land. He was typical of what the early Jewish Zionists had demanded and perceived of Israeli youth. I learned that Dov was already something of a hero, having thwarted an attack by a group of Arab infiltrators into his Kibbutz, La Hav, on the Jordanian border. Dov had killed all three terrorists before they could accomplish their mission. But he was very reluctant to speak of such events; his sister bragged openly about her brother's exploits.

Aviva explained that we had to be leaving but David explained that they wished for me to come and stay with them in their home. But where would I sleep? Bracha could sleep with them and I could have her bed in the bedroom. Tsipora and David shared the couch in the living room. It was a thoughtful gesture that I gratefully declined but they insisted that I think about it. After all, there was Shah to consider and, eventually, Lydia would be arriving if the Larry Frisch film ever came to fruition.

That evening, Ilka and Aviva suggested that I might consider ben-David's offer to stay with the family in Tel Aviv. My singing friends would be off to America for a month of engagements, the car would be put into the shop for much-needed repairs and the bus into the city was not the most reliable mode of transportation. If I stayed with the family I would be in the city and close to entertainment and nightlife that I sorely missed. In truth, I had seen very little of Israel other than my experience in Nazareth. So the following day I returned to the home of ben-David to work out the details for my coming to live with them. A couple of days later, Shah and I moved into the flat on Rehov bin-Nunn.

As agreed, I got the bed, Shah got the balcony and although they refused any reimbursement, I explained that I could not, under any circumstances, accept their hospitality without contributing to the household. In that I got my way.

The next two weeks proved to be most hectic. I got in touch with Larry Frisch to inform him that I had moved into the city and I gave him my change of address. He was now much more cordial and informed me that without a doubt we would begin shooting in two weeks. The contracts were already drawn up and I could come by the studio and sign them at any time. That afternoon I made my way to Geva Studio by bus. If you have never traveled in a foreign country by public transportation and without the knowledge of the language, you haven't lived. Everyone on the bus who knew two words of English offered to help get me to my destination. But no two people gave the same directions. It finally boiled down to accepting the directions from that person whose face looked most trustworthy; usually a pretty young woman. That proved wrong. I spent an hour in the hot sun sitting at a bus stop waiting for a bus that had long since been discontinued. I arrived at the studio late in the afternoon and Larry gave me the grand tour. It wasn't what I had expected. It was one building in which there was a small sound stage and half a dozen offices, a product of German repatriation. Most of the equipment had yet to be plugged in to see if it functioned. In many cases, the operations manuals had been lost or misplaced and no one had the foggiest idea for what the machines were intended. The production staff was busy doing all sorts of tests with the camera and film in order to make certain that there would be no foul-ups once the actors and crew got on location.

A Vulcan Odyssey

My contract for the entire film was a laugh. I was to be paid two thousand dollars for my total participation in the film *Pillar of Fire*. The length of shooting was vague but Larry gave me his word that it would be probably three, perhaps four weeks at the most. I signed on the dotted line.

A few days later a young actor living in the same building with the ben-David family came by to see if I would like to spend the day at the public pool. It was a local hangout for many of the performers from the local theatres and there was a good chance I would get to meet some of the actors with whom I would be working on the film. So off we went to the *bat-yam* (swimming pool. You may not like the book but you're learning Hebrew!)

I am my father's son in one special way; I know of no one who worshipped the sun like my dad. Some of my earliest memories of my father were of him playing handball at Coney Island or in the park, stripped down to the waist with his skin tanned to the color of bronze. And whenever the opportunity arose, I could not resist taking off my shirt and letting the sun do its bronzing on my body. I always felt good when I had a tan. But let me say that my father never exposed his body to the Israeli sun!

I sat around the pool in my shorts for the better part of the morning, meeting all sorts of interesting actors and artists and discussing differences between theatre in Israel and the United States. After lunch, I lay down on my towel and took a short nap for a couple of hours. Around four o'clock, my actor friend suggested that we head on home saying that he thought I had taken a bit too much sun. But I felt great and although I knew I had gotten a bit red, I was not prepared for sun poisoning!

That night my skin began to blister and I experienced excruciating pain in my back, chest and legs. Before the night was over, David had to fetch a doctor for me. I was burning up with fever. And of course, my first thought was whether or not I would be well enough to begin work on the film in less than two weeks. The doctor brought a jar of gooey stuff and a number of applicators and gave Tsipora and Bracha instructions on how to medicate my burns. He gave me a shot to bring down the fever and wrote a prescription for pills that would prevent infection. My face was swollen so badly that I could not see and my lips were a mass of blisters. I was one hell-of-a sight. Poor Shah was confined to the terrace because I was in no condition to share my bed with him.

I lay there for the next couple of days with nothing on; even the sheet inflicted pain. Whenever there came a knock at the door, I covered myself just enough so Tsipora or Bracha could medicate me. The heat in that apartment was almost unbearable. There was no air conditioning and we were having a very early summer. On the second or third day I managed to get up out of bed and have a bit of tea at the table. During my absence from bed, Tsipora had decided to store some winter clothes in a metal container that fit under the bed. She generously salted the clothes with raw camphor and shoved the container back under the bed. That night, the fumes from the camphor under the bed poisoned me and with the cramps in my stomach I could not straighten my legs. There I was with my knees up around my ears and blisters popping all over my body. I looked like a victim of a blow torch incident with the doctor standing over me and inquiring if by any chance I had taken God's name in vain. Under the circumstances, his levity went way over my head.

The fact that the picture had to be pushed back another week to accommodate Michael Shilo who was playing the Israeli lead, did not hurt my healing process one little bit. Michael was appearing in a show in Tel Aviv and it would be impossible for him to commute from the Negev locations to the theatre in Tel Aviv each evening. My burns were ugly but nicely on the mend. If I could survive my bout with the camphor, I philosophized that I was not meant to die in the Holy Land.

While confined to my sickbed, I had plenty of time to think about Lydia. We had been separated for over two months. I had written to her a number of times explaining my tentative plans but after signing the contract with Frisch, I wrote for her to come ahead to Israel and I arranged a one-way ticket for her passage. Her reply contained both good and bad news. Yes, she would come but not before another month. She had been commissioned to do a sculpture in Geneva and could not possibly finish the job before that time. I had my doubts that I would ever see her again. I began to think that she was a mere figment of my imagination, someone I had conjured up in my dreams.

* * *

I was still peeling dead skin from my legs and chest when the production sent over the script and a note telling me that I would be picked up at my door the coming Saturday evening, after sundown, for the trip to Beersheba. I could not drag Shah down to the desert but Ben-David came up with a solution. He knew a man who worked at the slaughterhouse in North Tel Aviv, just a few blocks from the apartment. If he would take Shah for a while, I could be sure that he got plenty of good red meat. We went around to meet him. I was not too pleased with the arrangement. The man was not very sympathetic towards animals (how could he be working in a slaughterhouse?) and I would have to pay him to care for Shah. But the entire compound was enclosed with a fence and Shah could have the run of the facility. I had no choice. Ben-David had offered to keep Shah on the terrace and Bracha had promised to take him out each day for a run, but I could no longer impose on the family. Again, I had to play the familiar scene of saying goodbye to Shah. The poor animal still loved me in spite of all the abuse I heaped upon him.

The trip to Beersheba took place at night so I did not get a chance to see any of the sights along the way. There were eight of us in the sedan and we had an opportunity to get acquainted along the way. I managed to nap the latter part of the trip and when I was awakened and informed that we would be stopping for a late snack, I was excited to get a look at the frontier town of Beersheba. I had not been prepared for the culture shock. As I emerged from the vehicle, I was immediately thrust back into the first century.

The restaurant was an adobe structure the likes of which I had seen in numerous biblical films. Tied up to a hitching post in front of the restaurant were a group of foul-smelling camels. Near the camels was a group of Bedouins squatting in the dirt by the side of the road drinking Turkish coffee. They were dressed in long traditional garb and Arab headgear. On the ground next to each man was a long rifle of very early vintage. Some of the men wore crossed ammunition belts over their shoulders and each man wore an ornate, curved knife in a sash around his waist. My first impression was that DeMille had arrived before us and was shooting a film using dress extras. But this was an honest to God scene from life and it boggled the imagination. As the group went ahead into the restaurant I could not help but linger and stare at the picturesque sight of these desert nomads. One of the actors came to fetch me.

"Will you look at the engraving on the handle of his knife! It's all done by hand," I said admiringly.

"You'd better come along. Everyone's waiting for you…"

But before we could move, the Bedouin with the exquisitely engraved knife addressed me. My companion spoke Arabic. "He asks why you are staring. It's considered quite rude, you know."

"Tell him that I meant no offense but that I was merely admiring his knife."

"I don't think you should..."

"Please, tell him," I insisted. The actor proceeded to translate and within a second, the Bedouin was on his feet and walking towards us. The actor explained to the group that I was an American actor on my way to work in a film being made in the Negev. The group all uttered a long "aaaaah" in unison, somewhat like a Greek chorus. Then, the Bedouin removed the knife from his waist and held it out to me. I got a close up look at the workmanship. It was a silver scabbard and handle all engraved by hand with intricate flowers and designs.

"Beautiful," I said. "Absolutely beautiful." I handed the knife back to the Bedouin but he made no move to retrieve it.

"That's what I was trying to tell you," said the other actor. "He is giving you the knife."

"Does he want me to buy it? Ask him how much."

"I mean that he is giving it to you. It is their custom. If a stranger admires what belongs to a Bedouin, he will give it as a gift. This makes what he has all the more worthwhile."

"But then he no longer has it."

"No matter. His friends will tell the story from campfire to campfire of how he gave his knife to the American actor. Now, why don't you thank him before you admire his clothes."

"Can I pay him for it?"

"That would be an insult."

"And if I refuse to take it?"

"Also an insult."

I thanked the Bedouin in English and my companion repeated it in Arabic and I tried it in Arabic a couple of times as we backed away from the group and entered the restaurant with me clutching my gift in my hot little hand.

"I hope I didn't create a problem," I said to the actor.

"No problem. But someone should have given you a crash course on Arabic etiquette."

I tried to take the edge off the seriousness of what I had done. "Well, at least now I know how you Israelis won the war."

"How's that?" asked the actor.

"You probably all stood up opposite your Arab enemies and yelled out how beautiful were their guns and when the offered them to you as gifts, you took them prisoners."

"Not quite," he smiled.

So what the hell, it was a bad joke.

* * *

Pillar of Fire got off to a shaky start. Although the technicians had been tinkering around with the new equipment for some weeks, they still had not worked out all the bugs. If it wasn't an actor blowing a line it was the film jamming in the camera. This was the first all-Israeli production so actors were not expected to know what they were doing the first time out. But they were all professional theatre performers and after one or two days, they were as comfortable in front of the camera as they had been on stage.

Our shooting days were from sun-up to sun-down with a two hour break at midday because it was just too damn hot to be working outside in the desert. I was still getting over my bout with sun poisoning so by the end of a day's shooting, I was ready to crash. And within a couple of days, most of the cast was down with a popular Israeli malady know as *shulshul*. It is the equivalent of that famous Mexican export, Montezuma's Revenge.

For those of you who are adverse to toilet humor, I suggest that you skip over the next few paragraphs. Since I have had stomach poisoning numerous times in my life, I find very little on the subject about which to laugh. On the other hand, in retrospect, I cannot help but smile at the vision of myself hugging a porcelain bowl as I heaved up my guts. Then, there is that charming vision of me sitting on the throne with my head in the sink and my body being wracked by spasms. If you haven't been there, just think of what you're missing. And of course, worse than the physical discomfort is the embarrassment that comes if one is having one of these seizures in the presence of someone of the opposite sex.

This diabolical Israeli secret weapon hit me just before noon on the second day of shooting. We were about two miles from Kibbutz Revivim and we had no facilities at the shooting site. I could tell that this malady was about to overcome me. I was feeling cold and clammy, I was sweating, and I was having extreme cramps in my lower abdomen. I immediately informed Larry that I needed to get back to the Kibbutz, that I thought I was going to be ill, and that I was sorry, but I could not finish the scene. He reluctantly called for a jeep to run me back to the Kibbutz. I am sure that he thought that I was just looking for a way to get out from under the hundred and ten degree sun.

The "facilities" on a frontier Kibbutz were most primitive. There was no "his" or "hers" with running water. Men and women shared the same facility and one had to take the precaution to lock the door from the inside when occupying a slot.

The "facility" nearest to my quarters was some fifty yards down a path from door to door. It consisted of a large hole in the ground over which was placed a concrete slab with two holes in it. Over the slab a hut was constructed made of corrugated tin. And on top of the hut was a tin roof which guaranteed that during a hot summer's day, no person in their right mind would want to be found dead inside such an oven. Between the two holes in the concrete was a piece of plywood board to separate one side from the other. Visual privacy was respected but two people sharing the same crapper had better be quite intimate.

The jeep dropped me in front of my quarters and mustering all the strength I could, I made a frantic dash down the path towards the john. And there, trotting down the path from the opposite side was this absolutely gorgeous Kibbutznik. We both arrived at our destination at the same time and both avoided eye contact. As I entered from my side, she entered from the other side. Our zippers were in concert. I shall avoid being too graphic as to what ensued next. Needless to say, the embarrassment was overwhelming. I was determined to stay in the foul-smelling prison until I was sure that she had finished and that I heard the door on her side slam shut. But was it possible that she had died on her side and I was suffering in vain? The heat had to be over a hundred and forty degrees and I held a handkerchief over my face to block out the overpowering stench. Still, there was no sound from her side. I watched a ferocious-looking, hairy spider spinning a web over my head. I decided that I could no longer brave the torture. Hiking up my trousers, I burst from the hut at the same moment my partner in misery decided to burst forth from her entombment. There we stood, frozen in time, swathed in sweat, staring into each other's eyes. God, how romantic! What had begun as love at first sight was now reduced to ships that crash in the night. I lowered my head, turned, and headed back up the path from where I had come. God was merciful in his infinite wisdom: I never saw that girl again even though there were only a hundred members in that Kibbutz. I had visions of her volunteering for a suicide mission behind enemy lines to avoid meeting up with me ever again.

In a couple of days, with the help of pills prescribed by the Kibbutz' nurse, I managed to stand up from my bunk, walk to the dining hut and consume some food. The following day I was strong enough to return to work.

Between long, talky scenes were intercut a number of stock shots from newsreel footage of the real war. But the stuff that we had to shoot there on location was all done with "live" ammunition. This was their first film and they could not afford to import a special effects technician from Europe or the States with blank ammo. One of the actors, Uri Zohar, a most clever theatre comedian but a little short on common sense, was intrigued with guns. Many a time I found myself eating desert sand as Uri decided to fire off a number of rounds from his weapon "just for fun." Ricocheting bullets were a greater danger to us than the scorpions and snakes that constantly crawled into anything we might momentarily place on the ground. This was show business at its finest hour. (I haven't a clue what ever possessed him, but Uri later went on to become an orthodox Rabbi!)

Three weeks into filming we got word that *Pillar of Fire* was closing down production, indefinitely! Geva Studio had only one camera in its arsenal. When an outside company was interested in renting the equipment on a paying basis, Geva gave priority to the paying customer. Since Geva was the co-producer on our film, no actual money for the use of the camera changed hands.

"What about me?" I bellowed at Larry as we stood toe to toe. "What about my money?"

"You don't expect me to pay you for work you haven't completed, do you?"

"But it's not my fault you're closing down production. Why should I be penalized?"

"You'll get your money," he said with confidence.

"When?" I demanded.

"As soon as we finish the film."

I was caught up in some Kafkaesque nightmare. "All right, you son-of-a bitch, I'll sue!"

When we got back to town, I contacted an attorney who was less than encouraging. Since this was the first Israeli film, there was no legal precedent on which to base a case. And even if he agreed to represent me, it could take years by which time the film would probably be finished and I'd have my money. The law in Israel offered no more protection than the laws in the United States. I was being screwed in order to keep me from leaving the country. Larry was afraid that I would take the money and split back to Europe. At that moment in time, that is exactly what I was planning to do. Meanwhile, my funds were running extremely low again and in a week, Lydia would be arriving from Europe.

The ben-David family greeted me warmly upon my return. They were terribly disappointed when I informed them that I would be taking my own place. I could not impose on them to house both Lydia and me at the same time. They were living in cramped quarters as it was.

I found a small, furnished flat on the corner of Frischman and Ben Yehuda, right in the heart of Tel Aviv. We would only be one block from Dizengorf which was the main street for restaurants with their outdoor seating especially for people-watching. Café Caseet, which was a popular sidewalk café and a hangout for actors and artists, was spitting distance from my door. I call it a flat but in truth it was merely a room with a toilet and bath facilities. There was no kitchen so we would have to eat all our meals out. There was a small terrace overlooking Ben Yehuda and there was no air conditioning. Since it was on the second floor and located on the corner, we could open all the windows and get a cross breeze…when there was one. And all this for only seventy-five dollars a month. I thought I had discovered a gold mine because in Israel, a popular way to rent a flat was to pay "key money." This could amount to two or three thousand dollars up front for a modest flat but it was refundable at the termination of the lease. In such an instance the rent would have been only a fraction of what I was paying. But I didn't have enough for "key money" and such a contract was usually for a long term. I didn't want to commit to anything that would take me beyond the conclusion of the film. After three months in the Holy Land I saw no future for myself in that country. Although I was managing to pick up a little of the language, it was obvious that I could not master it sufficiently to work in the theatre, the only work for which I felt qualified. So the flat on Frischman and Ben Yehuda, payable from month to month, suited my transient plans perfectly. My only other problem that had to be resolved was what to do about Shah. I could no longer afford to keep paying the man at the slaughterhouse for his keep. I explained this dilemma to ben-David who seemed to have a solution for just about everything. This time was no exception.

Ben-David's son, Dov, was in town visiting from his Kibbutz. It was suggested that Shah return to LaHav with Dov where he could live a very productive life. Since LaHav was the object of many insurgent Arab attacks, a dog of Shah's breed and size would be a most welcome asset to the Kibbutz. He could be trained for border patrol and he would be well cared for. My only alternative was to sell Shah to the man at the slaughterhouse who indicated that he had grown attached to the animal. I had to deliberate about what I was going to do. It would not be my decision alone; he was Lydia's dog as well. She adored that animal and I did not have the heart to send him away without her seeing him one last time.

The day of her arrival I took the train to Haifa. I was in a state of total anxiety as she stepped from the boat. She was definitely much more beautiful than I had remembered. We stood in the customs shed clinging to each other as if our separation had been years instead of only three months. Under her arm was tucked the better part of her worldly possessions; the violin. Who would think that a violin could cause so many complications? The Customs Officials were determined to grill Lydia about the instrument. "Where did you get the violin? Do you have a sales receipt? Do you play it? Do you plan to stay in Israel? What is the value of the violin in dollars? In Israeli lirot? Swiss francs? Do you plan to sell it? Why not?" The interrogation went on for almost an hour before they stamped her passport and made a note therein that she was in possession of the instrument. The whole interrogation boiled down to the contingency that if Lydia sold the violin while in the country, upon leaving she and the buyer would be subject to Israeli sales taxes.

As soon as we arrived at the flat I could tell that she was disappointed. I don't know what she expected but I tried to explain, first in a little

French, then in a little English, that I had not been paid for the work I did in the film and that when the money arrived we could decide whether we wanted to remain in Israel or return to Europe. I explained that it was only a temporary accommodation and that seemed to relieve her mind. Meanwhile, I had floated a loan from my dad to under-write our stay until I was able to get the remainder of my money from the studio.

I took Lydia to meet ben-David and family. They immediately fell in love with her. And because her mother was German she had a small command of that language, enough to communicate with the family that understood fluent Yiddish. So there they were, carrying on in Yiddish and German, with a smattering of Hebrew, and in a pinch, French and English. They were communicating.

Lydia's first few days were marred by our having to say goodbye to Shah for the last time. Lydia cried when she saw him and I swear that he remembered her. He tried to jump into her lap while she was standing and nearly knocked her down. He whined and barked and did everything but cry real tears at the sight of her. Damn, but he wasn't making things easy! I paid my bill at the slaughterhouse and with Shah on the end of a rope we walked back to the apartment of ben-David. Dov was waiting for us with a jeep he had borrowed from the Kibbutz. He assured Lydia that we could visit Shah any time we wished and that he would always be our dog. I'm not sure that psychology worked because as Dov led Shah down to the jeep, Lydia and I were wracked with sobs. We saw Shah one more time when we attended Dov's wedding at Kibbutz LaHav. Although he had gone through extensive training as a border patrol dog, he still had that puppy demeanor when he saw Lydia and me, and all the commands in the world from Dov could not keep Shah from going airborne at the sight of us. He had gained a bit of weight from a diet of white cheese but Dov made periodic trips to the slaughterhouse in North Tel Aviv to get meat scraps for him. To this very day I still think of Shah. A better friend no man ever had.

I could not wait to show off Lydia to my theatre acquaintances at the *bat-yam*. In a bathing suit, Lydia was a ten plus long before anyone ever heard of Bo Derek. She drew a crowd wherever we went. At first, I was pleased at how quickly everyone took to her but then I began to feel a twinge of jealousy set in. I'm not sure if it was because of all the male attention she attracted or because she was stealing my limelight.

Whatever the reason, I could not avoid the way I felt and instead of trying to rationalize away the feeling, I began to pout like a little boy. This was a side of me that Lydia had not yet seen and a side of me that I didn't know existed. But each night, when the two of us were alone, all the negative vibrations of the day seemed to melt away as we resolved our differences between the sheets. It seemed that the two emotions over which I had no control were, one, my deep love for her, and two, my almost obsessive, violent jealousy that was a bi-product of that love.

By day, we passed our time at the public pool and by night we sat on Dizengorf in an open-air café and watched the parade of Sabras, Olim Hadashim (new immigrants) and tourists. It was not a very productive lifestyle but Lydia and I could not seem to get off the honeymoon. In the afternoons, when the heat was oppressive, we took refuge in the cinemas which were comfortably air-conditioned. And within three weeks of her arrival, I heard from Larry Frisch.

With numerous rewrites of the script, it would not be necessary to return to the Negev where temperatures were now in excess of a hundred and twenty degrees (not counting inside the john!) The remaining scenes would be shot inside the Geva Studio. That was a relief but there was still the issue of my contract that I felt had been breeched by the production. Larry and I finally sat down and worked out the details. I would be paid the fifteen hundred dollars still owed to me and for each day I worked until the end of the film, I would be paid a hundred dollars a day. But I wasn't taking any more chances: I wanted the money owed to me immediately and before each day's work I would be paid in cash. This was the only guarantee that I would not be screwed over again. Larry accepted and we went back to work.

When we finished production, Lydia and I took stock of our finances. After paying off the money I had borrowed, barely a thousand dollars remained. I explained to Lydia that we could use the money to purchase passage back to Rome and hope that the dubbing business was in full swing. We would have to make a decision soon.

I guess this is as good a time as any to confess that *Pillar of Fire* was a horrible piece of Zionist-conceived Israeli propaganda. It was the story of a young American Jew who feels compelled to go to Israel to fight during the War of Independence. He meets and falls in love with a very plain Kibbutznik (played by a well-known Israeli singer, Nehama

Hendel) who is the girlfriend of the commander of the outpost where they are making a stand against overwhelming Arab odds. The American falls in love with the girl, the girl falls in love with the American, and the commander conveniently gets killed! End of story. Oh, yes, the American and the girl win the war!

One afternoon, while seated outdoors at the Café Caseet, a middle-aged Israeli approached Lydia and inquired if she had ever done any fashion modeling. The man produced his card and explained that he was a manufacturer of a women's line of clothing that was almost exclusively for the export market. He explained that his new fall line would need to be photographed, worn by an attractive model and if Lydia was interested… There was something about this guy that didn't sit well with me and I should have followed my first instinct and sent him on his way. He addressed Lydia as if there wasn't anyone else at the table, completely ignoring my presence, like he was on the make. Lydia looked over to me for some sign of support. I asked the man if he spoke French, and when he assured me that he did not, I addressed Lydia in my broken French.

"If you want to do it, why not?" I encouraged her.

"But I've never done any modeling…with my clothes on," she laughed.

I know it was said in jest but I suddenly had a flash. "For that kind of modeling he'd have to pay a lot more," I tried to go along with her jest.

I turned to the ragman. "I'm her manager. How much do you pay?" I asked in English.

"Her manager?" he asked, completely caught off guard.

"That's right."

"I usually pay models fifty a day…"

"Dollars?"

"Lirot," he replied. That was the equivalent of about twenty-five dollars American. I laughed and repeated it in French to Lydia. She immediately picked up on the laugh.

"That's what hookers get on Hayarcon," I said. "You don't want a first class model. You're in the wrong part of town."

The ragman was getting very annoyed with my intervention. "Why don't you let her speak for herself?"

I got to my feet and raised my voice so that everyone could hear at the surrounding tables. "I'm her husband and you are rude trying to buy my wife for fifty lirot!"

The ragman began to stutter as he turned a deep shade of scarlet. "I'm sorry...I didn't...I wouldn't...I'm a married man..."

"Then you should know better."

He backed away from our table and stopped almost to the edge of the flow of foot traffic on the sidewalk. "How much by the day...just to model clothes...with a photographer?"

"One hundred dollars American each day."

"But I would need her for three days. You're asking too much."

"Ah, but she's worth it," I smiled.

The ragman turned and walked away. It wasn't fifteen minutes later that he returned with a counter-offer of four hundred lirot for the three days. We finally agreed to four-fifty. I was quickly catching on how the game was played. The ragman gave us instructions on how to get to his factory in Natanya, handed over an advance of one hundred lirot, and left. Lydia was ecstatic. She threw her arms around my neck and smothered me with kisses. It had been a great game and she enjoyed every minute of it.

During the following few days, I instructed Lydia on how to pose for the camera. As an artist, she understood how to show the best lines of the garment. Aside from a few butterflies in her stomach on the first day, the shoot came off as scheduled in three days. But after three weeks, when we still had not received the remaining three hundred and fifty lirot and after some half a dozen calls to the ragman, I decided to go out to Natanya to collect. It turned out to be a big mistake.

The ragman accused me of using Gestapo tactics to extort money from him. I was infuriated at the implication. I must have hit him hard enough for him to take a rack of dresses with him as he landed in a heap on the floor. Before a number of his employees were able to come to his aid, I was pummeling his face with my fists and shouting obscenities. When they finally dragged me off, the ragman was yelling for someone to call the police. I suddenly came to my senses and vacated the premises.

I doubt that anyone had called the police because nothing was ever heard from the ragman again. Lydia never got her money and I continued to fume at the thought that she had been ripped off by that son-of-a bitch. There was no recourse through the law and I was possessed with the thought of getting even. Without telling Lydia, I enlisted the aid of a young acquaintance, Eric, who owned a car. Late one night, we drove out to Natanya and I set fire to the ragman's building. I don't know how much damage I inflicted but I'm sure it exceeded the 350 lirot he owed Lydia. In introspect, I could never figure out why the police didn't hunt me down and question me since I left a trail as wide as the Chisholm. I can only reflect that the ragman had so many enemies that it would have been impossible to figure out which one had torched his factory.

One would have thought that I had learned my lesson after dealing with Larry Frisch but I was still naïve enough to accept people at their word. I guess the word is "stupid." But I was becoming aware that I would have to learn to walk away from altercations and not resort to violence that could get me into deep trouble. It was not an easy lesson to learn or practice.

During the next few weeks, Lydia and I worked to create a fashion portfolio, she as a model and me as a photographer. We found a small manufacturer with whom we worked a tradeoff; he supplied the dresses and we gave him copies of the photos. All the photos were exteriors since I could ill afford to rent a studio and lights. I met a young man, Danny, who was confined to a wheelchair from polio, and he had a photography lab in his apartment. He was only too happy to have me share the lab and I promised to pay him if and when Lydia and I were successful in getting some accounts. We shot all over the city, even in the slaughterhouse, and together we created some very avant-garde photos. But my work was a bit too *nouveau* for such a young country and the photos that actually got us some accounts were the ones I considered quite common and unimaginative.

The amount of work we were able to generate did not pay for the amount of work we put into building the portfolio. We were able to pay the rent and buy chemicals and paper for Danny's lab, but food and an occasional evening out came from my fast depleting funds. I was growing more and more malcontent and agitated with each passing day. Who was I kidding? The photography and modeling was just not going to work. Slowly, I slipped into a depression and Lydia and I ceased to communicate. I don't know what precipitated the incident but Lydia and I had a pisser of a fight during which I threatened to destroy her precious violin! Granted that it was an ill-chosen choice but little did I expect the results. The following day, when I returned home from the lab, Lydia was gone!

To this day I can remember the feeling that enveloped me as I opened the apartment door. Before I even entered, I knew that something was amiss. I could just feel it in my gut. That Lydia was not there to greet me was most unusual. Instinctively, I opened the closet door. All her clothes were gone! I rushed into the bathroom; her toilet articles were gone. I opened the cabinet where she stored the violin. It too was gone!

I immediately went to the apartment of ben-David. They had not seen her since our last visit. Was something wrong? No, I assured them, everything was just fine. Meanwhile, there was a gnawing pain in the pit of my stomach. If the pain would only subside I was sure that I could rationalize the whole situation and figure out where she might have gone. But the pain would not diminish and I went aimlessly from one café to another, from one acquaintance to another, inquiring if anyone had seen her. Carrying her photo, I traveled north to Ein Hod, the artist community near Haifa. No one had seen her. I spent days aimlessly walking the streets of Haifa, showing her photo to café and storeowners, all without success. I began traveling from one Kibbutz to another and for the next two weeks I traveled from one end of the country to the other. Lydia had vanished from the face of the earth. I could only surmise that she had left the country. But she had no money; only that precious violin and a few lirot in her purse.

Back in Tel Aviv, I sat in the Café Caseet with Danny. He and his wife were terribly upset to learn that Lydia had split, that the two of us were having problems. I was at the end of the trail. I could not continue searching without some sort of lead.

Previously, on numerous occasions, I had met Lydia at the Café Caseet where she sat with a young American girl by the name of Lynn. There was something about this girl that rubbed me the wrong way. She was constantly bitching about everything and on numerous occasions I suggested that perhaps she would be happier if she were to pack up and leave Israel. Lynn and I mixed like oil and water. To be quite honest, she was quite attractive but it was her personality that brought out the worst in her. She did nothing to hide her dislike for me. She was rude and made cutting remarks that brought out the worst in me.

On this particular evening, as I sat with Danny at the Café Caseet, the last person in the world I wanted to see was Lynn. But there she was coming down Dizengorf and heading right for my table. She invited herself to join us. What could I say?

"How's Lydia?" she asked after indulging in a bit of small talk.

"Fine," I lied. "Just fine."

Without changing the pitch or the emotion of her voice, she said, "Lydia wants to see you."

"What's that supposed to mean?" I was slow on the uptake.

"It means that I know where she is. I also helped her to pack, for what it's worth," she smiled as if she took great pleasure by inserting the knife. "She's staying with some friends of mine at Beit Hashita, in the Galilee."

"You knew all the time?"

"Of course," she reported matter-of-factly. "Personally, I had hoped that she'd never get in touch with you. I think you're a pig but there's no accounting for some women's taste, is there?"

"I should kick your fucking heart out, you know that."

She smiled. "But you won't. You're so fucking predictable you make me ill. I'll tell you something…you're a loser, right down to your socks. And Lydia is…well, something very special. I thought I had her convinced that you weren't worth a second thought. Now, I'm through with her. You can tell her I said so." And with that, she got up and walked away from the table.

Early the following morning, I was on a bus heading north to Afula in the Galilee.

* * *

Beit Hashita was one of the oldest Kibbutzim in all of Israel. It was a Kibbutz of the political left, Mapam, and its members numbered over a thousand. The countryside around Beit Hashita was rich and fertile and the members raised olives and citrus. They had their own canning factory, one of the few in the Kibbutz system. By Israeli standards, this Kibbutz was modern and quite progressive. Geographically, it was about ten kilometers from Afula and some thirty kilometers from the Sea of Galilee. Just a few miles to the north, one could stand on top of a mountain and see Jordan on the one side and the Mediterranean on the other. The whole width of the country at that point was about ten kilometers across. The town of Afula was famous for its prisoner of war compound where hundreds of Arab prisoners were being incarcerated. Periodically there would be a break from the compound and the countryside became a hive of activity with Israeli police and military searching out the escaped prisoners. Within twenty kilometers from Beit Hashita was Nazareth, the town with which I had a passing acquaintance during the riots some months before.

The bus went as far as Afula where I could change buses for my destination. But I was impatient so I thumbed my way to Beit Hashita. It had taken me the better part of a day to make the journey and I was fatigued from the heat and the dirt of the road. The living quarters and office buildings were set back about a kilometer from the main road. I proceeded along the dirt road that was bordered by vast orchards of oranges, lemons and limes. I could discern very little activity at the evening hour but I could hear music coming from a large building centrally located. This was the communal dining room that served as a theatre, meeting and social hall. As I entered, a group of professional dancers, probably from Tel Aviv, was in the process of entertaining to the rhythm of drums and Shepard pipes. I caught the attention of one of the Kibbutz members and asked if he knew where I could find the French girl, Lydia. He led me to a rather heavyset woman who introduced herself as Shlomeet. She was in charge of the *ulpan*, the Hebrew language school that was attended by new immigrants planning to make their homes and futures in Israel. Shlomeet informed me that Lydia could be found in the infirmary. She had contracted a foot infection, nothing serious, and that she had been expecting me.

The infirmary was a small building that accommodated some ten cots, dormitory style. Lydia was one of the three female patients in the dorm and I could pick her out immediately in the fading light of the day. Silently, I walked over to her bed and knelt beside her. Her eyes were closed and I watched her napping for only a few moments before she became aware of my presence. She opened her eyes, saw me kneeling by her bed, and softly, so as not to disturb the other patients, she began to weep. I held her hand to my lips and tried to reassure her that everything was going to be all right. We remained clinging to each other late into the night when Shlomeet came to turn on the night-light and look in on her girls.

"There is a cot over in the second men's hut by the ulpan. You can sleep there tonight." She handed me a set of clean sheets, a towel and soap. "The showers are only a few meters from the hut. Any of the men will be glad to show you." Shlomeet looked quite severe and unfriendly but she turned out to be a very gentle and caring individual. We valued her friendship and counsel through the entire time we remained at Beit Hashita.

The following day, Lydia and I had time to consider a number of alternatives regarding our lives together. We both agreed that the city, without a working knowledge of the language, was not practical. Did I want to remain in Israel or did I want to return to Italy? It was a question that I could not answer at that moment. I needed time. So Lydia suggested that we take advantage of the hospitality offered by the Kibbutz. She and I could have our own hut, which we could fix up any way we desired. Our first home. Our meals would be provided in the *heder ohel*, dining room, and there would be free laundry and medical. We would be expected to work six afternoons a week but we were expected to attend, regularly, Hebrew classes six mornings a week. The ulpan was a three month crash course and those students who finished came away with quite a good working knowledge of the language.

As soon a Lydia was able to get back on her feet, we were assigned a hut in the ulpan. We found a few pieces of wood that served as a bookcase, an old dresser, and some material that Lydia used to fashion some drapes and a spread for the bed. It was a very difficult and primitive existence. The work in the orchards was long and tedious. Some days we labored in citrus and others in olives. And each morning we were dedicated to learning the language.

The ulpan was made up of some twenty-five students from all over the world and all walks of life. One did not have to be a Jew to immigrate to Israel so there was a conglomeration of Catholics, Protestants, Moslems and Hindus, as well. The preponderance of Jews was from Russia, Poland, England, France, South Africa, Australia, India, South America and North America. We were an odd lot, each trying to communicate with the other in his own language until slowly, slowly, ever so subtly we were able to make the transition to Hebrew.

My work details varied from day to day. If I was not assigned to the *pardes* (orchard) it was possible to find myself working on a garbage truck, a most undesirable duty. I thought that if I was assign collecting garbage it was a sort of punishment until I learned th: man who headed the detail was an ex-high school principal from Canada who had migrated to Israel some years before and was now in charge of all education for the children of the Kibbutz. He was a visionary who believed that it was unfair to ask a person to do a menial task unless he himself was prepared to undertake the same task. He showed true leadership, I thought.

On some days I was assigned to the stables where I shoveled *zevel*, good old horseshit! And Lydia worked in the dining room preparing food. Our lifestyle was simple at best but I don't think that we could have survived those first few months without the ulpan. We were soon to learn that among the residents of the Kibbutz were writers, architects and political activists. Most of them held menial jobs during the day and their intellectual pursuits were limited to evenings. Physical labor was the backbone of life in the Kibbutz.

What seemed like an ideal way of life had a most obvious flaw in its structure. The Kibbutz was not only responsible for feeding the country but it represented outposts which were militarily responsible for repelling enemy attacks in times of hostilities. In effect, the string of Kibbutzim along the borders of the country designated the geographic parameters that defined the country. Without these outposts the country would have been overrun with infiltrators and terrorist groups. So the children of the Kibbutz were depended upon and trained as defenders. From the earliest age they were able to understand their ultimate responsibility. The ideal situation for life in the Kibbutz would have been for every member to have all the luxuries known to their counterparts in the cities: television, entertainment, American style dress and music. As magazines and the media brought Europe and America closer to rural Israel, it became obvious that it was going to be nearly impossible "to keep 'em down on the farm after they seen Paree." The Kibbutz was responsible for the education of each child right through college. It was no cheap proposition. But the irony existed that a youngster sent to one of the universities in the cities was exposed to all the comforts of modern city life. In many cases, by the time a student had completed four years of college, he was alienated from Kibbutz life. It was definitely a dilemma that the Kibbutz system faces to this very day.

The next couple of months at Beit Hashita passed very quickly. Lydia was befriended by the Kibbutz architect and she spent much of her spare time at his office learning whatever one learns in an architect's office. The germ that was planted during this period of her life would eventually determine the course she would later pursue. I managed to find some art materials on a trip to Nazareth and Lydia began to do some light painting and sketches to amuse herself. Everyone who saw her work agreed that she was most talented. I would not be the least bit surprised if some of the paintings she did many years ago are still being exhibited in some of the homes of Beit Hashita.

So "homey" was our existence that Lydia even managed to acquire a pet, a foot long lizard that took to living on our screens and kept the cabin free of flies and other insects. It was an ugly looking, horny, green thing that moved with the grace of a ballet dancer in slow motion and had a tongue that could strike with the speed and accuracy of a bullet. I had an aversion to that beast but Lydia carried him on her arm when we were invited to visit other cabins. I called it "her green scab."

One morning, Lydia was called from class to report to the architect's office. She retuned a few minutes later and summoned me back to our hut. The architect, Shlomo, was on his way up north to a sister Kibbutz that had been shelled the previous day by Arab mortars and small arms fire. It was Shlomo's job to go up to the Kibbutz and assess the damage and draw up plans to rebuild that area destroyed by the attack. Shlomo had requested that Lydia and I join him on the trip. She was to help him with his evaluation while I was to photograph and document the damage.

Shlomo had been assigned a private car with driver and he spent the entire trip pointing out the historic sites along the way. He was a wealth of information and he enjoyed sharing his knowledge with anyone who would listen. The trip only took a couple of hours to Kibbutz Gadot. The damage was immediately evident; houses were completely leveled and bullet holes were peppered all over those buildings still standing. The members of the Kibbutz seemed to go about their business as if nothing had happened out of the ordinary the previous day.

A committee of four member of the Kibbutz greeted us. They took us on a guided tour of the small community as Shlomo assessed the damage. As we walked among the ruins, Lydia became engrossed in conversation in French with one of the committee. They spoke too rapidly for me to understand so I occupied myself with taking photographs of the damage.

At lunchtime, Lydia informed me that the young man with whom she was speaking French had recognized her from the detention camp where she and her family had been interned just after the war. Lydia's mother, being German and a vocal supporter of the Nazis, was targeted by the communists for execution when the war ended. Late one night, Lydia's father spirited the family across the border from France into Switzerland where they were interned in a camp by the Swiss authorities. Most of the internees were Jews fleeing the aftermath of the war and the young French Jew, the one from the committee, had been an internee in the very same camp where Lydia and her parents had been interned at the end of the war. It was truly a small world.

After lunch, Shlomo asked me to join him as Lydia had an assignment in another part of the compound. We walked to the edge of the Kibbutz that was enclosed by a double field of barbed wire known as "no man's land." On the other side of the wire was a small mountain and with the naked eye, one could discern a number of gun emplacements. We stood on a high ground looking up at the hill.

"Do you see those bunkers?" asked Shlomo. "The U.N. swears that they are merely an Arab 'rest home' for military retirees. I'd like to get some shots of those gun emplacements but I wouldn't suggest you be too obvious or you could get shot. I won't mind if you refuse…"

"No problem," I assured him.

Shlomo turned and went back to the compound looking for his committee. How the hell could the U.N. call those bunkers a rest home with all their guns sticking out halfway across the valley? I asked myself. I walked along the Israeli side of the wire. There was no cover from where I could photograph without being observed. By now I had acquired a long lens for the Mamayaflex and I proceeded to mount the lens on the front of the camera. Turning my back to the Arab position I could hold the camera in such a way as to look into the viewfinder without appearing to be taking pictures. One of the Arabs on the hill must have also owned a twin lens reflex because I suddenly became aware of a loud thud from across the valley followed by a whoosh of air and an explosion just beyond where I was standing. It took me a few seconds to register that we were in the process of being shelled!

I turned and made a mad dash down the hill towards the center of the Kibbutz. My first thought was to find Lydia but a Kibbutznik with an automatic weapon was directing traffic and I was ordered to follow the flow of people into the nearest shelter. I was herded underground as a barrage of shells peppered the area.

The bunker was foul smelling for lack of air. I had been in such a bunker when we were filming *Pillar of Fire* back at Revivim. It seemed that all bunkers had a drainage problem because there was two or three inches of water collected on the concrete floor. Everyone sought to get onto a bunk or raise their feet to get them out of the water. There were about thirty people crowded into an area intended to accommodate half that number. Only one lantern was lit (I imagine in order not to contaminate the already smelly atmosphere) and we sat in the semi-darkness singing songs and wondering what was happening overhead.

It was after sundown when the all clear sounded and we made our way up out of that stifling hole in the ground and into the warm night air. I had to find Lydia. The flow of traffic was towards the dining hall and I pushed my way through the milling bodies who were also searching for loved ones from whom they had been separated.

It was good to see Lydia and Shlomo seated together in the lighted dining hall talking over tea. We greeted each other and I pulled up a chair to join them. I no sooner put my weary ass to the chair when I was approached by a member of the committee.

"Are you all right?" he inquired, obviously more than a little concerned.

"I will be as soon as I get out of these damp clothes," I assured him. The water from the bunker had caused the pants to dampen up to the knees.

"Have you seen a doctor?" asked the committeeman.

"There's no need. I feel fine," I said.

"And the leg?" he asked.

I looked down and saw that what I took to be the dampness from the water seeping up my right leg was actually blood. I couldn't explain it because I felt no pain and had no sensation of being hit. The committeeman raised his arm and caught the attention of a medic who had been circulating among the crowd. He came over to where we were seated and when he saw the blood, he removed a knife from his pocket and slit my pant's leg up the side.

"Are you in pain?" he asked.

"No. None at all."

"Were you in contact with anyone who was wounded?"

"Not that I know of..."

The medic placed the knife between my leg and the inside of the boot. "What are you going to do?" I asked.

"Not to worry," he assured me. "I only cut away the boot."

"Ruin a perfectly good pair of boots? Why not just cut the laces? I've had these boots for years, from when I was in the Marine Corps. Unless it's absolutely necessary, I'd like to save them."

He cut away the laces, peeled back the boot and removed it. I could now see a small hole in the leather of the boot just above the inside of the ankle. Almost immediately upon the removal of the boot, I began to feel a slight throbbing sensation around the ankle. The once white work sock was soaked with blood.

"Well, I'll be damned," I said. "I never felt a thing." I peeled back the sock and there in the flesh of my ankle was a small piece of metal protruding, perhaps no more than a quarter of an inch. By now Lydia and Shlomo were trying to give me moral support as a crowd of curiosity seekers had gather around. The medic said that he had to get his bag from the other side of the room. In his absence I reached down and touched the protrusion. There was no sensation at all; if anything, only a slight numbness. What the hell, I thought, and I grasped the metal between my thumb and forefinger and tried to dislodge it. It came out of my leg with a bit of coaxing and was followed by a flow of thick, red blood. I handed the small shrapnel piece to Lydia. "You can have a necklace made from it," I joked. The medic had returned.

"I see you've already operated," he quipped.

"It wasn't in very deep," I assured him.

"Any pain?" he asked as he probed the area with his fingers.

"I'm not sure. Perhaps a bit of throbbing, that's all."

"You're very lucky. One of our members wasn't so lucky," he said,

"Is he badly hurt?"

"He's dead."

I have always wondered whether it had been my fault, whether my standing up there on no man's land with a camera in hand hadn't actually drawn the fire that caused the death of that man. Shlomo tried to assure me that I had nothing to do with that man's death, that it was an unfortunate coincidence and nothing more. I wasn't convinced.

The medic sprinkled some yellow powder on the small wound and wrapped it with a bandage. "If you come by the infirmary I'll give you a tetanus shot..."

"I had one a few months ago when I left the States." I hated needles. I turned to Shlomo. "Don't we have to be getting back," I pleaded.

He looked at his watch. "It's quite late. He's right. We'd better be getting back." He turned to the medic. "The shot can wait until we get back to Beit Hashita, can't it?"

The medic assured us that it could wait but made me promise that I would check into the infirmary for observation the first thing in the morning. We gathered up our things and took to the road.

The following morning, per instructions, I reported to the infirmary and received a tetanus shot. There was a small amount of pain just above the ankle and by the time work call rolled around after ulpan, I had all I could do to put my weight on that foot. But I limped out to the olive grove and put in my time along with everyone else. The next day I knew something was definitely wrong. During the night the leg had swollen and taken on a myriad of colors, blue/purple/yellow, all around the wound and I could feel a definite throbbing pain as I tried to stand. Lydia helped me over to the infirmary where the nurse took another look. Sure enough, just a few millimeters from where I had removed the shrapnel, the nurse discovered a smaller piece of metal imbedded in my leg. She wanted to give me a local anesthetic but by now the skin area around the ankle was so numb that I assured her I could not feel any pain. She probed the tiny hole and I could feel the instrument but no discomfort. She found what amounted to only a tiny sliver of metal and assured me that with the foreign object removed, I would feel relief within a matter of hours.

The next morning my temperature hit a hundred and four! My leg had swollen to twice its normal size and the pain was unbearable. With help from Lydia and a couple of students from the ulpan, I hobbled my way over to the infirmary. The nurse immediately admitted me and placed a call for a doctor.

I have only a vague recollection of what transpired over the next five weeks. I do remember waking up a number of times but I had no idea of how long I had been asleep or where I was. On one occasion, I remember hearing voices and when I opened my eyes, the dorm was filled with people and I could hear Lydia crying. Then, I slipped back into sleep. Perhaps it was fatigue that lowered my resistance or the fact that the wound in my leg had been exposed to contaminated water in the bunker, either of which could have added to the impending infection. But the blood poisoning was spreading fast and there was a consensus of medical opinions that my leg might have to be removed. I do remember that over the next few days, whenever I awoke, there was a sickly smell in the room as if something had crawled up alongside me and died. The stench was sickening. I tried to fight the fatigue that was wracking my body but I had no strength and could not keep from slipping back into unconsciousness.

It was Lydia who bore the brunt of my predicament. By the tenth day, it fell upon her to make the final determination as to whether or not the leg would go. And the attending doctor reminded her, in no uncertain terms, that if the infection continued to spread, I could very well die. But Lydia was determined to get one more doctor's opinion. She had heard of a Russian woman doctor who was attending at Hadassah Hospital in Tel Aviv who had worked as a field doctor during the war on the Russian front. It was reported that she had seen all kinds of infections and was literally able to perform miracles. At the eleventh hour, the woman doctor was called in. (I don't remember her name so I'll call her Doctor Naomi.) For the next few day she attended to me day and night, administering shots of antibiotics, placing drains in the festering wound, and cutting away pieces of dead skin. The first indication that there was any hope was when my temperature began to drop. Then, as if I had been in a long sleep, I opened my eyes and announced that I was thirsty. For the next couple of weeks my leg was wrapped in compresses and I could still feel the deep throbbing from the infection but Doctor Naomi insisted that we were winning the battle and she was sure that the leg could be saved. I later learned that the doctor had literally stayed by my bedside, night and day, throughout my ordeal that had lasted almost five weeks. And then, one day she was gone and we never heard from or about her again. Some time later, when Lydia and I were in Tel Aviv, we went by the Hadassah Hospital only to learn that Doctor Naomi had moved on, address unknown.

In the Kibbutz, unless you are dead, you carry your own weight. I was no sooner on my feet than I was assigned to light work duty. In a few days my strength had returned and the pain had subsided. Two weeks after I was back on my feet I was called into the office of the Kibbutz administrator.

I have mentioned before that Kibbutz Beit Hashita was considered quite progressive in its politics and in its economic outlook for the future. It was the first Kibbutz, to my knowledge, to implement a canning factory for some of its produce and I know that it was one of the first communal farms that was successful in raising fish in man-made ponds for local consumption. At least once a month we ate "zebra" which came from a short, fat, little animal that was identical, in my recollection, to an animal called a "pig." But pork was not part of Jewish dietary laws and the zebra was now giving us bacon. A rose by any other name...

Beit Hashita was now about to embark on its most adventurous experiment. The land between Afula and the Jordanian border consisted of great plains of what we call "scrub grass" in America. The Kibbutz was about to import two hundred head of cattle from Yugoslavia. This particular breed was known to thrive in the northern part of that country on vegetation quite similar to that found in the great valleys in the eastern part of Israel. Also being imported were four Brahma bulls that the Kibbutz hoped to cross with the smaller Yugoslav breed, thereby developing a cow that would produce meat for the population that was almost starved for beef. It was a daring concept that had been developed over a number of years and the time had come to initiate the plan.

It was decided by committee that two fulltime cowboys would be responsible for herding the cattle over the valleys and mountains and then return them each evening to be corralled. This was considered to be a plum job in the Kibbutz and it was being offered to me. After all, what American boy had not dreamed of herding cattle across the great plains, living in the wide-open spaces and sharing the camaraderie of one's fellow cowboys? How could I turn down the chance of a lifetime? How indeed!

At first report of my good fortune, Lydia rejoiced with me. Her jubilation was short-lived. I had to rise each morning at five in order to be driven by jeep out to where the cattle were penned. The other "cowboy" was a moody, tight mouthed, bearded Kibbutznik who answered to the name of Moshe. His English was almost perfect but he preferred to address me in Hebrew, when he spoke to me at all. In time I was to learn that Moshe was put out on the range with the cattle because he had some kind of a social problem. His father was a prominent medical surgeon in Tel Aviv who had arranged for his son to live in the Kibbutz, away from people. Some months before Lydia and I had arrived, there had been a mass escape from the prisoner of war camp in Afula. On that day, Moshe was working in one of the orchards near the edge of the Kibbutz. One of the escaped prisoners had made his way from Afula and had come upon the orchard at Beit Hashita. Moshe had first sighted the Arab across the barbed wire entanglement that ringed the orchard. The Arab felt perfectly safe from Moshe as long as he kept the barbed wire between himself and the Israeli. But the frustration of trying to reach the escaped prisoner was too much for Moshe. Suddenly, he threw his body into the barbed wire in an attempt to get his hands on the Arab. The entanglement tore great pieces of his flesh but he seemed to be impervious to the pain and continued to pursue the escaped prisoner.

When a search party came upon Moshe, he was calmly sitting upon a rock smoking a cigarette and half bleeding to death. Nearby, on the ground, was the dead Arab who had been strangled to death. And Moshe was the man with whom I was to be sequestered indefinitely!

My little adventure on the range had tried Lydia's patience to the limit. For the first couple of weeks I would arrive back at our hut with such pain in my legs and back that I could barely sleep. Sitting on a horse for twelve hours a day is a little different than riding through Prospect Park in Brooklyn for a couple of leisurely hours. Rarely did I arrive back to the Kibbutz before nine at night and I was always too tired to indulge in small talk with Lydia or even to ask about her day. It seemed as if we just shared a bed. And all the while I was working with the cows, Lydia had been relegated full time to the dining hall where she spent her days mopping floors or washing dishes. We went on like this for some six months. Something had to give.

I must admit that sitting on a horse watching two hundred head of dumb animals is not the most stimulating job to which a man can aspire. My great revelation was that a cow can do nothing today that he did not do yesterday and he will not do anything tomorrow that he did not do today. I would sit on my horse staring out across the wasteland

and wondered who the hell would want it? There was nothing there but rocks and briar and scrub grass. And for this, men gave their lives! It was way beyond my comprehension.

Lawrence on the Jordanian border with 200 head of cattle 1959

One day, as I sat reading some engrossing novel and paying no mind to the cattle, about twenty head wandered across the border into Jordan. When I looked up and saw what had happened, I was petrified. I was not about to risk life and limb for a bunch of dumb cows. If a border patrol were to happen by, I could rightfully be shot as an infiltrator. I fired a couple of rounds from my rifle and in a matter of minutes, Moshe came riding up. I did not have to do too much explaining as the situation was obvious. But instead of reading me the riot act, Moshe merely smiled and took off across the border. Within half an hour he returned with the delinquent cattle, smiling all the way. That crazy Israeli was hoping to draw fire from a Jordanian patrol so he would have reason to return fire and possibly put a couple of notches on his Sten gun. I could see that my time in the Kibbutz was drawing to an end.

Moshe and I were finally called in from the range with all the cattle while the Kibbutz evaluated to what extent the plan was working. Many of the cows were about to drop their calves and it would be better if they did so in a controlled environment. For me, it was good to get back to the backbreaking task of working in the orchards. My rear end had developed calluses and saddle sores and if I never saw another horse again, it would be too soon.

Lydia and I finally got back into a routine that was somewhat normal. But neither of us was very happy on the Kibbutz and we agreed that it was time for us to move on. After all, it had been eleven months since our arrival. We had some leave time accumulated and we decided to spend it in Tel Aviv. The few dollars we had in the bank in the city was not enough to consider returning to Italy so our first thought was how were we going to sustain ourselves. And how could we earn enough money to save up for passage back to Europe.

Lydia was more fortunate than I as she immediately found work as a waitress in a new restaurant called The California. It was owned by an oddball Israeli by the name of Abie Nathan, who made something of a name for himself in later years by crossing the border into one of the Arab countries and demanding to meet with the Arab leaders in the hopes of obtaining some kind of peaceful co-existence. Everyone thought that Abie was very brave or extremely stupid and naïve. I opted for the latter. He could have easily been shot. In any case, Abie had always had the hots for Lydia and when he opened his new restaurant, a job as a waitress was a small price to pay for a chance at getting into her pants.

Our problem about where to live was solved at Café Caseet where Lydia and I were greeted with great fanfare by a number of actors and artists that had wondered what had become of us. One of the actors, Chaim, suggested that we could stay with him and his wife until we found a place to live. We did not want to be an imposition but Chaim assured us that he had more than enough room and that it would be no imposition at all. Lydia and I slept on the living room couch as Chaim and his wife were the most perfect hosts. (As a side note, Chaim went on to portray Tevye in the film, *Fiddler on the Roof*, which made Topol an international star. To us he was just good old Chaim Topol.)

Through a friend of a friend of a friend, I heard about a job working on a fishing boat. The pay was equivalent to five dollars American a day with food and lodging. A meeting was arranged for me and the owner of the Menorah, a fifty-one foot monster of a fishing boat out of Tel Aviv harbor. Working on a fishing boat sounded exciting and an adventure that I had not dreamed of before. The owner of the boat agreed to contact me when they were ready to shove off. Meanwhile, someone at the restaurant told Lydia about a small room in the basement of a building that we could have for almost nothing. The room was just big enough for a bed and a dresser and clothes would have to be hung on the back of the door, but the price was right. And if I was going to be out at sea, Lydia assured me she did not need more than this monastic accommodation. On paper, if we both kept working, we could see a light at the end of the tunnel…

A few days later the owner of the boat sent word for me to meet him at the Tel Aviv harbor that night. The weather had been foul for the past few days and the Menorah would not be coming dockside but I would be picked up by dingy. No one seemed to know how long I would be away, anywhere from two weeks to three months depending on our success at sea. I dreaded the thought of being separated from Lydia again but I had no option. Our relationship had deteriorated terribly and I was afraid that we were very close to the edge. The night I left, it was raining and gale force winds were kicking up the sea. I should have stayed ashore!

I didn't get seasick until the dingy made it out beyond the breakers. Once on board the Menorah, I met the Captain and then proceeded immediately to the rail and barfed. Shades of my experience on the S.S. Italia when I sailed from New York. Who was it that said that if you feel seasickness coming on, the best thing to do is eat something, throw it all up, and you'll feel great? Bullshit! I barfed continuously for the next three months. I couldn't hold anything in my stomach, which was a damn shame because I was the only person on the boat who would eat shellfish. Jewish law prohibits the eating of lobster, crab and shrimp and the Mediterranean was just loaded with all three. Our nets were always loaded with shellfish and I managed to find a bucket in which I could cook up a potful. I kept the cooked shellfish in the refrigerator locker below deck and nibbled on cooked shrimp each and every day we were at sea. We traveled from Tel Aviv, up the coast of Lebanon and across to the Greek islands. We worked four hours on and four hours off around the clock, seven days a week. I had thought that life in the Kibbutz had been difficult but compared to this, it was a piece of cake. If we were unfortunate to pick up a shark or two, then our four hours off were spent repairing the damage the sharks did to the nets. We grew to hate the sight of a shark and often, after working around the clock hauling and repairing nets, the sight of a three foot shark in our net drove us into a frenzy as we bludgeoned it to death with clubs. Men who have been deprived of sleep for an extended period of time can easily be reduced to behaving like beasts.

Our engineer was a young Yemenite. More than sharks and shellfish, he feared the Arabs. At least once or twice a week we would see an Arab gunboat off in the distance heading straight for us. The Yemenite would immediately crawl in behind the engines of the boat and begin praying for all he was worth. The Captain was a cantankerous Frenchman who took great pleasure in using his ship-to-shore to call for air cover. Within a matter of minutes, we could see French fighter planes with Israeli markings on the wings, come swooping in low over the water as the Arabs would veer off in another direction. I learned that if the Arabs ever decided to board us, they would kill the Yemenite engineer. It was just one of those unwritten rules of the Mediterranean.

On numerous occasions we had come into Tel Aviv harbor to drop off our catch and pick up supplies but each time, the sea had been so rough that we had to anchor outside the harbor, unload our catch into flat bottom boats, take on supplies and return to sea. We never got a chance to go ashore. I was dying to get in touch with Lydia but there was just no way. Finally, after almost three months the sea calmed and we were able to pull into port. I had no sooner gotten on shore than I got sick from the lack of motion. The crew went immediately to a locker room where there was access to fresh hot water and soap. I had not had a fresh water shower in three months! During our stay at sea we had bathed hanging over the side of the boat like shark bait or using a makeshift shower on deck that dribbled salty seawater. The dirt on my elbows and knees was literally imbedded into my skin. I used yellow soap and a stiff brush to try to get off the dirt but nothing helped. As I felt the pleasure of that hot water consume my body, I swore then and there that I would never again set foot on the Menorah.

Three months at sea had netted me the equivalent of four hundred and fifty dollars but we still came up short for our return passage back to Europe. While hanging around the Café Caseet, I learned that one of the oil companies, Rosh Zohar, was hiring men to work as *shomer,* guards for surveying teams down by the Red Sea. The pay was twice what I had been making on the Menorah and Lydia and I agreed that this job served us better than the one at sea. I could get up to Tel Aviv on Shabbat (Saturday) to see Lydia, which was an added incentive.

Rosh Zohar was located some fifty kilometers east of Beersheba near the Dead Sea. During the day the temperatures could soar up to the hundred and thirty degree mark. My job was to carry a rifle, always situating myself on a high point, and keep guard over a small group of surveyors who were charting the desert. The worst part of the job was the afternoon sandstorms, *Chamseen*, that seemed to come up out of nowhere with blinding winds that would pin us down, sometimes for hours. If we were lucky we would find a Bedouin camp and take refuge with them. Perhaps "lucky" is a bit euphemistic if one has never experienced Bedouin hospitality. My nose had never been subjected to such vile odors. The food consisted of a base of goat meat and cheese, both of which happen to drive me up the wall. And most of the women washed their hair in camel piss to bleach out the color. With the sun beating down all day the inside of a tent smelled like a city dump.

I had been with the surveying team for about four weeks when I happened down to the edge of the sea after experiencing a severe sandstorm. I was covered from head to toe with a fine layer of sand. The rest of the team had headed back to Rosh Zohar and I would soon follow. As I stood at the shoreline, I wondered what it would be like to immerse myself in water with a salt content so high that I would not be able to sink. There was no one around so I stripped down to my skivvies and cautiously edged out into the tepid water. True enough, I lay on my back and floated but could not sink. If I wanted to get my head under water I literally had to swim with all my might to fight against my own buoyancy. I didn't stay long in the brackish water because it was not particularly clean. I noticed that there was a very fine film of oil floating on the surface and as I made my way to the shore my body was covered with that slick. I later learned that any living thing that perished in that water, such as insects or vegetation, would decompose upon contact and the oil would separate and rise to the surface. With the heat of the afternoon hovering above a hundred and twenty degrees, I dressed in my work clothes and headed back to camp. I couldn't wait to get a fresh water shower as the briny water had raised a rash that attacked every crevice of my body. And by late that night, the rash had turned to small bubbles and it was all I could do to keep from scratching myself raw. We had no medic on site so I got a lift into Beersheba to check into the Hadassah clinic. But it was closed for Shabbat so I took a communal taxi on to Tel Aviv. By now the itching had subsided and I went directly to Lydia's basement apartment. It was empty. Her clothes were gone and she had vacated the premises. I went around the corner to the Café California where they were just closing down. Lydia had left a note for me explaining that I could find her at the Weitzman Institute in Rehovot, some ten kilometers from Tel Aviv. There was an address but with the city closing down for the Sabbath there was no way for me to travel. I checked into a cheap rooming house for the night and the following morning I set out for Rehovot.

The house where Lydia was staying belonged to a very wealthy American couple. Mathilda had been a friend of Lydia's at art school in Geneva and coincidently they ran into each other at the Café California. Mathilda's husband, Arthur, was a very wealthy American who was the CEO of one of the largest film distribution companies in the world. They were both strong supporters of Israel, especially the Institute where they donated vast amounts of money for medical research. Mathilda was a scientist who spent part of each year donating her time to the Institute. So when she and Lydia renewed their friendship and Mathilda learned of the hardship that Lydia had endured with me, she invited Lydia to come and stay at her home in Rehovot.

By the time I arrived on the scene, Mathilda and Arthur had already returned to the States and Lydia was living alone at the Institute. She assured me that Mathilda knew of my situation and that she had extended by proxy an invitation for me to stay in her house with Lydia. It appeared that for once our luck had really changed. We could take the time to figure out our next move without worrying about where we were going to live and how we were going to eat. Mathilda had arranged for us to order in food and sign for it. I felt obliged to do some chores around the house like taking care of the lawn and pruning back the trees, much to the consternation of the Yemenite gardener who thought that I was moving in on his territory. After three weeks of living high on the zebra, we received word that Mathilda and Arthur would be arriving in a few days and that they were both quite anxious to meet me. Lydia and I fantasized that if I could get into Arthur's good graces, there was a chance he might recommend me for some film work that his company was involved with in Europe. Any place; it didn't matter. All I wanted to do was work.

Mathilda turned out to be a beautiful, charming young woman who one could not help but like immediately. Arthur, on the other hand, was a very quiet and reserved middle-aged man. The two did not seem to go together. Mathilda seemed to gush when she talked and Arthur sat like a great sphinx with a Cheshire cat smile on his face. Mathilda seemed fascinated with the stories of Lydia and my adventures in the Holy Land and before the first evening was over, I was convinced that I had at least one ally in our hosts. Their stay was only for four days and not once was the subject of my working for Arthur ever broached. But on the evening of the last day of their stay, Lydia had prepared dinner for the four of us. As we sat around the table, Arthur suddenly seemed to come to life as he dominated the conversation.

"What are you planning to do?" he asked quite bluntly.

"About what?" I asked.

"About your life, boy," he said in a somewhat fit of exasperation. "Do you have any plans? Any goals?"

"Of course I do. I'm an actor and a damn good one. All I need is a break."

"An actor?" he said as if he had just swallowed something distasteful. "One would think that anyone with the slightest amount of intelligence could realize that being an actor is not a profession, it's gambling. Is that what you want to do with the rest of your life?"

He was shaking my confidence. "No, sir. But it doesn't have to be like that. I know lots of people who have made a good living in the theatre and in films. Why do you have to equate me with someone who can't make it?"

The question was moot. "I wouldn't know about that," he replied. Right then I knew that my chances of depending on him for a break were nil. "I have a subsidiary company in Rome. I could arrange a job for you there if you're interested in the business end of filmmaking. I can always use a bright young man," he said.

I hesitated. I looked over at Lydia for some sign of support. Why didn't my friend Mathilda intercede on my behalf? Not one person at that table suggested for a moment that I just might be the most talented person the face of the planet. It didn't mean a friggin' thing.

"Well, think about it," said Arthur. "We'll be back in a couple of weeks and you can give me your answer then."

Lydia and I spent the next two weeks weighing the pros and cons of Arthur's offer. After all, being an actor was not the only thing in life even if I did feel that I was one damn good actor. Sometimes one had to compromise, to settle for second best, in order to do the right thing. If it took giving up acting to make a decent life for Lydia and myself, so be it. But there would always be that question in the back of my mind: why couldn't I provide for the two of us doing what I felt I did best?

Arthur did not return to Tel Aviv as planned but wired that if I was interested, he would make plans for me to fly to Rome and begin work for his company. I wired back and told him that I was ready to accept his offer. Naturally, Lydia would have to remain in Israel until I was able to get settled in Rome. But as soon as I got a decent apartment and was able to set aside enough money for a ticket, I would send for her. Our parting was most painful. There were tears and promises of being together forever once I was able to get established in Europe. There was a lot of lovemaking and kissing and holding. But all the while, I had the distinct impression that once I left Israel, I would never again see Lydia. It seemed to be written in the wind.

CHAPTER SEVEN
A STAR IS BORN

I arrived in Rome during August, a time of the year when all the Italians leave Rome and all the tourists enter. The weather was unusually hot and muggy, prices in restaurants and stores skyrocketed to take advantage of the tourist trade, and very little Italian could be heard on the streets. Upon my arrival, I immediately called the office and asked to speak to Robert Hashmi whose name Arthur had given to me. But I was informed that Robert Hashmi was not in Rome and was not expected to return until the end of the month, some three weeks hence. I explained that Arthur had arranged for me to come to Rome to work for the company and that I was expecting someone to meet me and explain where I was to live and what my duties would be at the office. I was put on hold and stood by the phone at the Central Station for an interminable period of time. Finally, a very friendly sounding gentleman got on the phone, apologized profusely that no one was there to meet me, and that if I stayed right where I was, he would come and fetch me right off. Within half an hour a car pulled up and I was spirited off to my quarters at the Residence Palace Hotel in Parioli, a very fashionable section of Rome. I tried to explain that I was merely an employee and that I was sure Arthur did not have it in mind for me to have a suite at one of the finest hotels in the entire city. Obviously, there was a communications breakdown and until my contact arrived back in town, I was to be treated like an Arab sheik. For the next three weeks I sat in my room in the hotel waiting for the world to come to an end. When Arthur heard that I was costing the company a small fortune for meals (for which I signed) and the price of that luxury suite, I was sure that the shit was going to hit the Italian fan. My contact, Robert Hashmi, did return to Rome and early the following morning, a car was waiting for me in front of the hotel to spirit me off to a cheap Pensione near the office and around the corner from the Bourghese Gardens. Signor Hashmi invited me to his lavish office to discuss what my duties would be. What had Arthur led me to believe

I would be doing for his company? I asked if he had spoken to Arthur about me but he assured me that Arthur was a very busy man with many things on his mind and that he, Signor Hashmi, was sure that Arthur would eventually get around to it. What a fucking dilemma! I felt as if I had been deceived and that Arthur had only sent me to Rome in some clandestine plan to get me away from Lydia and out of Israel. I couldn't believe that Arthur had not even mentioned me to Signor Hashmi who had just returned to Rome from New York where the two men were together almost every day for the past three weeks! I had been duped.

The following day I was given a small office and told to read over the press releases for a number of films that were soon to be released by the company in Italy. I was to submit to Signor Hashmi a one-page recommendation on how our company could best promote the films in question. One of the films co-starred an ex-classmate of mine from the Dramatic Workshop in New York, Harry Guardino. I got a twinge of jealousy at Harry's success because I was stuck behind a desk and totally out of the acting loop.

It was agreed that I would be paid fifty dollars a week in Lire. It was not a very impressive amount and surely not on a scale with what an American would make living in a foreign country. I was being paid as an Italian worker, which was fine if I were living at home with my family and everyone was chipping in to support a household. After a couple of weeks of being sequestered between the office and my room at the Pensione, I was crawling the walls. I was on a dead end street with no relief in sight. I was obviously given a job that didn't amount to a hill of beans because when I submitted my one-page recommendations to Sg. Hashmi, he placed them on his desk and dismissed me with a wave of his hand sending me back to my office.

One night, after work, I decided to splurge and treat myself to a good Italian dinner. Within walking distance of the Pensione was the restaurant, Il Pescatore. The food was purported to be excellent and the prices outrageous. What the hell, I thought, I deserved some relief from my dreary existence. Seated alone in the restaurant, I savored my broiled fish and pasta as a guitar-playing minstrel serenaded the clientele. I was engrossed in people watching when I heard someone call my name. As I turned, I saw a rather attractive woman approaching my table with her arms outstretched and her red hair lovingly framing a round, warm face. I had but a moment to register from where I knew her when she enveloped me in her arms and kissed me warmly on the cheek.

"How long have you been in Rome?" she asked. I suppose she reacted to the quizzical look on my face because I could not for the life of me remember where we had met or who she was. "Annalena," she said. "Annalena Limentani. You don't remember me?"

Of course I remembered her, but not as this glowing ball of femininity who was embracing me in front of God and everyone. When last I saw her she was close to death and now she was filled with life and had blossomed into an Italian beauty.

"Forgive me, Annalena," I stumbled, "but it has been almost three years and you've…changed. You look fantastic!" I put my arms around her and returned the greeting.

She explained that she was with business friends and that she could only talk for a few moments but that we must get together the following day for lunch and I must tell her all. And then she was gone. I had intended to get in touch with her and Mike Billingsly upon my arrival in Rome but with my new resolve to abstain from acting, I was afraid that I would be tempted if I exposed myself to those members of the acting community. It was a big mistake and I was determined to make amends as soon as possible.

The following day I left the office at noon and did not return until three that afternoon. Annalena and I sat in a café in the Piazza Hungaria and filled in all the gaps of the past three years. She had successfully recovered from her bout with death three years previously and she had gone on to become a very successful theatrical agent with Kaufmann and Lerner, a subsidiary of the William Morris Agency in New York and Hollywood. She represented a number of well-known American and European actors and was considered "the agent" in Italy. I was most happy for her success and was caught up in her enthusiasm. But as I related my present situation, I could tell that she was most disappointed with my resolve to give up my career. I was quick to steer her off the conversation and onto less personal subjects. She told me that she had never forgotten that it was me who she saw when first she returned from death three years before at that hospital. And her mother had often asked what had become of me. I would have to come to the house for dinner and tell them all about my time in Israel. We made plans to have lunch together again and if I wasn't busy over the weekend, we would have to get together for dinner as she wanted to show me "her Rome."

For the next week Annalena became the savior of my sanity as I continued to rot at my menial employment. One day she called me at the office and invited me for lunch. I could tell that something was on her mind but she took her time to make her case.

"A friend of mine is preparing a film from a very lovely script," she said matter-of-factly. "The company is looking for a young leading man…"

"Shouldn't be any problem," I intoned. "Rome is full of actors."

"It's a demanding role…a fantasy about a young sailor," she added.

"How about Mark Damion?" I suggested. He was a young expatriated American living in Italy whom I had met some years before.

"No, too pretty. They need someone who can age twenty years from the beginning to the end of the story."

"Well, I wish I could help, Annalena, but I don't know that many actors in Rome."

After a long pause she said, "Would you mind reading the script? Perhaps you could come up with some ideas."

Now, I didn't need a building to fall on me to tell me where this conversation was heading but I was still determined that if I was to save my marriage to Lydia, I would have to stay where I was and prove to Arthur that I could make something of my life. But I did promise to read the script.

The script in question had been roughly translated from Italian to English but I could get the general idea of the story and the characters. It would not be a great film but it could be a small gem if the director knew what he was doing. As I read the plot and saw the character evolve, I imagined myself in the lead role. Under any other condition I would have jumped at a chance to read for the part but I was married to my present situation for better or for worse. That evening I went by her office to return the script to Annalena. Everyone else had gone home and we were alone. I placed the script on her desk and sat down.

"You've got to give up that lousy job," she said quite bluntly. "What the hell are you doing there, anyhow? It's not for you. I could tell that from the first night I saw you at the restaurant. If it means so much to you to make a success of your marriage, then at least be happy in what you're doing. I could pick up the phone this minute and call the Production Company and sight unseen, you could have the lead in this film!"

"You know I can't do that. What about Arthur and Hashmi? One phone call from either of them and I would be *persona non gratis* all over Europe in five minutes."

"Do you think that Arthur gives a second thought about what happens to you? You're out of Israel and that's his only concern. Stop being a child. You want it in writing?"

I knew she was right but I didn't want to admit that Lydia could be a party to this situation. "When do I have to give you an answer?" I finally asked. It was Friday night and the production company was leaving for location Monday morning and they still had not cast the lead in the film. I had to make a decision.

Saturday morning I returned to the office and cleaned out my desk. I stopped by the switchboard to see if Robert Hashmi was in his office but when I was told that he wouldn't be back until Monday morning, I jotted down a short note, thanked him for letting me use the office and said that I was moving on.

I spent Saturday afternoon at the production office meeting the director and producer. There was still a dilemma that had to be resolved; one of the leading characters in the film had to be cast. The script called for the character to be of Spanish descent but I thought that a black actor would add a bit of color to the role. The idea was immediately taken up by the director, but where to find a black actor in Rome?

The only person with whom I had been in contact since my arrival in Rome had been my old dancing teacher from New York when I was studying at the Dramatic Workshop. Archie Savage was appearing at Bricktop's on the via Veneto and he was a definite part of my show business roots. Whenever we were together, Archie never criticized or passed judgment on me for all the mistakes I had made along the way and he proved to be a most reliable friend whenever the chips were down. Now it was my turn to return his friendship. That evening I dragged Annalena, the director Renato Dall'Ara, and the producer, down to Bricktop's Bar. Before the evening was over, Archie had been signed for the film. The following day, Sunday, we left for Livorno.

My contract was for five weeks; two weeks in Livorno, two weeks on the Italian Riviera and one week at the Ichet Studios in Milan. But we no sooner arrive in Livorno than the rains came. We sat in our hotel rooms, staring up at the heavens while the producer fingered his rosary and counted. By the time my contract had terminated, we were still sitting in Livorno waiting for the weather to clear. And the weather was not the only disaster. The director Dall'Ara had cast my leading lady, Lissia Kalenda, in that role because she was sharing his bed. And the producer had a girlfriend who was playing the other female lead. At first, I felt sorry that we were victims of the weather but I soon realized that we were victims of a couple of erections because neither of the two girls could act their way out of bed.

I guess that now is as good a time as any to dispel any notion that I was being paid like a big Hollywood star. My salary came to the total sum of three hundred dollars a week in Italian Lire. I also received seventy-five dollars a week for expenses. It may not sound like a fortune but when you consider that I was earning fifty dollars a week sitting behind a desk, I was now enjoying a new found prosperity. And here's the kicker; Annalena refused to take any commission on my salary.

On days off, which were many, what with the rains, Archie and I would venture into town to spend the day shopping at one of Italy's most renowned flea markets. I bought material from which I later had a couple of suits made. Archie was the master of bargaining when it came down to the final price. The word spread around Livorno that two American actors were there to make a film and each evening when we went out of our hotel, we were mobbed by groupies wanting to get a look at the American "stars." Archie attracted women like bees to honey. His chocolate colored skin and his finely chiseled features just seemed to be the right combination and women of every size and shape came running. But Archie did not go that way and he channeled any interested ladies my way. In no uncertain terms, if there is a correlation between too much sex and blindness, I was a candidate for a tin cup and cane for the time we spent in Livorno.

All was not peaches and cream between the director, Dall'Ara, and myself. I did not profess to know everything there was to know about acting but it did not take long to realize that this Italian lover might know pussy but he didn't know squat about how to direct a film. His concept of great acting was for me to stand in front of the camera and wave my arms with violent gestures while emoting my lines. I kept countermanding his orders while he ordered one retake after another. On one occasion, I could take no more of his unimaginative approach to a scene so I just walked off the set and returned to my room at the hotel. Let me say here and now that I have always regretted that display of temperament and I was never again to repeat that mistake although there were times when biting the bullet was tantamount to suicide. As I sat in my hotel room, the sun finally burst forth and instead of rolling film, Renato placed a call to his producer and I placed a call to Annalena and both were on their way to Livorno while the cast and crew sat around twiddling their thumbs. There was a screening that night after the cinema had its last showing, and we were able to ascertain how the film was going. It wasn't as bad as I imagined but it was obvious that I was acting up a storm and God bless Renato, he immediately saw the problem himself. We agreed to work together to bring a more natural character to the screen. Meanwhile, Annalena renegotiated my contract to cover the remaining scenes to be shot and the next morning she was on her way back to Rome. In Italy, an actor was not covered by a union contract so in order to protect me from being screwed by the production company, I was paid in advance of shooting each week. When the money stopped, so did my talent.

In order to mend bridges, Renato suggested to the producer that I get an extra hundred dollars a week because I was working day and night without compensation for overtime. It was a gentlemanly gesture on his part and we went on with the filming each with a new understanding and respect.

Archie and I managed to figure out ways to get into trouble whenever time allowed. Lissia, my leading lady, was the sweetest little eighteen year old you ever wanted to meet. And the idea did enter my mind to try to jump her bones if and when the opportunity ever reared its ugly head. What the hell, an erection has no conscience.

But after doing a couple of love scenes with Lissia, it was obvious that she had never been versed in the finer things of life such as bathing, soap and deodorant. On a couple of occasions, when the weather turned extremely warm, Lissia gave off an odor that could choke a horse. After discussing it with Archie, we decided to send her a box of soap, the real good stuff with deodorant in it, in the hopes that she would get the message. She didn't! And I was getting pissed that we still had to do a number of very passionate love scenes with her smelling like rotting fish. I never criticized the fact that she did not shave her legs and that it appeared that there was a flock of birds nesting under her arms. I don't know what possessed me but I had to strike a blow for those of us who believe in personal hygiene. The following day would be a big love scene. That evening Archie and I went to one of the good Florentine restaurants in Livorno and ordered one of their specialties, a humongous T-bone steak. I explained to the waiter that I wanted the steak covered with raw garlic and that if I could see one sliver of meat through the garlic, I would send the whole thing back to the kitchen. When the steak arrived it was a veritable Mount Blanc of garlic! I ate every morsel on the plate but late that night, in bed, I began to sweat, got nauseous and heaved up a ton of garlic. The following morning I showed up on the set all smiles and ready to do my big love scene. I could smell the garlic emanating from every pore of my body. Archie was doubled over with laughter because even the crew gave me a wide berth as I passed by. Let it be known that it was Lissia who got the last laugh. Although I was a walking garlic disaster, she never noticed a thing. I suppose she imagined that I had changed my cologne to an odor not unpleasant to her. It took me days to get the smell of garlic from my skin by way of my sweat glands.

Lissia Kalenda and Lawrence in *Mobby Jackson*, Livorno, Italy 1961

I arrived back at our hotel late one evening after a long day of shooting. There was a message from Annalena for me to get in touch with her immediately. It took hours to get through to Rome and Annalena had been long asleep when I finally made contact. She informed me that she had received a cable from Arthur and Mathilda saying that they would be passing through Rome on their way to Israel, and that Arthur wanted me to meet them. I put Annalena through to Renato and he promised that he would work around me in order that I could catch the train to Rome to meet with my "friends."

I was plagued with the thought that perhaps I had misread Arthur and that there was a chance that he had actually sent me to Rome to give me a chance to break into his company. The trip to Rome was endless. As I waited for their plane to touch down, I rehearsed all the things I wanted to say to him, including an apology for running out on him, should the occasion call for it.

But Arthur did not greet me when he got off the plane. He preceded right past me on his way to the bar. Mathilda took me by the arm and played the role of diplomat. Over drinks, Arthur read me the riot act. My actions reaffirmed his impression of me; I was a loser and I did not deserve a girl like Lydia. If I had any intentions for reconciliation, I would report to the office the first thing in the morning, apologize to Signor Hashmi and maybe, just maybe, he would return me to my job. I must admit, the man really had a way of bringing out the worst in me. I listened without saying a word and when he finished, I reached into my pocket and took out a roll of Italian Lire. I peeled off what I considered was enough to cover my airfare from Israel and threw it on the bar.

"Thanks for all your help," I said. I turned to go.

"You'll never see Lydia again," he warned.

"Perhaps you're right. Maybe it's better for her this way. I can't compete with you. I don't want to. I'm finally doing what's best for me and damn the lot of you!" I caught the next train back to Livorno and the following day I resumed work on the film.

* * *

After some ten weeks of shooting we wrapped in Livorno and the company moved on to the town of Imperia, a small fishing village located to the north on the Italian Riviera. The weather continued to plague us and what was to be a three-week shoot dragged out to seven. The evenings turned miserably cold and some of the night shots had to be done in the rain to get the desired effects. Annalena called me to say that she was taking her vacation the following week and that if it was all right with me, Renato had extended to her the courtesy of the company and she could spend a week with us on location. It was a godsend! We would soon be winding down the film and I needed some time with Annalena to discuss the possibility of finding more work and where I might find a place to stay once I returned to Rome.

I suppose one cannot fight against that which is ordained. Annalena and I ended up sleeping together. I know that I needed a lot of TLC but I could never understand why she chose to bed down with me. After all, she had her choice of a bevy of international actors from which to pick and surely I was no great shakes when it came to my career. But for whatever reason, Annalena and I served each other well and that week on the Riviera was like an extended holiday. Annalena assured me that there would be more work in the offing and that *Mobby Jackson*, the film I was currently doing, would only enhance my career. She suggested a very nice apartment in Parioli once I returned to Rome. She had covered all my bases.

Somewhere it is written that "idle hands are the devil's workshop", or something like that. With all the free time between shooting days, I managed to indulge myself with side trips into the countryside. There was something about Italy that captivated me and appealed to my romantic nature. How I ended up in San Remo I will never know but there was an old and very majestic casino that caught my eye and I decided to try my hand at the game of roulette. It was a weekend, work had shut down on the film because of inclement weather, and I was in no rush to get back to Imperia. I must have sat at the gaming table for a good six hours, finally coming away with a handful of Italian Lire worth the equivalent of five hundred American dollars. I had devised a system that I was convinced was foolproof; I couldn't lose.

The following week, I recruited Archie to come with me to the casino to implement my system. He would play at one end of the table, I would play at the other end, and we would progressively move our bets over the numbers. I was on a mission. When last I met with Annalena, she was in the process of putting together a consortium to open a nightclub in Rome. Each participant would put up fifty thousand dollars and there would be ten investors. I could taste the excitement of being a part of such a venture but I was short by about forty-five thousand dollars. And there it was, just sitting at the roulette table in San Remo waiting for me to pick up my winnings. Archie and I played through the night and early into the next morning until my entire savings had totally disappeared; five thousand dollars. We were so broke that between us we didn't have enough money to purchase tickets to get us back to Imperia, so we boarded the train in San Remo and moved from car to car just ahead of the conductor until we arrived at our destination. As I reflected back over the years, my little foray into the world of gambling was a stupid endeavor.

In our seventeenth week of shooting we moved to Milan. Our Pensione was situated right off the Piazza Duomo where the mammoth church with its ornate spires and architecture was most impressive. I don't think I ever saw so many pigeons in my life! But the cold weather had set in and Milan is a miserable city when it's cold. Ichet Studios was some half hour drive through the city and where the tourists only got to see the Duomo and La Scala, we got to see some of the seediest parts of that cosmopolitan city. All the remaining scenes to be shot were interiors so we were not affected by the inclement weather. Just two more weeks of shooting and *Mobby Jackson* would be history. The little production company was fast running out of money and instead of looking for other sources of financing, pages were literally lifted from the script even if it left great holes in the story plot.

One of the scenes to be shot at Ichet was to take place in a waterfront dive in which I get into a barroom brawl with another sailor and the place is reduced to shambles. The scene started with a girl dancer doing her solo dance. The girl's name was Patrizia and although I have seen better-looking dancers in my life, she had a lot of enthusiasm and was perfectly charming. She was appearing each evening at one of the local nightclubs, Il Pipistrello. And Patrizia just adored Archie and took to following him around like a pet puppy. So great was her charm that she was able to extract from Archie a promise that he would bring me down to the club that evening after work. I was more than perturbed that Archie would volunteer my services when we were working twelve to fourteen hours each day. But he accused me of behaving like a big "Hollywood star" and suggested that I come off it. Besides, I owed him after our fiasco in San Remo. So that evening I dragged my weary ass down to Il Pipistrello to watch Patrizia do exactly what I had been watching her do all week on the set.

The rathskeller type club was situated in the basement of a building in a part of town that catered to the low end of the tourist trade. Once inside the club, one descended a flight of stairs into a long room where the dance floor took up most of the space with tables and chairs situated along the walls. The bandstand was at the far end of the room where Patrizia had arranged a table for her two celebrities. From where we were seated we could observe everyone who entered the barn-sized room by way of the stairs. The room began to fill within a few minutes of our arrival and I made Archie promise that he would get me out of there as soon as the show was over. We ordered a bottle of wine and watched the couples as they moved around the dance floor. Suddenly, my attention was drawn to the stairs where two of the most luscious looking women were making their way down into the club with their companions. One was dressed in powder blue with hair to match and the other was all in pink. I was partial to pink and told Archie that I was prepared to make him heir to all my worldly possessions if he would only get me an introduction to the one in pink.

"You mean CreeCree?" he asked all knowingly.

"Is that the little darling's name, CreeCree? How absolutely charming. Sole heir to all my worldly possessions," I repeated.

Without another word, Archie got up from the table and disappeared into the crowd. A few minutes later he returned to the table.

"It's all arranged. During the next dance you're to cut in. But try to be cool, man. She's with a date. And by the way, she only speaks French." I smiled at the thought of how disappointed Archie was going to be when he found out that my estate was penniless. As the music changed, Archie nodded to me and I got up and proceeded across the dance floor to where CreeCree was dancing with her date, a gorilla dressed in a suit. Dare I cut in? I thought. But when she saw me from the corner of her eye, she said something to her partner that sounded like "an old friend", and I found myself in her arms. She was wearing a backless, almost frontless little creation and smelled of spring flowers. Her skin was cool to my touch and as I spirited her around the floor I could feel a wee bit of activity commencing between my loins. She was not the most demure girl I had ever embraced and she danced with her body literally wrapped around mine. I could feel every crack and crevice of her lovely young body. No doubt about it, I was getting an erection…and so was CreeCree! When it finally dawned on me that this precious thing in my arms was actually a man, I created a space between the two of us through which once could drive a Mack truck. As I held "it" at arms length, I could only think of what punishment I was going to mete out on Archie once I got my hands on him. As I led CreeCree back to her companion, the last thing she said to me was, "Please don't tell the man I'm with. He doesn't know." From the look and the size of the guy CreeCree was with, either he was in for the shock of his life or CreeCree was on her way to the hospital for a prolonged stay. When I got back to the table, Archie was gone. I looked around the room and caught sight of him at the other end of the room, double stepping it up and out of the club. He could hardly contain himself as he was doubled over with laughter and just as I was about to take off after him, the lights dimmed and the show was about to begin. It took two hours of a second rate show to take my mind off of my promise to murder Archie that night.

* * *

Returning to Rome was like going home. Ironies of all ironies, Annalena had arranged an apartment for me on the residential side of the Residence Palace Hotel where I had been dumped when first working for DEAR Films. The apartment was ample, being fully furnished and having a working fireplace, a closet sized kitchenette, a terrace and my very own *bidet* in which I could wash my socks. I had managed to save a couple thousand dollars even with my losses in San Remo. Annalena had convinced me to send her a check each week so I would have a small nest egg by the time we finished with the film. She had a good business head but she hadn't counted on Alicia Purdom freezing all the accounts of Kaufmann and Lerner. Alicia and her spouse, Edmund Purdom, were in the process of going through a divorce and in order to keep Edmund from taking off and leaving the country, her attorney froze the client account for the whole agency. I was indefinitely broke. But Annalena came to my rescue and advanced me enough money from her personal account to get me by until things eased up at the office.

There was still one loose end in my life that had to be resolved. With Annalena sitting by my side, I placed a call to Lydia in Israel. My heart was beating like the world's largest base drum as I heard the phone ringing in Rehovot. Then, I heard her voice as clear as if she were sitting in the next room.

"Lydia, it's me, Lawrence."

There was a long pause as she gained her composure. There wasn't an ounce of warmth in her voice. Arthur and Mathilda had done a good job.

"I'm not coming to Rome," she said. "Arthur has arranged for me to go to school in London to study architecture."

"Is that what you really want?" Please say "no", I thought.

"I'm sure it's what I want."

I wished her well and hung up the phone. Annalena held me in her arms all night as my mind retraced the three years Lydia and I had shared together. Our fantasy had finally and unquestionably run its course…

CHAPTER EIGHT
AND THE SHOW GOES ON

Rome in the early sixties still retained much of the romance and mystique that Hemmingway referred to in some of his early works. The sounds of music could be heard wafting from every window and storefront. Italians had a great pride in those things that were *proprio Italiano* (uniquely Italian). The center of Roman social life was the activities along the Via Veneto with its outdoor cafes and the hustling *paparazzi* (photographers) trying to get that one shot of a visiting celebrity in an off-guarded moment. The film renaissance in Rome had attracted name stars from all over the world: Elizabeth Taylor, Eddie Fisher, Richard Burton, Guy Williams, Jack Palance, Alan Ladd, Keenan Wynn, Guy Madison, Lex Barker, David Niven, Barbara Steele... My God, the list was endless. Any night of the week one could sit in front of the Café de Paris and watch the celebrity parade go by. The restaurants were filled to overflowing as the actors and writers and performers dined on the town. For an American looking for a bit of home, there was Jerry's Bar. And for the Polynesian enthusiast, there was Jerry's Luau, one block up and around the corner from the Veneto. A little off the beaten path and around the corner from the Fontana Trevi was the Piccolo Budapest where one could savor a bit of old Hungary as the violins cried with the sounds of gypsy music. For those of us who lived in Parioli, there was a wonderful restaurant called *Il Camineto* (the fireplace) where one could savor such dishes as Osso Bucco and Fettucini Alfredo and fresh melon with prosciutto. Most of us who lived in the American colony had to make do with a way of life that was simple and Italian. But those who were passing through, who were in town for one film and were staying at the Grand or the Hilton, they paid dearly for everything. And in many ways, it ruined it for those of us who remained behind because waiters and hookers were spoiled by the rich foreigners who threw money around as if it were going out of style. It sometimes pissed me off that "my

Rome" was being raped by the high rollers who would soon leave and create a financial vacuum that the locals could ill afford to fill.

I had been back in Rome about a month when Annalena called to tell me that Fillippo Ratti was preparing a film in which I would be perfect for the lead. The afternoon I had my interview I was a nervous wreck. I had been sitting around for the past month considering the possibility that I might never work again. I managed to pick up a few days here and there at the dubbing studio but I had a passion to get in front of the camera again. Now I was up for another lead and I was determined to get this role. My Italian had come a long way and I felt comfortable in conversation. I discovered that the greatest mistake American actors made when coming to live in Rome was not making the effort to learn the language. Italians enjoyed and appreciated it when a foreigner made an attempt to speak their language. It opened many doors.

When I walked into the production office of Sergio Cortona, an old friend, Franco D'Este, warmly greeted me. He had been an actor on *Mobby Jackson* and was now the writer of record on this new film, *Rapina al Quartiere Ovest* (Rape of the Western Quarter.) As fate would have it, Franco had recommended me for the leading role in his new film. The film community in Rome was indeed small and word traveled quickly from one production company to another when a new personality came on the scene. Again, the budget was quite small and the salary being offered was commensurate with what I had made on my last film but my first concern was to be working in the hopes that eventually I would be recognized as a commercial entity and move up to bigger and better films.

Rapina was a gem of a film and Filippo Ratti was a director of some renown having had a number of successful films to his credit. But Fillipo had been stricken some years before with tuberculosis and he was just now making a bid to return to the scene. We hit it off immediately and I could tell that if this man had an ounce of talent, this was a perfect showcase for him.

Basically, the film comprised two stories, one of a cold-blooded killer (played by me) and the other story of a family trying to stay together against all odds. The end of the film brings the two stories together when the father of the family finds some money from a bank robbery that I had pulled off. After being torn between keeping the money and turning it over to the police, the father opts for the latter that leads to a shootout with the police and me. In a reckless chase scene, a car runs down the little boy of the family and he and I share the same ambulance on the way to the hospital.

I'll admit that I did nothing for the telling of the story but you'll just have to take my word that Franco did a masterful job on the script and the rest would be up to Fillipo.

The director and producer both agreed that I would be much more menacing if my hair was bleached blond. I had visions of losing all my hair due to some mistake in the bleaching but Annalena and Franco convinced me that it was a simple process. I must admit that someone had a good eye because the effect of me with bleached blond hair was startling and I did not have to do too much to portray villainy. What I didn't like was the two trips a week to the hairdresser for touchups, and of course, the crowd of gays that I attracted whenever I happened onto the Veneto.

The film was scheduled for five weeks of principal photography and Filippo brought it in exactly on time and on budget. He was a competent director and did a great job but unfortunately the budget placed many restrictions on him. When it went into distribution there was not sufficient capital to hype the film and it quickly faded from public view. *Rapina* did nothing to advance my career but it surely did nothing to hurt it.

* * *

Located some hundred meters down the street from where I was living was the American Palace Hotel where a group of us sometimes congregated for our evening toddy. I had become very friendly with an American film editor who was staying at the hotel, by the name of Gene Ruggiero. He had been the film editor for the Academy Award nominated film, *Oklahoma*, and he had a list of credits as long as my arm. Gene had a young assistant working with him by the name of Tim Zinneman and when a vacancy in my building became available, I called Tim and he moved in. We became fast friends and Tim sometimes called on me to translate when he was having trouble communicating with his beautiful Italian girlfriend, Anna. I also took the time to show Tim some of the basics of photography in which he was most interested. And when Tim's dad arrived in Rome, I was invited over to meet his father,

Fred Zinneman, who had been the recipient of an Academy Award for his direction of the film, *High Noon*. Here was a chance to show a first rate director what I was capable of delivering as an actor. With Tim's help I arranged for the Zinneman family to view *Rapina*. It was still in the rough cut stages but the producer and director were both eager to have such a qualified and famous authority as Fred Zinneman view their work.

The evening of the screening Tim's father invited me to join the family, along with Tim's girlfriend Anna, for dinner before we went to the theatre. Since it was a private screening we were not in any particular hurry and we proceeded to enjoy a fine dinner with plenty of Italian *vino*. By the time we got to the theatre I noticed that Mrs. Zinneman was feeling no pain. By the end of the two-hour screening, the Zinnemans were biting the bullet to get back to their hotel. The film was painful to watch without music, sound effects and the correct sound levels. I don't think that Mr. Zinneman was very impressed with our efforts and he and his family were eager to leave the premises. Unfortunately, Mrs. Zinneman missed the top step of the second floor studio stairwell and she didn't stop bouncing until she hit the bottom of the landing. There were just some days when I wished I had never gotten out of bed and that evening was one of them. I guess it wasn't meant to be and if I want to wane philosophical about the whole evening, Mr. Zinneman missed out on a good deal: me!

During this time in Rome I befriended an American by the name of Joe Justman. Joe had moved to Rome with his family just for a change of scenery and I considered his home my home away from home. Joe had been in the film business in one way or another for half a century and it seemed that he knew just about everyone who passed through town. He was a very gracious person and his hospitality was a mile wide.

On one occasion, Joe mentioned to me that a friend of his, Terrance Young, a director from England, was in town to direct a film with Alan Ladd and that if I got in touch with Terrance and used Joe's name, perhaps he would be able to find a role for me in his film. I immediately phoned Cinecitta where it was purported that Terrance was in pre-production, but the chain of command was too deep and I could never get through to him. After a couple of weeks of trying I got Terrance's home number from Joe. I called the house a couple of times around the dinner hour knowing that is usually the best time to reach someone if you're persistent. But I was getting a bit frustrated that my efforts were in vain, so I decided to call Terrance at seven AM on a Sunday morning!

It was only a small role but I cherished it because Terrance went on to direct the James Bond epics shortly thereafter. He later told Joe, "Any actor who has the balls to call a director at seven o'clock on a Sunday morning deserves a job." The film was *Duel of Champions* that failed to catch on in the States. But for me it was one of those windfalls that actors only dream about. I was signed for only one day's work. The following day the company would be leaving for Yugoslavia for exterior shooting. My scene demanded the use of many extras and I had a rather early makeup call because I was supposed to have a very nasty looking scar down the side of my face.

Worked only one day, paid for ten weeks in *Duel of Champions*, Rome, Italy 1961

I sat around all day in makeup and costume waiting for my big scene and between the time we got the first establishing shot of me, some minor disaster befell the company and they had to close down production for the day. I was only getting a paltry hundred dollars for the day but it was decided that since the company was leaving the following morning for Yugoslavia, they would keep me on the payroll to insure that I would be available when they returned to Rome to finish my scene. We worked six-day weeks on location so for the next three months, until the company returned from Yugoslavia, I collected six hundred dollars a week! And by the time they finally got around to shooting my scene, Terrance was no longer connected with the film. Granted I didn't get rich from the six hundred dollar-a-week annuity but it sure was a nice feeling to know that I was wanted.

About this same time I met another American actor who was passing through Rome by the name of Jimmy Dobson. He had been living and working in Munich, Germany, for the past two years on an obscure American television series called *The Vikings,* as casting director and sometime actor. It was one of those epics that no one seems to remember but it must have had some success because it ran for two years. It starred an old acquaintance of mine from New York, Jerome Courtland.

Jimmy was passing through Rome on his way back to the States after the production closed down and we met at Jerry's Bar on the Veneto. During our conversation he asked if I might know of a good photographer because he needed some current headshots and wanted to use some of the Rome landmarks as a background. It would be something different that would catch the eye of casting people back in Hollywood. I suggested that if he wanted to take a chance, I would be glad to take his pictures for the price of film and printing. It was like casting bread on the water; who knew when he might return to Europe to cast another film?

Jimmy and I spent a full day together where I photographed him with some of the world's most famous landmarks in the background. I worked with natural light and used the technique of blurring the background in order not to detract from the subject, but one could still discern the Coliseum or the shadows of the Caves of Caracala. A couple of days later, when Jimmy saw the proofs, he was elated. He must have ordered a dozen finished photographs for which I charged him exactly what the lab charged me. He tried to lay some money on me for my time but I explained that I enjoyed the challenge and that perhaps someday I would return to photography and if he knew anyone coming to Rome that needed pictures, he could give them my number. Actually, my remark was said in jest and I was really not prepared for what happened about a month later.

It was about three o'clock one morning when I heard the phone ringing from way off in the deepest recess of my mind. I was in a sound sleep and I was always reticent to answer late night calls because it usually meant bad tidings. But in this case it was an actor calling from Champino Airport. He had just arrived in Rome and had been instructed by Jimmy Dobson to get in touch with me immediately upon landing if he wanted me to do his photos. Three o'clock in the morning was a bit literal but I guess it was no more so than an actor calling a director at seven o'clock on a Sunday morning when he was looking for an acting job. I set up an appointment to meet the actor at Jerry's Bar and instructed him to bring what pictures he had in order to ascertain if I could do any better. A few days later we spent the day photographing at a number of historical sight that I felt complimented this actor's personality. I had no idea what to charge as the actor wanted to order half a dozen finished shots. I decided to set a flat rate and the actor assured me that I was definitely cheating myself and that my work was worth much more than what I was asking. But at that time, I had no idea that this could be the beginning of a very profitable little business.

A few days later I got a call at a much more reasonable hour from another actor who had just arrived in Rome and wanted photographs. Jimmy Dobson also recommended me to him and before I had finished with his session, I heard from a young actress, Fay Spain, who also needed shots. Even if I was only going to be doing one or two sittings from time to time, I would have to set up some kind of business plan. I decided to do the photography sittings for just the cost of the film and the lab work. In those days in Rome, that would run about ten dollars which included four rolls of film, or forty-eight shots. After that, if the actor wished to purchase any of the photos, he would pay twenty-five dollars for each original shot. From a pre-shooting interview with each potential client, I could determine what they needed to enhance their portfolio and what they could possibly afford to pay. Say I was looking at a client that needed five different headshots that included changes of wardrobe, location and mood. From the proof sheets I would pick out what I considered to be five of the best shots along with five mediocre shots and have them all blown up to proof size, five by nine inches. In most cases the client would pick the five good shots, rejecting the five decoys. The system turned out to be about ninety-five percent foolproof. Since the client paid for all my expenses, whatever I made was profit. And since I worked out of my hat, there were also no taxes! But what I didn't count on was that the photography business began to snowball. Actors were telling other actors about the photographer in Rome who didn't charge for the sitting and if one didn't want to purchase photos, there was no obligation. Before I realized what had happened, I was averaging ten sittings a week. Word got around the colony that my work was of very high quality and I began getting accounts from people other than actors. The photography was beginning to afford me a high standard of living in the Italian economy.

* * *

My social life was centered around the pool of the Cesare Augustus Hotel in Northern Rome. The actor, Jack Palance, and his family were frequent guests at the pool and he and I became friendly over a period of time. Sometimes when Jack and his wife, Virginia, had things to do during the day, I would pick up Cody, Holly and Brook, who were just tots at that time, and I would bring them up to the rooftop pool where I would baby-sit. One day, Jack introduced me to a very distinguished gentleman who was wearing an eye patch. As we sat around the pool, I learned that the gentleman was the director of Jack's next film, Andre deToth who had been born in Hungary. When I mentioned to Andre that my grandfather had come from Budapest, we became fast friends. I also mentioned that I had worked on a number of films in Hollywood as a fencer and I proceeded to drop a number of names of stunt men I had worked with. He immediately picked up on my background and asked if I would be interested in choreographing the fencing for the film he was preparing to do in Yugoslavia, *The Mongols*. I hesitated to respond because the photography was going so well that it didn't make much sense for me to branch out into another field. But Andre also mentioned that there might be a part that I could play. Would that interest me? Within days I was invited down to the production office of Royal Films and after a short interview, I signed the contract to act in and choreograph *The Mongols*. My contract was to be for five weeks in Belgrade.

I put the photography business on the back burner and caught a plane to Yugoslavia. The money was not great, probably half of what the photography was netting, but actors are like racehorses: when the starting bell sounds, they are off and running.

Belgrade was not the romantic, intriguing city that I imagined it would be. In fact, it was very depressing since Tito had recently nationalized almost all small businesses and the people had lost their initiative to work. Aside from my pay that was to be deposited weekly in my bank account in Rome, I was drawing the equivalent of twenty-five dollars a day in *dinars* to cover my expenses. It was more money than I could spend if I tried. The merchandise in the stores was of such poor quality that I had no desire to purchase anything. If one wished to shop, there was a government export store where one had to pay with hard currency (American dollars or English pounds) and the quality of merchandise was of the best. But I did not plan to spend my dollars when I was loaded down with dinars that were worth nothing outside the country. I would figure out a way to get some value from the worthless money.

Immediately upon my arrival I was hustled out to the University to audition some of the best fencers in the country. They would make up the better part of my crew. I chose ten of the best to help set up the battle scenes and in turn, they would teach other fencers the routines. In one battle scene alone, we had two thousand men simulating sword combat.

There was reluctance on the part of the students to get very friendly with outsiders because of the political tension at that time. But it didn't take long before I was being invited into their homes to meet their families and got a feeling of life behind the Iron Curtain. I empathized with these young people because they were the cream of Yugoslavian youth and once they had completed their educations, there was very little for them to look forward to in the way of employment. Many expressed a desire to leave their homeland to live abroad, mostly in the U.S. I don't know how many of them made it but the desire to get out of their own country was prevalent.

I soon learned that working with Andre was not all peaches and cream. He was a Hungarian tyrant and he had a very strange way of exerting his authority. I remember the first day of shooting. We arose at five in the morning for a three-hour trip by car into the countryside. The Yugoslavian cavalry had been turned over to the production and there were in excess of two thousand extras on horseback dressed as Mongols or Polish soldiers. Jack was playing the role of Genghis Khan, Anita Ekberg, the Swedish beauty, was playing a Polish woman who had been captured by the Mongols, and I played a Polish officer, one of many, whose job it was to rescue the fair Ekberg. Imagine the scene of all those people assembled out on the plains of the Yugoslavian countryside, it was almost mind-boggling. And as the actors were getting their makeup and costumes, all hell broke loose. In true Italian fashion, someone had forgotten to bring the cameras from Rome! So there we sat for three days waiting for the cameras to pass through all the bureaucracy and paperwork of customs. I had heard that Jack Palance was a veritable tiger to work with and that he often displayed a very short fuse. But in spite of the mass screw-up, Jack remained cool and friendly at all times.

When we finally got the cameras, Andre set up the first scene with Jack. Rehearsal went off well and then the cameras began to roll. Andre insisted on doing sixty "takes" of that first scene! Everyone waited for Jack to explode but to everyone's surprise, he did the scene with the same professional enthusiasm each and every time. At the end of the day, Andre announced that they would print the first take! I thought Jack would kill him. That evening, when Andre and I were alone discussing plans for the upcoming battle scenes, I asked why he had tested Jack in that manner. "Control," was his answer. And later, when I asked Jack why he stood for Andre's obviously degrading behavior, he said that he took it out of "respect." I don't think I would have stood for it, but then, I was not a star and Jack was.

Jack Palance and I were casual friends up until the time we worked together in Yugoslavia. Then, on one occasion he saved my life, after which we really bonded. While the *Mongols* was in production in Belgrade, another film company came into town and was working out of the same studio, *Koshutyak*. The other film starred Louis Jordan and Sylvia Syms and was called *The Virgins of Rome*. I had decided to use some of those Yugoslavian dinars to purchase tickets for a box at the local opera for a performance of Don Quixote as it was considered to be one of the premier performances of the season. Changalovic was singing the title role. I knew that Jack was an opera buff so I invited him, Louis and Sylvia to join me for the evening. It turned out to be one of the finest opera performances I have even seen.

A Vulcan Odyssey

After the show, Louis invited us all for a late dinner at the Sportsmen's Club, probably the best eating establishment in all of Belgrade. Over after-dinner drinks Louis threw down the gauntlet.

"I believe that the Virgins of Rome can beat the Mongols at a game of volley ball," Louis told Jack.

"You're joking," said Jack. "It wouldn't be a contest."

"A small wager?" asked Louis.

And so it was that after dinner and back at Jack's hotel he took me aside and asked, "What do you know about volley ball?"

I hadn't a clue. I knew that there was a ball involved and there was a net, but that was the extent of my expertise. We put our heads together and Jack finally came up with a solution to save the Mongols from defeat. "How about some of those fencers of yours? There have to be at least a few volleyball players among them."

The next day I recruited a handful of giant college athletes all of whom swore up and down that they knew how to play volleyball. Jack and I were confident that the Mongols could cream those Virgins. The game was set for the coming Sunday at a remote park outside the city. My players assured me that they knew the location and they would get there on their own. They showed up on time and ready to play.

Jack Palance taking time out from filming *The Mongols*, Belgrade, Yugoslavia 1961

The Virgins team looked like midgets compared to the ringers I had recruited and I could tell that Louis was concerned that he had overplayed his hand. When the game was over, the Virgins had kicked the Mongol's asses! The score wasn't even close. I was embarrassed for my guys and as we packed up to head back to Jack's hotel to be subjected to the Virgin's jibes, I stood there with my players while everyone else climbed into their cars to return to the city. No one had offered to give my guys a lift back to town. I walked over to where Jack was seated alone in his limousine waiting for his driver. I stuck my head in the window.

"Hey, Jack, you've got some pull around here. How about seeing if you can get some wheels for my guys to get them back to town. After all, they did come out here at our invitation."

It must have been the tone of my voice because Jack jumped out of his limo ready to take on the world. "Get in here!" he yelled out at the students. "G'wan, get in."

I waved them over and they climbed into the limo but there was no more room for Jack or me. The driver promised that he would drive the students back to town and then return for us. Everyone else had taken off and only Jack and I remained in the park with about fifty spectators who had stayed for the game and were milling around to get a close look at the American movie star. Jack was pissed as he looked over at me with fire in his eyes.

"You know, you've got a big mouth!" he spat.

"What the hell are you talking about? You're the one who told me to put a team together. What's the big deal about arranging transportation for them? Damn it, don't be such a big shot!"

"Who the hell are you calling a big shot?"

"You, damn it…" The next thing I knew, Jack and I had squared off at each other ready to have a go at it. Did you ever notice that on the screen, when Jack has a scene in which he gets angry, his nostrils flair? Jack stood over me by a good three inches and as I held up my fists I swear I could see the back of his eyeballs through his flared nostrils. I was too scared and humiliated to back down now that we had attracted a sizeable crowd of onlookers anticipating bloodshed. Jack and I began to circle each other looking for an opening to throw that first punch. Then, out of the corner of his mouth he hissed, "You know, we look like a couple of asses."

"Yeah," I agreed. "What do we do?"

"C'mon," he said. "Let's get out of here." And with that he threw his arm over my shoulder and the two of us turned and headed for the park entrance, through the crown of disappointed onlookers, to where the limo would pick us up. And I know that Jack saved my life that day for if he ever hit me he probably would have killed me.

(While editing this book I learned that Jack Palance had passed away yesterday, November 10th, 2006. Although we had not been in touch for many years, he will be missed and my condolences go out to his family.)

Through Louis I learned that one of the cast members of the Virgins was packing up and heading back to London the following day. I don't know whatever possessed me but I felt compelled to buy some small gifts for Lydia and I imposed upon this actor to deliver them for me. We met at the Grand Hotel, a misnomer if there ever was one, for a drink and he informed me that we would have to call it a short evening because he had an early flight. I turned over the trinkets and Lydia's phone number in London to the actor and to show my gratitude, I ordered a bottle of Slivovitz, a national drink of Yugoslavia. It was supposed to be a plum brandy but it tasted more like something left over if someone pressed the liquid out of some old furniture. We soon learned that Slivovitz was a sneaky drink. My drinking companion was trying to get rid of his surplus dinars so he ordered another bottle and we called for the band to come over to our table for a private concert for which we tipped them handsomely. At about midnight we realized that if he was going to catch his early plane, we had better call it a night. But when we tried to get up, we both realized that we were paralyzed from the waist down. Of course, the only solution was black Turkish coffee and to kill the taste, we ordered another bottle of Slivovitz. At about three in the morning the management rolled us out into the street. We said our goodbyes, he turned towards the Metropole and I towards the park through which I would have to navigate to get back to my hotel. I was aware of everything I was doing but my legs were betraying me. I used parked vehicles and passing buildings for support. But once I got to the park, I was on my own. I was doing fine until I hit the wire intended to keep pedestrians off the grass. Down I went in a heap where I lay on the cool, green grass looking up at the brilliant stars in the purple sky. As I was trying to count the stars I became aware of the presence of an intruder, a rather large dog of questionable breed. He sniffed me over from head to foot and convinced that I was something he had never smelled before, he proceeded to pee all over me. It was in this condition that I arrived back at my hotel only to find the front door locked. I rang the night bell and when the porter finally came down and saw me, he shook his head, turned off the night-light and went back to his bed.

I was confined to my room for the next week with all sorts of stomach maladies. My chief concern was that the production company might decide to begin shooting the battle scenes while I was incapacitated. But luck was with me during my recuperation and I was neither called for work as an actor nor as choreographer. The first evening I recovered enough to entertain food, I ran into Jack's brother and sister-in-law in the dining room. John and Mary were having dinner with a very tall and attractive Yugoslav woman by the name of Delfina Tomasavic. I was invited to join the threesome.

I quickly learned that Delfina was staying at our hotel...under house arrest! I couldn't believe that such an attractive women could do anything that might bring down the wrath of the State Police. She had been born into Yugoslav royalty that existed before Tito's rise to power. His first order of business was to do away with the monarchy and confiscate all holdings of the rich in order to keep his promises to the people that he would share the wealth under the new regime. But Delfina's father had seen the writing on the wall and sent his brother to Brazil. Then the senior Tomasavic began to divest the family's holdings and diverted the money to bank accounts set up by his brother. By the time Tito had completed his takeover in the name of the new Communist state, the Tomasavic holdings were next to nil. Delfina's father was arrested and put in prison where he languished for five years. He finally killed himself.

At this time Delfina was married and had a daughter, Giardena. When the marriage began to dissolve, Delfina decided to leave the country and took up residency in Milan, Italy. She had lived there for some five years, afraid to return home for fear of retaliation from the Tito regime for her father's actions. But when Delfina's grandmother took ill, Delfina's greatest desire was to see the old lady, perhaps for the last time. Delfina went to the Yugoslav Consulate in Milan to see about permission to return home. The authorities assured her that all was forgiven and that she could return home without fear of reprisal. She packed up the child and returned to Dubrovnik, her hometown. But her homecoming was marred by the sudden illness of her child who suffered from a thyroid condition. Rather than trust the primitive medical facilities in Dubrovnik, she boarded a train with Giardena intending to take advantage of one of the good Catholic hospitals in Milan. When the train arrived in Trieste, the border between Yugoslavia and Italy, Delfina was informed that her passport was not in order and that she would not be allowed to leave the country until the proper paperwork was provided. The authorities agreed that the child would be permitted to proceed, so Delfina called ahead to the Sisters at the hospital to meet the train and make sure that Giardena received the proper medical attention. Meanwhile, the authorities assured Delfina that it was just a formality and that she would probably be able to leave the country in a matter of days. When I met her, she had been sitting for three months waiting for authorization to leave the country. And all the while Giardena was being taken care of by the Sisters.

I was very moved by her story that gave me an insight into the mechanics of the totalitarian government. Delfina was an innocent victim, a pawn in some bureaucratic foul-up that had kept her from being united with her five-year-old daughter for over three months. There was nothing anyone could do to help other than give her moral support. Each evening Delfina and I dined together, sometimes with John and Mary, other times with Jack. She was a lovely, charming woman who spoke no English but had a perfect command of Italian. We got along famously and enjoyed each other's company.

My five-week contract was now into its tenth week. The weather at night had turned cold so I purchased some sweaters and a jacket at one of the local department stores. It gave me a chance to unload a bushel of dinars and I figured I could always pass the clothing on to some of the students that were working for me on the film.

One evening, I came down to the dining room to find Delfina engaged in a serious conversation with John, Mary and Jack. It seemed that one of the Italian crewmembers had heard of Delfina's dilemma and had offered to marry her to get her out of the country. It was a good plan except that he wanted five thousand dollars for this act of charity. We were all incensed that the Italian had the balls to actually hold her up for money. I went ballistic and by the time I had settled down I heard myself saying that I would marry her without any payment! Everyone thought it was a great idea and Jack agreed to be my best man. I don't know what was going on in my head. I was already married! But who the hell would know that unless I said something so I just kept my mouth shut and put Delfina to work applying for the necessary papers from the Yugoslav authorities while I pursued permission from the American Consulate. I wanted everything to go right because once I was out of the country, there would be nothing else I could do to help her. The Consular officer told me, off the record, that he was familiar with Delfina's case and that he thought I was doing the right thing. That made me feel a lot better because I realized that there could be severe repercussions if I was caught sticking my nose into another country's internal affairs. The Consular officer assured me that he would give me all the protection of the United States government that he could and that once Delfina and I were married, there was nothing the Yugoslav government could do to prevent Delfina from leaving the country. Once we had cleared all the formalities with both governments we planned to be married the following Monday. Sunday evening, when Delfina and I were returning to the hotel from a small dinner party given by some of her friends, we were intercepted by another friend who informed us that the State Police were at the hotel with a warrant for her arrest. We found a taxi and rode around the city for hours, another good way to spend some dinars. We had breakfast at some obscure restaurant that opened early for workers and then we proceeded to the city hall where we were to be married. A number of Delfina's friends had already arrived…along with some members of the State Police. But they made no attempt to keep us from entering the building.

Marriage in a civil ceremony in Yugoslavia was really quite touching. "Everything that belongs to Lawrence now belongs to Delfina. Everything that belongs to Delfina now belongs to Lawrence. And everything that belongs to both of you now belongs to the State." With those tender words we were pronounced husband and wife. At the last minute Jack had to report to the studio for work so he could not serve as my best man but he sent his brother instead. It was a bit ironic because Johnny and I really did not care for each other and here he was, best man at my wedding. Something told me that this marriage was not going to last forever.

After the twelfth week of shooting on the film I went to the office to pick up my expense money for the following week. I was informed that the company had run out of money and that if I didn't care to stay on, I was free to return to Rome. I couldn't pack fast enough. It made very little difference to the plot of the film that I suddenly disappeared in the middle of the story. That's the way things were done in many Italian productions and it was that kind of haphazard production that finally led to the downfall of the Italian film industry.

* * *

My absence from Rome had not hurt my photography business. There were some dozen messages posted at Jerry's Bar from prospective clients. I fell right back into the swing of things with the photography without missing a beat. Between the photography and a periodic dubbing gig, I was managing very nicely. Unfortunately, my relationship with Annalena had greatly deteriorated. She had ceased to be my agent because my demands were too great and she had other more important clients with whom she had to devote her time. Shortly after my return from Yugoslavia I heard that she was seeing one of the American muscle men that had come to Rome to play in one of the Hercules films. A while later, I heard that she unsuccessfully attempted suicide. I did manage to speak to her briefly on the phone but she gave me one of those "busy agent routines" so I let it slide. I never saw her again but I think of her from time to time and it saddens me that we had not remained friends.

Two weeks after my return from Yugoslavia I received a call from Delfina. She was in Milan with her daughter! They had finally let her go. She invited me to come and visit her and Giardena and I accepted the invitation. As it turned out, Delfina was a very wealthy woman in her own right. She owned her own apartment on via Lario near the center of the city, she had a closet full of expensive clothes and Giardena attended a private and very expensive Catholic school. Delfina insisted that I be her guest as we dined in the finest restaurants in the city, attended La Scala for the opera and took in the theatre. We never broached the subject of divorce because I had no other plans for marriage. But Delfina was so grateful for my helping her to get out of Yugoslavia that she mistook it for love and began making plans for our life together. She was a very warm and loving person and we eventually consummated our marriage. But I never intended to give her the impression that we would stay married forever.

Aside from Delfina's work as a translator, she had a sizable monthly allowance each month from the investments her Uncle had made in

Brasilia where he had opened a number of very successful health spas. Delfina loved to spend money and it was partly this desire to have fine things that eventually led me to the realization that she was way out of my league. As a young man I was filled with a sort of false pride about my manhood. I always felt that I could make enough money to take care of my own needs. I never thought in terms of supporting a family or being responsible for another person's life. My failure to be able to support and take care of Lydia should have told me that with my lifestyle, I was not going to be able to take on the responsibility of marriage for a long time to come. Delfina had a compulsion to show me her gratitude by showering me with gifts. At first, I thought it was a fun gesture and didn't realize that she was actually courting me. In my blindness I accepted her offerings and compounded a very touchy problem. My first trip to Milan lasted only a few days and when I returned to Rome I was filled with a sense of accomplishment that I had been, in a small way, responsible for reuniting Delfina with her daughter. After that visit, we spoke to each other daily by phone. She visited Rome on a number of occasions and I went back to Milan for a few visits. We were playing at being married.

I received a letter from my father saying that he was coming to Rome with some of his handball buddies from the "Y." I had not seen him for more than three years and I missed him very much. Upon his arrival we dined and toured around the country for some ten days. I took him down to Ischia, a small island near Capri that the tourists had not yet discovered. Our first night on the island we met a couple of ladies, one a middle aged woman and the other, her secretary who was considerably younger. The four of us teamed up and spent our days on the beach and our evenings hopping from one club to another. When I think back, I realize that my father was not very assertive because the woman he was with absolutely adored him. My father could have made me a very happy man and provided for me for the remainder of my life had he put a move on that woman. Her name was Maria Ferrari and she was the sister of the famous car manufacturer, Enzo Ferrari.

Back in Rome, we decided to eat at my very favorite restaurant that was within walking distance from my apartment. Il Caminetto served some of the best Italian dishes in Rome and the prices were reasonable because they catered to the local Italians and not the tourist trade. When

I first returned to Rome in the fifties, Il Caminetto was just a small family storefront but the quality of food they served caused it to grow into a very popular local eatery. During nice weather, one could sit outside under the cover of an umbrella but it seemed that there was always a wait for a table. On this particular day, we decided to get an early start and arrive before the lunch crowd. As we came to the entrance I heard someone calling my name and I turned to see Delfina making her way through the maze of tables. She was quite a sight to behold, all six feet of her with her four-inch heels and beehive hairdo.

"I've been trying to call you for days," she gushed.

I was really quite surprised to see her. We prattled on in Italian until I realized that my father was just standing there not understanding a word that was being said.

"Oh, excuse me, Delfina. This is my father," I said in Italian.

Her eyes widened and I could see that she was overwhelmed. She took one step forward and embraced my dad to her ample bosom, all five foot nine of him. My dad was completely caught off guard and turned beet-red as he was being smothered in her breasts. In a moment, Delfina returned to her friends and promised to call me so we could have dinner together.

"Who was that?" asked my father as he regained his composure.

"Your daughter-in-law," I said as I passed him heading for the door. When I entered the restaurant, I looked back and he was still standing outside glued to the pavement. It seems that I had failed to mention to him that I had remarried and for all he knew, I was still married to Lydia. It was a long dinner that evening as I tried as best I could to clear up his confusion.

Robby thought that the pool at the Cesare Augustus was the greatest thing since the Coliseum. I had hoped that some of my celebrity friends would be poolside, as I wanted to impress my dad. I was not disappointed. Jack Palance gave him a very warm reception, as did Andre and other members of the colony. As we drank in the Italian sun, I noticed that most of the young men were congregated down at the far end of the pool. The object of their attention was a raven-haired beauty wearing a black bikini that barely covered her ample breasts. I have always been something of a connoisseur of women with ample bosoms and this one was, without a doubt, magnificent. I slipped into the tepid water and as I swam close to the target area, I could tell that her admirers were all stifled by the same problem; the lady in question appeared to be speaking French. I said a small prayer of thanks to Lydia and proceeded to introduce myself. As her admirers drifted away in deference to my linguistic advantage, she revealed to me that she also spoke perfect English!

KATIA CARO, Rome, Italy 1961

Katia Caro was only sixteen years old going on thirty. She was from the famous horse racing village of Maison Lafitte just outside of Paris. She was working in Rome as an actress and to date, she had done the leads in some ten films. I could not vouch for her acting ability but her physical stature must have had something to do with her success. That evening, she joined my father and me for dinner and after dropping my dad off at his hotel, Katia and I went to my place and made beautiful love all night and well into the following day. I could not believe that this nymphet had chosen to share my bed and I felt no sense of guilt in having had sexual relations with this gorgeous minor. Katia had left school at the age of fourteen to pursue an acting career at the encouragement of an agent in Paris. At that tender age she had already co-starred with the French idol, Jean Marais, and was brought to Rome to star with Ugo Tognazzi, and Italian star of the fifties and sixties. From there her career had taken off in a flurry of questionable publicity regarding wild parties and bizarre sexual encounters. But I was so captivated with this adorable creature that I was impervious to her faults and proceeded to fall madly in love with her.

When my father and his cronies moved on, I found myself spending all my spare time with Katia. It was by no means an easy relationship. Most of the time we related as adults but there were times when my little Lolita was more than difficult to understand. When I looked at her I saw this fully mature, sexual being, but in reality, she was only a child of sixteen. And Katia looked to me as her deliverer from all her worldly problems, of which there were many.

Katia's mother was something of a shrew that had exploited her own daughter when she saw that there was money to be made off her looks. But Katia had turned out to be headstrong and constantly defied her mother, which caused an estrangement between the two. Living on her own in Rome was not the healthiest of environments and Katia soon fell in with the *Dolce Vita* set. It was not long before she was being used as nothing more than a cheap receptacle for stars and directors. She was fortunate to work all the time but she contended that she was talented, that she was an actress, but no one was interested in her ability in front of the camera. I guess I empathized with her. In those days, unless you were an American star brought over from the States by a reputable production company, most of the films being done were exploitive pieces of trash designed to cash in on the free flow of money that came from international co-productions. Rome was a veritable cinematic zoo.

A Vulcan Odyssey

I guess there comes a time when a man has to stand up and be counted. My time had come. I had two options: I could marry Katia, or preferably, I should adopt her. She had turned seventeen and needed the security of a person upon whom she could depend for both her professional and monetary stability. She confided in me that she was in debt up to her lovely ass; she owed more than twenty thousand dollars! I was astonished, to say the least. Most of the money that she owed was for clothes that she could ill-afford and she had a compulsion to just spend money she didn't have. I suppose under normal circumstances I could have married her and disavowed any liability but under Italian law, I would have become liable for her debts. We discussed the situation and we both agreed that before we could think of marriage, we would have to make a concerted effort to satisfy her creditors. I didn't know how the hell we were going to find twenty thousand dollars but at least she was willing to hold off being married and said that she understood my situation. Meanwhile, I got another film that took me down to Southern Italy and a little village called Roccorazzo.

This was one of the most interesting projects on which I had worked. It was called *I Briganti Italiani* (The Italian Brigands) and it starred Ernest Brognine and an international cast of stars of that era. One of my all time favorite actors had always been an Italian actor who came to the United States as a young man and was wasted by the major studios in all kinds of trash. He was never able to realize his full potential as an actor but when he finally returned to Italy, he achieved the recognition he rightfully deserved. His name was Vittorio Gassman and working with him was a lesson in acting for all of us who were fortunate enough to be cast. And of course, the highlight of the film's talent was in the person of the great character actor, Akim Tamiroff, who was cast in a "cameo" role. If anyone ever wanted to spend a more glorious time than to listen to the tales this man had to relate about his career, it would not have been possible.

Ernie Borgnine was then married to the spitfire actress, Katy Jurado. When the two of them would get into it, Ernie would fire up his Ferrari (that was given to him by Dino DiLaurentis for his participation in Barabas) and drive the treacherous back roads of that rural village. We could hear him winding up that engine from any place in the town and everyone would remark that "Ernie and Katy were at it again." After a few weeks in Roccorazzo, I was going stir crazy. I missed Katia and it took hours to place a call to Rome to speak to her. I finally suggested that she come down to the location for a few days of R and R.

Everyone on the location was completely captivated by her beauty and wit. She was able to go from Italian to French to English without missing a beat in the course of a conversation. Katia, Ernie, Katy and I would play cards until the early hours of the morning. It was a lovely time in that peaceful little Italian village and Katia and I had plenty of time to make our plans for the future. I had decided that we would marry and that I would just have to figure out a way to resolve her financial dilemma. Then, of course, I would have to contact Delfina so she could initiate divorce proceedings. Everything would work out fine.

Upon her departure, Katia informed me that she would be making a trip to France to visit with her mother in Maison Lafitte. There was also a matter of some female disorder that was plaguing her and would have to be taken care of while in France. We promised to write and I assured her that I would call just as soon as I got back to Rome.

The director of *I Brigante Italiani* was quite well regarded in Italian cinema for his work over the years. But time was running out for Mario Camerini and what appeared to be a fine film on paper turned out to be something of a financial disaster for its producers. I had a most unusual role in the film that could have opened many professional doors for me had the film been a success. Unfortunately, I went down with the ship, so to speak. For a while I was beginning to believe that all these mediocre films and their failures had a direct correlation to my talents as an actor. After all, it seemed that everything I touched turned to shit! Of course, I could not take responsibility for those films in which I did not have the leading role. But it was still difficult to not take some of the responsibility and it took me a long time to accept the fact that coincidently, I just had a series of films that were not very good. and for which I could not take the blame. I was thankful that at least I had a chance to be working in the profession of my choosing.

Upon my return to Rome I called Delfina. I needed to discuss our situation face to face so she caught a train and was in Rome the following day. We spent a couple of days together before I was able to muster up the courage to broach the subject. I knew she cared for me and no matter how I handled the situation, she was going to be hurt. I am not proud to admit that I was a wimp when it came to addressing the issue. Finally, the scene between the two of us turned out to be most painful for us both. She cried and told me that she was hoping that with time I could come to love her and that she was willing to be patient. She pleaded with me not to ask her to file for divorce. I felt the trap closing and I began to panic. Perhaps I was wrong. I should have picked up the phone and told her, by long distance, that I wanted a divorce and that was that. But no, I had to do things by a set of rules dictated by my moral conscience that constantly put me behind the eight ball. I sent Delfina back to Milan with nothing resolved. I vowed to myself that I would call her in a few days and tell her to begin divorce proceedings immediately. Meanwhile, I was speaking to Katia by phone every day. I kept inquiring when she planned to return to Rome and she kept avoiding giving me a direct answer. But since she was under doctor's care I did not press the issue feeling that when she was finally discharged, she would return.

About the middle of January I got a call from Jimmy Dobson from Munich. He had returned to Europe to cast a film for the King Brothers called *Captain Sindbad*, starring Guy Williams, of Zorro fame. I had recently worked on a film in Rome with Guy called *Damon and Pythias* for MGM. I had never been to Germany, probably because I had some mindset relating to the incidents of the last war. Had it not been for the Sindbad film, I doubt that I would have ever set foot in Germany. And the photography business had never been quite the same since my return from Roccorazzo. So I decided to take the job in Germany that Jimmy had offered me. It was winter in Europe and the making of films in Italy had all but come to a standstill. The money I would be making in Germany could be used to pay down the debts facing Katia. I threw some clothes in my station wagon and took off for Munich, Germany.

CHAPTER NINE
DEUTSCHLAND UBER ALLES

The King Brothers were living legends in their own time. There were Frank, Maury and Hymie. But the real brain behind the success of the King Brothers was Mama King. She was the ruler in the matriarchal dynasty and indeed the King holdings were staggering. Rumor had it that Frank King had Mafia connections and that is how the family got its start. Then there was the rumor that Papa King was a bootlegger during the depression and with his underworld connections he was able to amass a small fortune. Frank was as bald as a billiard ball and I always referred to him as "the Buddha," but never to his face. As the story goes, when Frank was a child, his father sent him down to the cellar to fetch a bottle of whiskey for a small party. Waiting in the cellar were some of Papa King's enemies who grabbed Frank and threatened to kill him. The child was so traumatized that shortly thereafter, he lost all his hair and it never grew back. The King stories proliferated but the bottom line is that in the film industry, they were able to produce successful films for decades.

Maury kept a very low profile and had a phobia about dirt. His brother Frank would tell stories about how Maury, when he was in the military, spent most of his time in the shower. I liked Maury. He was a very gentle and sensitive man.

Hymie was rarely to be seen. It was said that Frank had him tied to a desk and only let him out when the film came in on budget and on time.

The work on *Captain Sindbad* tested everyone's stamina. February in Munich was bitterly cold and it was almost impossible to keep the sound stage where we were working at a reasonably warm temperature. Since this was a sea story with water constantly raining down on the cast, we were wet from morning till night. The entire film was shot on stage; even the scenes aboard ship. The technicians used large tanks filled with tons of water that, when tipped over into large chutes, caused the water to cascade down onto the ship giving the impression that we were indeed in a raging sea. Most of the cast came down with colds that persisted throughout the run of the film. And if the water and cold weren't enough, we had animals to contend with. In one scene, an elephant ran amok and damn near destroyed the set. First one up the ladder was Frank King yelling for someone to stop the elephant before it ruined his picture. After the smoke had cleared and the elephant was safely removed from the set, Frank wanted to know if I got any pictures of the havoc with my new Leica. I told him that the only pictures I might have gotten were of his ass because I was up the ladder right behind him. There is nothing so awesome as a charging elephant on a motion picture sound stage!

I must admit that the King Brothers were a set apart when it came to Hollywood. Those in the industry who knew them swore that Frank could determine if a film was going to be a success by how much the script weighed. If the film fell behind, Frank would arbitrarily tear out a handful of pages and return the script to the director telling him that they were no longer behind. But for all their crassness and what appeared to be their lack of sensitivity, they managed to win themselves an Academy Award for a little gem called *The Young Bull*. It was written by Dalton Trumbeau, whom no one would touch because he had been black-listed by the McCarthy purge. Putting all politics aside, Dalton was an excellent writer and the King brothers recognized his talent when they produced his film. I learned to have great respect for the King Brothers.

As the twenty-sixth of February rolled around I became very lonely because I had no one with whom to share my birthday. My letters to Katia had gone unanswered and I was missing her very much. I decided to place a call to her mother's home in Maison Lafitte. Her mother spoke perfect English but preferred to defiantly speak to me in French. She seemed reluctant to speak to me at all and when I insisted on speaking to Katia, she informed me that Katia was no longer in France, that she had married and had moved to America! I was stunned. Was the old lady lying to me? It had been three weeks since I last spoke to Katia, just before I left for Munich. We had made plans for her to join me in Munich after which we would return to Rome. Had she known all along that she had alternate plans? My thirty-first birthday was a real bummer.

(Let me jump ahead for a moment. Some years after Munich, I was working in Los Angeles and a friend mentioned that he had met this really "hot woman" at the pool of the International Hotel on Sunset Strip. This friend said that after talking to her for a while, she mentioned my name. The downside was that my friend surmised that she was a hooker. It was Katia. The next afternoon I went to the hotel pool and there she was, a bit road weary but as beautiful as ever. She was very reserved as we talked about our careers and the waters over the dam. It appeared that after two children, her marriage did not work out and she came to Los Angeles to try to pick up the pieces of her career. Unfortunately, she was not able to make any inroads into acting and when one disappointment followed another, she ended up working in an upscale whorehouse in Beverly Hills. I could see in her eyes a kind of pain that I had never witnessed before. At the time she was no more than twenty-three years old but she appeared to be much older. Things had not gone well for her; she had lost the right to see her children, she was alone in a strange and vicious city, and her pride was all she had left. We didn't connect and as I saw her for the last time, I felt very sad for this forlorn child. Some months later, I learned that Katia had killed herself. I still have a photo of her that I took in Rome, and from time to time I am compelled to look at it and think of what might have been.)

While working at Gazelgasteig Studios I was attracted to a very stunning lady whom I first saw in the commissary. She was quite tall with blond hair and she carried herself with great confidence. When I first saw her, I persuaded Jimmy Dobson to introduce us. He knew everyone. Her name was Monika Ahrens and she was quite a well-known personality in Munich. At that time there was only one television station in town and Monika was the Katie Curic of German news. She did everything: news, sports, the weather. She had recently finished starring in a film with Theodore Bikel called *The Dog of Flanders,* and she was currently doing a play at the Kammerspiele Theatre. She also had a singing contract with Telefunken Records. Monika spoke perfect English, French and Spanish, as well as her native German. And to top it off, her stepfather was the world-renowned conductor, Herbert von Karajan. This lady was class with the capital C and I was coming off a bad fall and she offered to catch me. We connected.

A couple of weeks before Sindbad wound down, we heard that the Mirisch Company was coming to town with a very big film. Rumors spread like wildfire and everyone in the Sindbad cast got their hopes raised high in anticipation of possibly getting cast in another film right away. When the casting call came down, I was one of the last to hear about it because I was spending so much time with Monika that I had drifted out of the talent environment. And then there was another major issue: Monika had missed her period! When word came down from the production office that I had an appointment with the casting people over at the Mirisch Company, I was a little preoccupied, to say the least. And I had heard through the grapevine that they were only interested in seeing British and German officer types. I felt that the whole thing would be just a big waste of time. But Monika encouraged me to go to the audition, if only to get me out of the house.

I met the casting director, Lynn Stalmaster, and he handed me a long monologue to look over. It was one of those scenes that was so well written that an actor would have to be dead to give a bad reading. When I finished my audition with Lynn, he took the time to ask me some questions about myself and I got the impression that he was sincerely interested in me for a role in the film. But there were some excellent English and German actors working on Sindbad who also felt that their readings went off well and after comparing notes, I came back down to earth.

Captain Sindbad finished on time (with a number of pages wrenched from the script) and I was planning to go back to Rome, pack up my things and return to Munich to marry Monika. I had moved out of the Moorbad Wetterstein and into Monika's one room apartment in the heart of Swabbing. We spent our days looking for a house and in the evenings we fought like cats and dogs. I felt like I was being manipulated into marriage because of the baby and Monika played the martyr to the hilt by saying that she really didn't mind having an abortion. To me, that was a dirty word. Not that I was against a woman's right to make that decision, but this was my baby and if I had any say, it was not going to be aborted. (For the short time I was with Lydia, she tried to get pregnant but it wasn't meant to be. On one occasion, she missed her period for a couple of months but it was a false pregnancy and we were both terribly disappointed. I was convinced that I was not able to make a baby so I wasn't about to see this one terminated. I guess things happen for a reason.)

A Vulcan Odyssey

Before I could leave for Rome, I got a phone call from Lynn Stalmaster. The director of the film, John Sturges, wanted to see me. I compared notes with some of the other actors who were still hanging around town in hopes of getting a shot at the new film. As far as I could determine, I was the only one of the English-speaking cast to get a callback. But I was still not about to get carried away with the prospect of another job so soon after Sindbad.

I read for Sturges, met Robert Relyea, his associate producer, and was told that I would hear something in a week or two. I mentioned that I lived in Rome and that I would be on my way back to that city and if they wanted to reach me, they could call me through my Munich agent. Of course, I didn't mention anything about my intentions to move to Munich and get married. If they hired me from Rome, they would have to pay me daily living expenses that could amount to quite a bit of money. It was an outside shot.

I said goodbye to Monika and took off for Rome. Either way, with or without the job, I would be back in two weeks. But tying up loose ends in Rome took a lot longer than I had anticipated. There was the photography business to be handed over to a friend in the hopes that he could make a few lire on the side. But truthfully, I had more than raped the market and what with the failure of the Italian co-productions, there were less and less actors coming from abroad in need of photography. Then, there was my apartment on via Archimede. It was a great pad and I hated to give it up. After two weeks, I phoned Monika to inform her that it would take me another ten days to get out of Rome and for her to be patient.

Four or five days later I got an urgent call from Monika. It seems that the people from the Mirisch Company had been trying to get in touch with me through my Munich agent. But the agent had left town on vacation and had not returned the calls. Monika said that Robert Relyea had called her to say that if I did not get in touch with the company within twenty-four hours, they would re-cast the role. I was dumbfounded. All this was news to me. Monika no sooner hung up than I was on the phone to Relyea.

"I hope you're not trying to hold us up for more money," he said. "We made an offer to your agent but she never called us back."

I assured Relyea that I had not been in touch with the agent and that if he would give me the information, I would give him an answer right then and there.

The name of the film was *The Great Escape* and it starred Steve McQueen and James Garner along with a wonderful cast of international actors. I was being offered a featured role, the part of a Canadian officer by the name of Haynes that was patterned after the technical director, Wally Floody. The salary was twice what I was accustomed to making and they were throwing in an added three hundred a week for living expenses. "German marks?" I asked.

"Hell, no. Dollars."

I didn't have to think too long. "I'll take it," I said.

"We want everyone here on the fifth of May to begin wardrobe and costuming. You'll be paid from that date on."

And that was that. I called Monika. Then I called just about everyone I knew in Rome. I placed a call to my father and then a call to my mother. By the time I was on my way out of Rome, it seemed that I had contacted everyone I knew on the planet. I had struck it big! I thought that this was the break for which I had been waiting. Monika informed me that she had found a house in Bogenhausen, a lovely residential community on the other side of the English Gardens and across the Isar River. I could not wait to see it.

The first week of production on The Great Escape was spent with many of the actors getting fitted out with RAF uniforms since we were British officers interned in a POW camp. There were only two Americans playing Americans: Steve McQueen and Judd Taylor. The other four Americans all played other nationalities: James Garner played a Canadian, James Coburn played an Australian, Charles Bronson played a Pole, and I was to play a Canadian.

On the first day, Sturges introduced me to the technical director, Wally Floody. He was quite tall with bloodshot eyes and a great mischievious grin.

"Stick with him day and night," instructed Sturges. "I want you to know everything about this man because your part is patterned after him." I was very impressed and flattered. Wally was the technical advisor on the film because he had been involved in some seventeen-escape attempts from various camps while a POW during the war but he himself never escaped. Sticking with Wally was not as easy as Sturges had painted it. Wally began to drink first thing out of bed in the morning. I'd meet him at the studio at eight or nine o'clock and we'd have "a wee toddy." By noon, I was six sheets to the wind and he was still going strong. After a few days I told Sturges that if I was not relieved of my role as babysitter, I would end up an alcoholic. But I did manage to get Wally's accent down even though there wasn't much cause to use it in the film. My contract was for five weeks. Steve McQueen arrived a couple of days after most of the cast. Along with Steve was his current wife, Neile Adams, a great dancer with whom I studied in New York. She introduced me to her husband who was on a comet to stardom and we had a good rapport because we learned that he had been two weeks and one platoon ahead of me in boot camp in the Marine Corp and we both got discharged within weeks of each other in 1950. Upon arriving on location, Steve was sporting a scab on his lip from a racing accident. I heard that he had a clause in his contract prohibiting him from doing any racing during the shooting of the film. But Steve's appearance did not stop us from starting to shoot the following Monday. We just worked around him until his wounds healed.

One of my favorite actors of all times was an Englishman by the name of Richard Attenborough. I had watched his career religiously and now I was going to have the opportunity to work with him. Of course, there was a bit of a disappointment when I learned that the role I had read for in the audition was the role that Dickie was going to play. My role was considerably smaller. During the first few days of shooting we were introduced to the camp, *Stalag Luft*. I was the only foreign actor to have worked at this studio before so I knew almost every inch of the area.

I was really surprised when I went out to the back lot and saw the transformation from the lovely pine forest to a full scale POW camp, complete with barbed wire, coolers and machinegun turrets. It was most scary and the realism was mind-boggling.

Some members of the company of *The Great Escape*, Munich, Germany 1962 (left to right) John Sturges (director), Charles Bronson, John Leyton, James Coburn and Lawrence Montaigne as HAYNES

A Vulcan Odyssey

Shooting of the film began with the arrival of the prisoners to the camp. This required a lot of "shtick" because a number of us tried to escape from the camp before the gates were even closed behind us. This was a good light touch to keep the film from getting bogged down in the dramatic realism of the situation. Sturges knew what he was doing and I learned a lot from watching him. He had come out of the old film editor school and knew exactly what he wanted in order to make the film cook. Personally, I believed that he was not very strong working with actors. John was not a very gregarious man and he didn't really communicate well. He depended upon his actors and their talents to take command of their roles while he, as the director, took care of the technical end. He must have known what he was doing because he had a list of successes over the years that were some of the finest films ever made, including *Bad Day at Black Rock, The Magnificent Seven, The Old Man of the Sea, Marooned,* etc. This was the consummate film director!

We were two weeks into production when word came down that all work calls were cancelled until further notice. Again, rumors proliferated. We had heard that Steve and John had a falling out and that Steve had been fired. Such was not the case. There had been a difference of concept in Steve's role and his agent had flown in from the coast to resolve the issue. Meanwhile, I sat at home and waited. The company waited for two weeks! The writers came in from Hollywood and the script got a quick facelift. When we were called back to work we were handed the new script with which to become acquainted. In the original script, my character, Haynes, did not escape from the camp. But in the new script I was to escape and finally die with a group of captured prisoners who were eventually executed as spies. I could not believe my good fortune. It now appeared that I would be working ten weeks instead of the original five!

There was no doubt about it. Monika was pregnant. Because she was quite tall it took some time for her to show but it seemed that one morning she got up and there was that belly for all the world to see. Our plans to marry kept getting postponed because the schedule on the film was so erratic. Sturges wanted the supporting cast on the set each day whether we were scheduled to work or not. This was most unusual. In most films the script was broken down so minutely that the production knew who was working from one day to the next. But Sturges sometimes worked on inspiration and if he decided he wanted to change a scene or use one of the other actors in a particular scene, we had to be close at hand. Sometimes we would sit around for weeks without being in a scene but we were being paid like clockwork and none of us had any cause to bitch.

My half-sister, Ada, had come to Munich to spend the summer with us. She was now a very headstrong fourteen. She and Sturges' daughter, Debbie, hit it off quite well and they spent a lot of time together. Charlie Bronson was like the camp babysitter. Looking at him one would not imagine that Charlie was crazy about kids but he would spend hours entertaining Debbie and Ada when we were confined to the compound. Charlie and I had done a film together back in the early fifties but we had never met because he was an actor and I was working as a dancer. That film was *Bloodhounds of Broadway*.

I guess I had been on the road too long because I had never seen the television series, Maverick, so I didn't know anything about the actor, James Garner. He was most congenial and seemed to go out of his way to kid around. One evening, the phone rang and Monika informed me that "it's Jimmy."

"Tell him I'll be right there," I said.

"It's not for you," she informed me. "He wants to speak to Ada."

Ada got on the phone, had a short conversation and then informed us that she was having dinner with Jimmy. She mentioned the name of the restaurant and as soon as she was out the door, I phoned for a reservation and by the time they arrived, there was Monika and I sitting across from their table. Hey, my kid sister was only fourteen and I didn't know James Garner from puppy poop. He just thought it would brighten up the kid's life if she had dinner with Maverick. It was all quite innocent and it gave Ada something to talk about to this very day.

There were a number of stuntmen on the shoot who ran with Jimmy and some of the stories that came down were priceless. There was a nightclub in Schwabing where many of the actors and stuntmen would hang out. An Israeli ran it by the name of Mario and he was a bull of a man. One night, the Roys (Sickner and Jensen) were at the bar having their usual one-too-many. Jensen bet Mario that if he was as strong as he claimed to be, they were willing to put up fifty marks to see if Mario could knock Jensen off the end of a bill that they both were standing on. Sickner laid a fifty-mark note on the floor and explained how each man would toe the note and if Mario could knock Jensen off the note, he would get it. Conversely, if Mario could not knock Jensen off the note, he would pay the Roys. Mario knew that there was a trick involved but he was willing to pay the fifty marks to see what it was. So Sickner picked up the fifty-mark note and walked over to the doorway. He laid the note down on the floor and closed the door so that the note protruded on either side of the door. Then Jensen toed the mark on his side of the door and Mario did the same on the other side of the door. The boys were near doubled over with laughter when Jensen suddenly went reeling across the room. Mario had put his fist through the door, knocked Jensen on his ass and collected his fifty marks!

My role called for me to work a great deal of the time with James Coburn. He was in Munich with his wife and they were having a lot of marital difficulties. I guess that accounted for Coburn's aloofness from the rest of the cast. He wasn't very friendly and went off on his own when the rest of us would get together for a night out on the town. His unfriendly demeanor was magnified by the fact that everyone else in the company was so friendly. The men of Stalag Luft were like a big club and we all did our share of partying together when the day's work was finished.

In August, Monika and I were finally married. I can't say whether or not either of us was in love with the other at that time but we both wanted the baby so much that we were willing to go through with it. We figured that the rest would follow if we were patient.

Shooting on the film had surpassed the ten-week mark and we were still not halfway through the script. Estimates ran anywhere from fifteen to twenty weeks. I had not been very frugal with the money I was making and we managed to spend it as fast as it came in. But with the report that we would be running over considerably, I was determined to put a bit away for a rainy day. When an actor had the good fortune to land a plum film like The Great Escape, it was easy to lose sight of the reality of the situation and think that it would go on forever. The last four weeks of shooting were on a distant location outside of Munich, so Monika and I packed our bags and took off for the village of Fussen, some two hours' drive from home.

The beauty of Fussen was like stepping through Alice's looking glass into a Disney world. There were two magnificent castles situated on opposite mountains in a valley and in the early mornings, the clouds would come down and touch the very tops of the castles' turrets. The setting was so romantic that Monika and I were caught up in the magic and we languished for the four glorious weeks that we considered our honeymoon. Our room was in a *Gasthaus* that overlooked a river on one side and the castles on the other. We took long walks when I wasn't off in the countryside shooting.

Then, one day, a group of actors dressed as Germans soldiers took a group of Englishmen and myself out to the countryside and executed us completing the last scene of the film. I could hardly believe it; I was terminated! After nineteen weeks and three days, I was again unemployed. The drive back to Munich was endless. Monika got carsick and I had to stop a number of times so she could throw up. By the time we got home to Morgenroth Strasse, we were hardly speaking.

During the shooting of The Great Escape I met an acquaintance of Steve's by the name of "Lucky" Lloyd Casner. Lucky had been a racecar driver on the European circuit and more recently was the owner of the American Racing Team, Camarady. Eight months before, he had been in a race in Vente Mille and after lapping the field with only one more lap to go in the race, another driver forced him off the road and he crashed. He spent the next six months in and out of hospitals having skin grafts done all over his body. Lucky was an outgoing sort of person who would strip down to his waist and proudly show off his scars at the drop of a hat. He was also a little bit crazier than I and we made a good pair. After the departure of the cast and crew of The Great Escape, I went through a couple of months of withdrawal. I would rise early in the morning, get dressed, grab a bite of breakfast and rush out of the house. But I had nowhere to go. After checking in with all the agents and local production offices, I was back to square one. There just wasn't any work for an American actor in Germany, especially when the Germans shot direct sound and didn't dub their films, as did the Italians. My German was passable to get by on the street but not good enough to pass myself off as a German if I was to be cast in a film. I was between a rock and a hard place. That's when Lucky decided that he had to get back into the racing scene. He was planning to go to Paris to see if he could get a ride with the Masseratti Team and asked if I wanted to come along. Sure, what the hell else was there for me to do? So we took off for France. Lucky got his ride with Masseratti and we continued on down to Le Mans for the big race. He got me connected with the pit crew and I managed to work with them during the big race. It was a most exciting experience and I had illusions of someday racing the big cars until Lucky put me in the seat next to him and drove me around the track at speeds up to a hundred and eighty miles an hour. I heard every nut and bolt in that car screaming and the car shook like some out-of-control ride in Luna Park. I followed Lucky around from track to track but I knew in my heart that I would never put my life on the line in one of those death machines. I liked to stay close to Lucky because he had borrowed a bushel of money from me and I had the impression that I would never see it again if anything happened to him. As it turned out, he couldn't pay me what he owed me and I finally ended up with a small racing car that he told me to sell to satisfy his indebtedness. That was Lucky. There wasn't a scheme or scam that he didn't consider sometime along his life's road and he didn't care whom he took down with him. He had me hooked on an idea of running fish from the Greek islands to European ports in refrigerator ships. All I had to do was come up with the ship. When I mentioned the idea to Anita von Karajan, Monika's mother, she came up with a ship owner who was willing to work a deal with us for the use of one of his ships. But when we got down to the bottom line, I didn't have an international bank credit that would afford me such an ambitious undertaking. So much for fish.

Then there was the idea of buying diamonds and selling them on the market where there was a premium for diamonds. Sounded good to me and while I still had a few dollars stashed away, I forged ahead full blast. During my time in Rome I had met a guy by the name of Leonard Bell. Lenny lived a very good life, traveling all over the world and returning to Rome where he stayed at the best hotels and ate in the finest restaurants. I had the idea that Lenny was connected with some sort of devious occupation that afforded him such an opulent lifestyle. If this was the case, it was worth a phone call to Rome to see if Lenny knew where I could purchase diamonds at a price. I know the idea was farfetched but many of the people that I met on the Continent had no visible means of support and there was just no way they could support their lifestyle without being involved in some nefarious scheme. But Lenny assured me that he hadn't a clue about how to obtain diamonds.

We talked for a while and I told him I was looking to get connected with something to do but he didn't have any ideas at the moment. If anything came up, he would get in touch with me. And that was the end of our conversation. As a last resort I had contemplated heading back to Rome but I had heard that there was very little production, almost no dubbing and actors were fast deserting the sinking ship.

Another friend from Rome was Walter "Piggy" Barnes. I had done his portfolio when I was doing photography and we became quite good friends. Piggy was a large man who had been All-American at Louisiana State and All-Pro with the Philadelphia Eagles. He had married a German girl form Dachau and when things got tight, they retreated to Germany where they would stay until Piggy could get a line on work. They were presently in Dachau, only a few minutes outside of Munich, and I'd see Piggy pretty regularly. We had worked on the *Sindbad* film together and we had been next-door neighbors at the Moorbad Wetterstein. Piggy and Britta, his wife, had decided to take a run over to Spain where he had heard that there was quite a bit of film activity. He owned a camper and a tent so his expenses were minimal. He asked if I'd like to come along with them to Madrid. Sounded good to me. Monika was due at any moment so I wanted to stay in town until the baby came but they assured me that they were not planning to leave for at least another month. That would be perfect.

Monika gave birth to a beautiful, healthy girl. Piggy and I had been up half the night drinking to the health of the baby and when the doctor reported that she had arrived, all I could manage to say was, "Is that all?"

We named the baby Laurence Jessica Lydia. Monika wasn't into trivial things like baby naming so I undertook the task. She would have shit a brick if she knew that her daughter was named after my first wife, Lydia. It didn't make any difference because the name of choice has always been Jessica. I called her Sica for the longest time but that disappeared somewhere along with time. When Monika arrived home from the hospital our house became a circus. One would think that my wife was the first woman to have ever given birth to a baby. We already had a housekeeper but now Monika decided that we needed a nanny to take care of the baby. And nanny had to sleep in. Then, Anita came rushing into town from Vienna to see her newborn grandchild. I've got

A Vulcan Odyssey

to admit, Jessica turned out to be the perfect baby. From the day she arrived home from the hospital she slept right through the night. The nanny had to wake her up for her nightly feeding which she appeared to sleep through. Everyone said that the baby looked just like her father and I modestly agreed. After all, she was perfect and beautiful.

About a month after the baby arrived, Piggy called to say that they were ready to head over to Madrid. He heard that Phil Yordan was preparing a film based on James Jones' novel, *The Thin Red Line*. There were supposed to be umpteen roles for men. I told Monika that I would be gone for a couple of weeks and that if I got held up, I would give her a call. Piggy and Britta left with their camper and I left the following day, driving a little racing Gordoni that I was hoping to sell in Madrid. We were car poor with three cars in the driveway. Driving that little sport car all the way to Madrid was an act of lunacy. Much of the road was cobblestones and the car did not have suspension for the open road. I had to stop every few miles to pee and my back began to kill me. By the time I got to Madrid, I could barely straighten up. I found Piggy and Britta in a tourist campsite just a few miles outside of town. It was a surprisingly comfortable setting with communal showers and bath facilities (that I was accustomed to from living in the Kibbutz). The van was for Piggy and Britta and there was a large tent for me. The manager in the office was extremely nice about taking messages. Piggy had already made contact with the production office and had interviewed with the director. He passed the information on to me and I rushed over to meet Andy Marton. He was a prince of a man and we got on just fine. I read for one of the leading roles, Lieutenant Stone, and Andy assured me that I was perfect for the role. I was back on cloud nine.

The production was based at the Hilton and all the American actors in town frequented the local bar. That first day I met a young man by the name of David Moss from Los Angeles. He was looking to get any kind of work on the film and didn't profess to be an actor. He was a bullfighter! Can you imagine, a nice Jewish kid from Los Angeles wanting to stick knives into live beefsteaks? It was David who introduced me to the Plaza de Toros de Madrid and the art of killing bulls. It didn't take me long to learn to barf up a day's meals while watching all that butchery. As I got to know David better, I learned that his estranged wife, who was also living in Madrid, was a girl by the name of Vera Ferguson. By coincidence, I knew a girl in New York by the same name but I knew it couldn't be her because my Vera Ferguson was probably still in New York breaking someone's balls! Wrong! Vera was right there in Madrid threatening to take David for everything he was worth in a nasty divorce proceeding. I was beginning to love Madrid. I also ran into an actor from the Dramatic Workshop in New York who had stayed with me for a short while in Rome, by the name of Phil Posner. He was doing a spaghetti Western that was winding down and he was looking to get a shot at The Thin Red Line. It appeared that Madrid had become what Rome was only a couple of years before. Through Phil, I met Steve Rowland who had this magnificent apartment on the Grand Via overlooking the entire city. He was looking for someone to share expenses and I jumped at the offer since I had a good feeling about working on the new film. I couldn't believe the amount of activity generated by the filming in that beautiful city. I couldn't explain why everything had moved from my *bella Italia* but I guess if you had to go some-where, Madrid would be it.

A few days after being caught up in all the activity going on around me, I had joined a group of actors at the Hilton bar for a drink before meeting Piggy and Britta for dinner. A guy by the name of Bernie came over to our table and introduced himself as being the production manager for the new film. He came on like a pushy little Willy Loman with a valise full of merchandise for sale. I immediately disliked him.

"You guys look like a talented bunch of men," he opened. "How would you like to work in a film? I need some men to be extras…" Can you imagine, this was his opening line? "I can use you and you and you." He pointed to three of us and I guess that was our cue to fall down on our knees and kiss his ass. I couldn't believe this guy; he was right off the wall. "Well, what do you say?" He was looking right at me.

"I say, why don't you kiss my ass!"

"What's your name," he demanded.

I should have known better than to give any information to the enemy but with Andy Marton's words still ringing in my ears, "Perfect to play the role of Lieutenant Stone," I had built up a false sense of security. Bernie Something-or-other walked away from our table mumbling my name over and over again as he went. The following day I found out that Bernie Something-or-other was not only the production manager but he was also one of the producers of The Thin Red Line! I was fired before I was even hired.

I had written to Monika to let her know that I was going to stay on in Madrid for a bit to see if I could drum up some work. If I could find employment I would send for her and the baby. One afternoon I returned to the tourist park and found a message for me to contact a Mister Henry in Brussels, collect. I didn't know anyone in Brussels. The manager who had taken the message could not give me any more information other than the phone number. Piggy and Britta had been in the city all day so they had not spoken to the Brussels party. I placed the call on the public phone and it took a couple of hours to get through. At first, I thought that someone was pulling a joke on me because the voice on the other end of the line sounded exactly like the distinct voice of one of my very favorite British actors, Jack Hawkins. The man introduced himself and said that he had gotten my name from Lenny Bell and that he would like me to come to Brussels to meet with him. I asked if he could tell me what this was all about but he said that he preferred not to discuss it over the phone. He was prepared to cover all my expenses. When could I travel? I told him that I would make all the necessary arrangements and wire him as to the exact time of my arrival. I guess I was pretty naïve to accept his offer to cover all my expenses but I was beginning to see a black cloud hanging over my head after screwing up my chances to work on that film. Now my mind began to do all sorts of weird tricks on me. Since Piggy and Britta were not around I had no one to bounce my ideas off. My first thought was that this "Mister Henry" was with the CIA and that they were looking to recruit me for some clandestine activity. It sounded great but for some reason, I couldn't imagine Lenny Bell with any connections to a U.S. Government agency. No, it had to be something different. After all, I had approached Lenny with an idea to smuggle diamonds and now someone who had been given my name by Lenny was contacting me. And if it was something to do with the diamond trade, why was Lenny so reluctant to help me when I approached him some months before? No, it had to be something else. My mind kept returning to the CIA. It was the only thing that made any sense. I was able to catch a plane later that evening for Brussels and merely left a note for Piggy and Britta that said I would not be able to join them for dinner and that I would see them the following day.

* * *

When I arrived at the Brussels Airport there was a message for me to proceed to the Amigo Hotel and Mr. Henry would contact me. I checked into the Amigo where a room had been reserved for me. I ordered a drink from room service and settled down to wait to hear from my contact. Suddenly, a thought hit me: drugs! Oh, my god, if this was some kind of drug-related operation, would I be able to just say "no" and walk away with impunity? Or was my presence in Brussels a silent acceptance of whatever it was that was expected of me? The ringing of the phone shattered my reverie. Mister Henry invited me to meet him in the bar...

My first impression on the phone in Madrid was correct: this man not only sounded like Jack Hawkins, he looked like Jack Hawkins! It was uncanny. He was a large man, as tall as me but much larger across the chest and shoulders. He had a good strong handshake and looked me straight in the eye as he introduced himself.

"I'm Henry," he said as he motioned for me to sit. "I suppose you're wondering what this is all about..."

"I have given the subject some thought," I casually replied, trying to fight the knots in my stomach.

"Have you spoken to Leonard lately?"

"Not for some months."

"And are you familiar with his activities?"

"No, not at all. But I will admit that I have always been curious."

"How so?"

"Well, Leonard has a very...splendid lifestyle. He always stays at the finest hotels, drives rented cars, eats at the best restaurants, and is always seen with beautiful women. He's a man to be envied."

"Would you like to do all those things?"

"To be candid, not if I had to deal in drugs," I replied getting right to the point. "That's where I draw the line. I'll consider almost anything except drugs and murder, but you might twist my arm on the latter if I were sympathetic to the cause. Drugs are definitely out."

"I'm glad to hear that," he said most assuredly. He smiled and I got the impression that he was enjoying this game of cat and mouse. "I can promise you quite candidly that what we do has absolutely nothing to do with drugs, prostitution or assassination."

"Then I guess that would rule out the CIA."

"Absolutely," he laughed. "We have nothing to do with any government agency." He suddenly changed the subject. "Are your accommodations satisfactory?"

It took me a moment to follow him. "Oh, yes. Quite."

He looked at his watch. It was a gold Rolex with a very ostentatious gold nugget band. I imagined it would have probably priced out at about ten thousand dollars in those days, give or take a few. "They have an excellent restaurant right here in the hotel. There are a number of good eating places in town but I'm waiting for a call..."

"No problem," I assured him as we got up and headed for the dining room. He was going to make me sweat. I could play his game but my first impression was to grab him by the throat and yell, "What the hell is this all about?" But I managed to keep my cool as we entered the dining room of crystal and velvet. The food was better than good, it was excellent. When the brandy and coffee were served, Henry leaned back and locked me with his eyes.

"By now I'm sure that you've surmised that what we do is not exactly legal. Therefore, I have to be sure that you can be trusted. You've shown great patience, which is definitely an asset. You come highly recommended by someone whose opinion I highly value. I consider myself a very good judge of human nature and I have a gut feeling that you can be trusted..."

I was being blown up like a Christmas goose and I loved every minute of it. I had passed the test and was now about to be passed into the inner sanctum of this highly secretive society.

"You might say that we are involved in the business of high finance. We are dealers of currency. We transport money from one country to another." He paused to let what he was saying sink in.

So far, I was terribly disappointed. "Is that it?" I asked, quite naively.

"Bear with me. Are you familiar with the term 'hard currency'?"

"Yes, I believe so. The American dollar and the English pound would be hard currency. The currency of those countries behind the Iron Curtain would be soft currency."

"Very good. But harder than the dollar and the pound sterling is... gold." He paused to let the word sink in. It didn't mean a thing to me. I had bought a gold coin for my mother in Germany and Monika bought me a pair of gold cufflinks, but "gold" per se was as foreign to me as some obscure foreign language. I had no idea what it looked like in commercial form and had never thought about it in terms of its monetary value. I knew that it represented the scenario for a number of Hollywood films, I could conjure up in my mind what gold dust looked like and I remember seeing pictures of gold bars in the vaults of Fort Knox in Kentucky. But I never had cause to question why gold was gold and what it meant in terms of the world monetary system.

"We're in the gold business," he informed me.

"Dealers?" I naively asked.

"Smugglers," he casually replied.

I thought he might be joking but after a long pause, he continued. "We're in the business of buying gold in Brussels or Geneva and smuggling it into the various countries in Southeast Asia. We purchase an ounce of gold for thirty-six dollars over the counter in the bank and once we deliver it, we get anywhere from a hundred to a hundred and twenty dollars an ounce. Gold is legal tender in some countries and not legal in others. In India, Thailand, Malaysia and Hong Kong, gold is used to fashion jewelry and religious artifacts and in some countries it is used in religious rituals where it is dumped into shark infested waters as a sacrifice to the gods. In these countries the governments assess a high tax on the purchase of gold bullion, sometimes as high as five hundred percent. We can split the difference between purchase price and the prices their governments impose."

It didn't take a rocket scientist to do the math. Gold smuggling could be a very profitable endeavor, I thought. "How does the gold get from Europe to the Far East?"

"Courier," he said. "We hire people to carry the gold on their persons." (Note: the timing here pre-dated metal detectors at airports.)

I was confused. "Gold is heavy," I said. "How much gold can a person carry and how do they keep from being detected when they go through customs?"

"We use a specially designed jacket that is worn under normal street clothes. It resembles a shooter's jacket with slots for shotgun shells, only each one of these slots holds a one kilo gold ingot."

My mind was racing ahead. One kilo of gold weighs 2.2 pounds so if a person carried, say ten kilos, that would be twenty-two pounds.

He continued: "A courier can carry up to thirty-five kilos a trip."

"Thirty-five kilos?" I asked in amazement. "That's almost eighty pounds. That's impossible!"

"The weight is evenly distributed over the body so it's really not all that difficult. The biggest problem is getting in and out of one's seat on the plane but other than that, it's quite easy." Again, that dramatic pause before the bomb. "Of course," he continued, "there is a small downside. The various Asian governments want to protect the market so they impose strict penalties on anyone caught smuggling gold into their countries."

Now we were getting down to the nitty-gritty. "Penalties?"

"Some countries impose prison terms of up to five years on persons caught smuggling gold. This is rare but we protect our couriers and we're committed to getting them the finest legal counsel money can buy. We've never had an incident where a courier was caught and served a full prison term. The authorities in almost every country in question are easily bribed and a cash donation here and a cash donation there and the courier is released, usually in the middle of the night, and escorted to the nearest airport. The one drawback is, the courier may have to spend anywhere from three to six months in a very primitive, overcrowded prison until release can be negotiated. As I've said, this is a worst scenario; it rarely happens. I don't think we've had three incidents of detection in the past five years…"

To be honest, this whole thing was way beyond my comprehension. What was I doing here? I had visions of spending six months in some rat-hole of a prison after being arrested for gold smuggling. I decided to get right to the point. "Are you offering me a job?"

"Actually, I was proposing that you work with us as a recruiter. We need couriers and from what Lenny told me, you're well traveled and personable and you could probably line up couriers all over the continent. It could be a very lucrative venture if you're interested."

I've always been partial to the word "lucrative" but from what I was hearing and knowing my disposition for failed ventures, this whole thing sounded very iffy.

"In two years I predict you could walk away with one million dollars! Of course, that's tax free."

"Iffy" just went on vacation. I was definitely interested.

Before I committed to any deal, Henry suggested that I make a trip to Singapore. And of course, while I was on my way out there, it would be practical for me to take a shipment just so I could understand the logistics. The seven digit number Henry had dropped on me the previous evening kept popping into my head and greed overtook common sense. I was ready for combat.

The following morning Henry picked me up in his Mercedes and we drove to the apartment of a tailor who made the jackets used to carry the bullion. I was measured and fitted and measured again. The jacket had to fit just right or the weight could cut off the circulation in the shoulder area and sitting on a plane for twenty hours, say from Geneva to Singapore, could present something of a physical problem. The jacket consisted of a vest with two large panels that would contain three kilos attached to the lower part of each side of the jacket. These panels rested on the thighs when in a sitting position. The zipper closed from bottom to top and held the jacket snuggly onto the torso and once on the plane, the carrier would go into the rest room and raise the zipper some ten inches. Then, he could return to his seat and position the leg panels so they would fall off to the sides of the thighs. This would take the weight off of the legs so as not to impede the flow of blood.

Later, Henry and I went to the bank carrying a gym bag. It seemed very strange to me that one could walk into a bank, go up to the teller, and ask for thirty-six kilos of gold, and no one batted an eye. Henry paid cash ($28,512) for our purchase and I loaded up the bag with the ingots. It was heavy. He took one handle and I took the other and together, we exited the bank. We drove back to his apartment and began to dress me for my impending trip. I had purchased a Hawaiian print shirt one size larger. Once I had dressed in the vest and loaded up all the pockets, I overdressed with the shirt. The two flaps at the bottom of the vest went below my belt inside my pants and rested on my knees. It was not the most comfortable garment I have ever worn. I thought I was in pretty good shape, working out at the gym on a regular basis, but this extra weight, almost eighty pounds, was not easy to navigate. I was thinking how it would be possible to recruit carriers that had to experience all this extra exertion if they were not physically fit. I guessed that hanging out at local gyms would be a good place to start. Once I was dressed and passed muster, Henry and I headed for the airport.

Needless to say, I was a bit nervous. We parked the car and walked into the terminal. I kept looking around to see if I had attracted anyone's attention. I felt as if the entire airport personnel had stopped what they were doing and were staring at me. They all knew, I could tell. I went up to the counter and checked my bag, gave my ticket to the clerk and was given a boarding pass. I was flying on Quantas, a popular airline in the Far East. Henry stayed with me until plane time and then we bid each other goodbye and I boarded. By now I had grown accustomed to the extra weight and was able to move rather freely down the boarding ramp. My seat was on the isle but seated next to me was a small boy of about ten and his mother. The woman took the seat by the window and the boy sat between us. No problems, so far. I was wearing loafer shoes and Henry suggested that I take them off while in flight as the feet had a propensity to swell because of all the extra weight on the body. So shortly after we were aloft, I worked my way down to the men's room where I raised the zipper on the vest. Then I returned to my seat and maneuvered the two lower pouches over to the sides of my legs and slipped off my shoes. I was actually quite comfortable despite all the extra bulk on my torso. But we weren't airborne for more than an hour when the little boy next to me had to pee. Now, getting up from the seat took a certain amount of strength and dexterity and of course I was concerned that one of the ingots might work its way out of the pocket and fall to the floor of the aircraft. But the kid sidled past me and returned to his seat without incident. We arrived in Tehran in about five hours and stopped just long enough to discharge passengers and take on a new crew. Then we were off to Karachi, another five or six hours away. Dinner was served on the trek to Pakistan and from there we headed for New Delhi, which is now Bangladesh. This would be our last stop before we arrived in Singapore, the end of our journey. I was beginning to feel confident that this whole trip was a piece of cake. As I reclined in my seat, my eyes closed for a light nap, I heard a commotion from the seat next to me. I opened my eyes just in time to see that the little boy who was seated next to me had panic written all over his face. He looked up at me, his eyes wide with fear, his breath quickening. He looked from me to his mother.

"Are you all right?" she asked.

"I think I'm gonna be sick," he replied.

Why he turned back to me, I haven't a clue. He could have stayed facing his mother, but oh, no, he had to turn to me as he tossed his cookies. I was a stranger. He could have barfed on someone he knew and cared about. "How could a ten-year-old kid barf up that much food?" I thought. He spewed all over my shirt, my pants and my shoes that were on the floor between us. Then he scrambled over me and down the aisle to the washroom. Along the way he told a flight attendant that I needed help. It was a smelly, horrible mess. Here I was, trying my very best to keep a low profile and this kid has everyone on the plane looking over at me. In those days the air conditioning on long distant flights was not as efficient as in today's planes and the cabin was heating up uncomfortably. In short order, here came the stewardess with a wet cloth attempting to wipe the vomit from my shirt and it was all I could do to keep her from touching me lest she discover that I was wearing a vest under my shirt. I grabbed her arm and wrestled the wet cloth from her, did a cursory cleaning of my shirt and when the kid came back, full of apology, I made my way to the rest room. I managed to clean up most of the mess but the stench was still with me. It's impossible to describe the condition I was in. We were now only about an hour out of Singapore and I smelled putrid. People all around me were making remarks as if there was something I could do about it. I heard someone say, "He must have been drinking. He threw up all over himself." I wanted to yell out, "It wasn't me. It was the kid," but no one would listen. Hell, he wasn't even my kid. It wasn't as if I'd encouraged him to barf all over me. And the kid's mother was beside herself with embarrassment but what could anyone say? And I was trying to be Mr. Cool, all the while scared to death that I had attracted so much attention that someone was going to take notice that I was walking like a person who was carrying eighty pounds of gold bullion. When we set down in Singapore, I stepped aside to let the passengers precede me to the down ramp. Where could I hide? And as I reached down for my shoes, I realized that they were full of…you guessed it…vomit. I had no choice but to put my feet into my smelly, vomit-filled loafers and try to be as inconspicuous as possible. Slosh, slosh, slosh. As I made my way down the ramp the crew parted to let me pass as if I had just passed gas in an elevator. As I made my way into the terminal I realized that the heat was oppressive and the smell of the air was almost as bad as the smell that was emanating from my clothes. I soon learned that Singapore had aboveground sewerage and during the summers the city smelled to high heaven. Not that it neutralized the smell coming from me but I wasn't quite as conspicuous as I could have been in any other city. As I entered the terminal, people were climbing over each other to get away from me. I went directly to baggage claim and from there to Customs where I was sure I would be strip-searched. But as luck would have it, the Custom officials waved me through without so much as a peek into my bag or an inspection of my person. They just wanted to get me the hell out of the Singapore airport.

* * *

My contact in Singapore was a young man by the name of Werner who was emphatic when he informed me that he came from Switzerland and not Germany. I could tell by the expression on his face that he was not very pleased to see me in my condition and as he guided me to the rear seat of his car, he placed a blanket over the seat to ensure that I wouldn't foul up his precious VW. Once at the office/apartment over on Cavanaugh Road in a very fashionable section of the city where most of the embassies were located, he helped me to unload the ingots, gave me a towel and showed me to the shower. Werner was quite anal retentive and everything had to be just so, as was the Swiss custom. The gold ingots were counted twice, then placed into a secret compartment in the closet floor and covered over with carpeting. The stench of vomit lingered in his car so that it had to be taken into the car wash and decontaminated. I could not get the barf smell out of my head so I asked Werner to pick me up a jar of Vicks, which I dabbed under my nose until my nasal sense returned to normal. Meanwhile, Werner wrapped up my travel clothes including my shoes and socks, and disposed of them in the trash along with the jacket used to carry the gold. Werner was most efficient. Then he drove me over to the Raffles Hotel where I would be staying for two days; a sort of vacation at company expense.

Raffles was world-reknown because it had been used in a popular Humphrey Bogart film, and it was where the Singapore Sling drink was invented. All the rooms faced in on a large courtyard of rich, green grass that was exquisitely manicured, along with exotic flowers and majestic palm trees. It was truly a storybook setting and my imagination ran wild as I expected to see Peter Lorre and Sidney Greenstreet when I entered the bar. My room was quite large with overhead fans whirling throughout the day and night (pre air-conditioning) and in the evening the guests placed their shoes outside their doors and in the morning retrieved them, all bright and shiny, as if by some miracle. After a good night's rest, I awoke without the stench of vomit in my head but was overcome by the smell of the city. I walked from The Raffles into the downtown market place and it appeared that I was the only person in the entire city that was bothered by the smell. I guess one had to live there for a while to get accustomed to it. The city was a hodge-podge of ethnic diversity. There were Malaysians, East Indians, Chinese and English, all intermingled in commercial ventures but living conditions were most definitely segregated. The English lived over by Cavanaugh, while the Malaysians, East Indians and Chinese lived in their own separate parts of the city. As I walked along the main boulevard, there were beggars everywhere, holding out deformed hands and arms begging for alms. I soon ran out of change. But I was attracted to a storefront that exhibited custom made clothes for men. I couldn't resist. As I entered the store an Indian clerk immediately greeted me with a winning smile. "Is there something I can help you with, sir?" he asked.

"I'm just shopping. Would it take long to have a suit made?" I inquired. "I'm leaving tomorrow."

"That would not be a problem," he informed me. "We could take your measurements now and have your garments ready for you by this evening."

That was impressive. He led me over to a table where there were bolts of some of the finest fabrics money could buy. My hands glided over the silk and wool fabrics as if I were being drawn by some magnetic force. I chose a silk blend, blue and gray mixture, and the clerk showed me photos of various styles I might choose from. I chose a single-breasted. I knew this was going to cost an arm and a leg and when I finally asked what it would cost, the clerk proudly said, "That will be forty-five dollars, American." Now, this was the year of 1963 but even so, there was no place on the continent or in the United States where one could have a suit made for forty-five dollars. I was hooked. I ordered six silk shirt with my name embroidered on the cuffs…in Chinese. Hey, go all the way, I thought.

A Vulcan Odyssey

I returned to the store later that afternoon for a final fitting and that evening the suit and six shirts were delivered to my hotel. Such a deal.

The following morning I checked out of The Raffles and Werner drove me to the airport. I had much to think about regarding my role with Henry and his band of merry men, whom I had yet to meet. As instructed by Henry, I got off the plane in Tehran to purchase a large bag of pistachio nuts and half a dozen jars of caviar. "Don't come back to Europe without them," he chided me. And instead of returning to Brussels, I flew directly to Geneva, Switzerland.

* * *

I took a taxi to the Hotel Richmond, situated right on the edge of Lake Geneva. My room overlooked the lake with the mountains on the far side. It was a most impressive setting. Here I was, just a few kilometers from where Lydia had been raised and where she went to school. I could not resist. I had to know how she was and what had happened to her. There was still that emotional connection to her that I could not shake, even after three years. With the help of the clerk at the front desk, he managed to find the family name in the village of Montreux just on the French side of the border. I placed the call around dinnertime hoping that I would find someone at home that I could speak to. Fortunately, Lydia's sister, Arlette, answered the phone. In my broken French I tried to explain to her who I was but she soon cut me off by informing me that she spoke English and that she was pleasantly surprised to hear from me. We spoke for quite a few minutes and I was pleased to learn that Lydia was living in London and going to architecture school with the help of Arthur and Mathilda. On the one hand, they had gone out of their way to break up my marriage and on the other, they were helping Lydia to achieve the best that life had to offer her. She had talents that had to be nurtured and I had not been in any position to give her the support she needed and deserved.

The meeting of my employers took place in the dining room of the Richmond. There was Henry, and Herbie Fry and Jacques. (Last names escape me.) Henry seemed to be the leader of the group, Herbie the brains and Jacques the Swiss front. I was to learn that if the shit hit the fan, it would be Jacques who would face the music since he was a Swiss citizen and had the most to lose if the gold business went tits up. I immediately took a liking to Herbie Fry. He seemed to have his head screwed on tight and when I asked questions, he was direct and straightforward. Henry had a habit of romanticizing everything and minimizing the risks, while Herbie was pragmatic and right to the point. He and I spoke the same language. I told the three that I would try to recruit as many people as I possibly could but that I was not giving them any guarantees. I thought that my proximity to the military bases in Germany might be a good source of volunteers but I would have to tread lightly as I didn't want military intelligence on my ass. Henry suggested that I contact some of my actor friends who might want to pick up some extra money and I agreed that this might be a good source. And so it went for a couple of hours before we finally concluded our meeting. Henry extended an invitation for all of us to have dinner together and then go to a show, so we met later that evening at some posh restaurant for an exquisite meal, at company expense. Then we went to a club for drinks and naturally, I fell in love with this most gorgeous stripper who took me home that night and banged me silly. The following morning I offered to pay her and she got terribly insulted and declined the money. I later learned that Henry had already picked up the tab.

* * *

Recruiting couriers was not an easy task; it proved to be impossible. I could not just walk up to any person on the street and inquire if they wanted to risk life and limb for a few hundred dollars and expenses by smuggling a load of gold into some far off country. I selectively chose a few friends who might be candidates but after careful consideration, I chose not to take a chance on recruiting them. I knew that Lucky Casner would jump at the chance to get involved but he was a loose canon and I knew I couldn't depend on him to show up at the destination with the gold. Lucky had a friend that I had met, Danny Philbrook, a sergeant in the Army stationed just outside Munich. I knew that Danny could use the money but he had a wife and two kids and if he got caught, I would never forgive myself. And all the while I was mulling over the details of how I would recruit couriers I decided to carry myself. I began making a couple of trips a month just to pick up extra money. I already had an inkling that my million-dollar dream was just that, a dream. But

A Vulcan Odyssey

I could still keep busy making a trip every other week to some far off destination.

Between trips I returned to Munich to check in with Monika and the baby. They were doing well but my marriage to Monika was on shaky ground. When Jessica was three months old, I suggested to Monika that she might consider returning to work. For the past year she had done nothing but lay around the house reading magazines and watching television. Once the baby had arrived, I just assumed that I could count on her to take a job in the theatre or return to the television station if only to help out with some of the heavy house expenses. But Monika claimed that the birth of the baby had left her unable to take on the responsibility of a job and until she felt stronger, she would just have to languish around doing nothing. I didn't tell her that I was busting my ass smuggling gold in the butt end of the Far East and she just assumed that I probably had another family somewhere other than in Germany and that was why I was away so much of the time. When we were together, we barely spoke. For me, life in Munich was pure drudgery and I returned less and less often, preferring to call Madrid home where I still shared the apartment with Roy Rowland. The downside is that I missed the baby terribly. She was growing by leaps and bounds and I was not there to experience the joy of fatherhood. When I was at home I spent hours taking photos of Jessica that I still carry with me to this very day. But I had to think first and foremost of making a living in order to cover my heavy expenses. Until something better reared its head, Switzerland and the Far East were my only options.

I had just finished my eleventh trip and dropped off my cargo in Singapore. I was taking a few days to shop and play at sightseeing. The evening before I was to leave for Europe, I got a call from Herbie Fry. Henry was under house arrest in Karachi! "Would I help?" he asked.

I caught the first plane into Karachi by way of Bangkok. I could have stayed forever in Thailand, it was that beautiful. But I was on a mission and I checked into the Metropole Hotel in Karachi and placed a call to Henry. He was so disoriented that he barely knew who I was but we made plans to meet away from his hotel for fear that the police would be following him. Henry had done a stupid thing. He had taken a woman of short acquaintance with him on a trip to the Far East. He was carrying forty kilos and he persuaded her to carry thirty-five kilos as "part of their adventure." At the airport in Karachi where they had a two-hour layover, the woman began to freak out from the discomfort of the weight and attracted the attention of the Pakistani police. Upon interrogating her, the police discovered that she was carrying a number of pieces of gold under her clothing. Then, to save her ass, she pointed her finger at Henry, who was immediately arrested. All seventy-five gold pieces were confiscated, a statement from the woman was taken and she was released to leave the country. Henry was placed under house arrest. He had retained legal counsel and we went to his office.

Mister Khan explained to me that the police did not really want to have a long drawn-out trial but there had been so much publicity in the press that they were under public pressure to pursue legal action. "If Henry would just disappear," he suggested. The government would just as soon take possession of the gold and kiss Henry goodbye. That's where the lawyer thought I could help. Would I be willing to go north to Peshawar where Mister Kahn knew the owner of a trucking company who could be persuaded to squirrel Henry across the border into Afghanistan? I would have to deliver to Shah Mohammed an envelope of an unknown quantity of American dollars and make arrangements to deliver Henry for the trip.

I caught a plane for Rawalpindi, some seven hundred air miles from Karachi. I stayed at the Freeman Hotel where I got deathly ill from some curry chicken and I spent the next two days puking up my brains. I should have stayed in Rawalpindi but I had to get on to Peshawar. I decided to rent a car for the last leg of my trip. It was a rugged hundred miles and when I arrived in that primitive town, I first had to find the home of Shah Mohammed. It seemed that everyone in Pashawar had the last name of Mohammed so it took almost a full day to find the right home. Then there was the ritual: first coffee and pastry, then small talk, and finally down to business. After making all the necessary arrangements with Shah Mohammed to escort Henry out of the country on one of his trucks traveling to Kabul, I handed over the envelope and drove back to Rawalpindi where I returned the car and flew back to Karachi. I had a few days to spend in that city before beginning my trek north. I was slowly recovering from my bout with food poisoning and I took to the streets for a casual stroll around the city. Outside the Metropole Hotel was a snake charmer that mesmerized the hell out of me. I thought snake charmers were only a Hollywood shtick but here was a guy dressed in a turban and little else, squatted down on a piece of carpet with a basket and a reed flute. He commenced playing and this cobra began to weave its way up and out of the basket, swaying to the whiney cries of the flute. When the cobra was extended to its full height, the snake charmer reached into his cloth bag and took out a mongoose that he placed on the carpet. Like a flash, the mongoose jumped up, grabbed the snake by the neck and wrestled it back into the basket to the cheers of the tourist that were throwing coins. It wasn't Ziegfield but it was entertainment.

The first evening I spent in Karachi, I left the hotel just after sundown and as I turned left along the main street, I was suddenly aware of a wave of human bodies reclining on the sidewalk as far as the eye could see. These were the poor and homeless people with no place to live other than on the streets of the city. I came away quite sad and disturbed.

Although I traveled light, I still managed to pack a pair of Levis and comfortable sneakers for walking. On the other hand, Henry refused to change out of his Gucci loafers and his custom Swiss-made suit. Police surveillance could see him coming a mile away but he was headstrong and I couldn't get him to "dress down." The morning of our departure we left his hotel with police milling around the lobby. I was sure they would either arrest or follow us but when we arrived at the airport, nothing. I purchased two tickets, we boarded without any problems and we were on our way. As the plane took off from the runway I could swear that there were a dozen policemen standing on the tarmac waving goodbye. They got the gold and I got Henry.

* * *

I arrived back in Munich none the worse for my misadventure. The gold business was now a thing of the past. During my short stay in Geneva the grateful bosses handed me an envelope that contained three thousand dollars for my ordeal, a far cry from the million I had anticipated. I had no idea where to go from here. I had severed my connections in Madrid, Rome was a thing of the past, and I was adrift in Europe with not much hope for the future. Things couldn't possibly get worse. Then, Monika informed me that Lucky Casner was dead! He had gotten killed at Le Mans while racing the twenty-four hour event. He never made the turn at the end of the Mulson straight and just disintegrated in a ball of fire.

I wondered what ever happened to his pretty German Shepard dog that was devoted to him.

And then came a fateful call from Herbie Fry. "I just wanted to tell you that Jacques has been arrested here in Geneva. Henry and I are both closing up shop and heading back to the States. I suggest you do the same," he advised.

"I've got a family here," I reminded him. "I can't pack up and take off just like that."

"Well, here's the situation. Interpol may have all our names and it's just a matter of time before they begin to put two and two together..."

"What's that supposed to mean, Herbie?"

"They could be serving warrants for our arrests."

"Oh, shit," I replied. "How bad does it look?"

"The sooner you can get the hell out of Europe, the better," he advised. "We'll be out of here this evening so take our lead and get out as soon as possible. I don't know how long Jacques will hold out before he makes a deal, in which case he'll implicate all of us."

He apologized profusely and hung up. So there it was; I had to get out of Europe and get out fast or I could be facing criminal charges. It was time to go home.

It was not easy to just pick up and leave Munich. Although Monika and I tried to maintain a courteous relationship, it was most definitely strained. But there was the baby, Jessica, to consider. By this time, money was short and I had barely enough to purchase a ticket to Los Angeles. A few months before my departure, Walter Barnes was going through a tough time and came to me for a loan. He was a good friend and I couldn't turn him down. I managed to scrape up two thousand dollars to help him out but there was no timeline for repayment. I told him that he would pay me back when he had it. Now, I had to depend on Walter to help me out of my dilemma. Instead of paying me back, he would make payments to Monika until he paid back the money he owed me. If I could have financially afforded it, I would have taken Monika and Jessica with me but logistically, it just didn't work out that way. It was some time later that I learned that Walter never made the promised payments.

I know it sounds cruel of me to leave my family without visible means of support and I'm not trying to make excuses. I remember that I was able to scrape up a couple thousand dollars to temporarily tide her over until I could figure out what I was going to do. It wouldn't have served any of us if I remained in Germany and was arrested by Interpol and subjected to a prolonged legal process. In all the time we had been married Monika preferred to stay at home with the baby instead of helping out by returning to work. We were both to blame for spending what money we had in a frivolous manner. We went through all the monies I had made on Captain Sindbad as well as The Great Escape. And even if I had been able to find work in Germany, I doubt it would have helped to keep our marriage intact. I didn't want to leave the baby. She was the light of my life but I rationalized that if I was not there, Monika just might get off her dead ass and find work. And in the final scenario, she could always turn to her mother, Anita, to help out. There were options and I had to hope that she would turn to one of them.

CHAPTER TEN
FIFTEEN MINUTES OF FAME

When I departed Rome for Munich, I turned over the photography business to my friend, Walter Maslow. Actually, it was no gift because by that time the dew was off the rose. Walter tried to make it work but there just weren't enough clients available for a viable business. We kept in touch and he preceded me back to the States by about a year. I called him from Europe and told him that I was on my way to Los Angeles and could he find me a place to stay when I arrived. He was living on Harper in West Los Angeles and offered me the hospitality of his small pad until I could get settled and find my own place. I took him up on the offer. It was a week after my arrival in L.A., on a Sunday, when I was awakened by a call from Marilyn Tosatti, another Rome acquaintance.

"Turn on the television," she charged without even a greeting.

"Wassup?" I asked through half-sleep.

"Just turn it on," she insisted. I could hear the emotion in her voice.

By this time Walter was awake and flipped on the set. President John Kennedy had been assassinated! Walter and I sat there in stunned silence. Welcome home, I thought.

* * *

After the shock of Kennedy's assassination subsided and everyone had mourned a respectful period of time, I began to make phone calls. Betty Atkinson had been John Sturges' secretary for many years and while working on *The Great Escape*, she and I had formed a close friendship. I called her to say that I was back in the States and she invited me out to the studio for lunch. She wanted John to know that I was back in L.A. because he was preparing a film and she was sure there would be something in it for me. Next, I called Frank and Maury King, the infamous producers of *Captain Sindbad*. I say "infamous" because I don't remember anyone who ever had anything nice to say about them. But when I walked into their office on Sunset Boulevard, they both greeted me with open arms.

"What can I do for you?" asked Frank as he ran his large hand across his clean-shaven head. He still looked like a Jewish Buddha.

"I've got to get an agent, Frank," and before the words were out of my mouth, he was dialing his phone.

"Paul? This is Frank King," he announced to the party on the other end of the line. "I've got a young actor in my office who worked for me in Germany and he just arrived in Los Angeles a couple of days ago. When he told me that he was looking for an agent, I immediately thought of you. He's a hell-of-an actor. Did you see *The Great Escape*? He played one of the major roles in it. And he did one of the major parts in our film, *Captain Sindbad*." Pause. "Okay, I'll send him right over."

That was Frank King. Direct, to the point, no bullshit. We talked for a bit but he soon shoved me out the door and pointed me in the direction of Paul Wilkins' office, some half mile up the Strip from the King Brothers Building.

I guess I expected some plush agent's office but in truth, it was a depressing hole-in-the-wall with an elderly lady sitting in the outer office. Her name was Dorothy and she greeted me as if I were the second coming of Christ. "Do you know that Steve McQueen is one of my favorite actors of all times," she informed me. "I've known actors over the years but that young man has 'it.' What was it like working with him?" she asked without shame.

"Great guy," I informed her. She hung on my every word. I told her stories about Steve and what it was like working with him and James Garner and Charlie Bronson and James Coburn. She was mesmerized. We must have talked for at least fifteen minutes and I was growing a bit anxious because I was there to meet her boss and she was getting off on war stories. But soon the door to the main office opened and as a client left, Paul Wilkins came out to greet me.

"Sorry to keep you waiting but I had a previous meeting. Come on in," and he ushered me into his office. He was a tall man, much taller than I, and he was gaunt but quite elegant. He wore glasses and he spoke softly but with great authority. I liked him immediately. "Frank King says you're a fine actor. So tell me about yourself..." and for the next hour I covered my short life, embellishing my career as an actor, both in the U.S. and in Europe. Paul listened attentively without interruption. I could hear the phone ring in the outer office but Dorothy must have been given instructions not to disturb us because our meeting went on uninterrupted. As I spent the hour trying to impress Paul, I noticed the photos on his wall of Robert Mitchum and Ernest Borgnine. I assumed they were clients or why else would their pictures be on his wall? When I had finished monopolizing the conversation, Paul took a few moments to get his thoughts together.

"Do you know that John Sturges is preparing a film at Goldwyn? We've got to get you over to see him as soon as possible." I told him I had already made plans to have dinner with John's secretary, Betty Atkinson. He was impressed that I had already taken some initiative. As he began to speak he was like a whirling dervish. "How's your Italian? Great. The director, Arthur Hiller, at Universal is preparing *Tobruk* and they're looking to cast a very important role of an Italian Officer." (I told Paul that I met Arthur Hiller when he was doing a film in Austria and I auditioned for him in Munich but I didn't get the job.) "I'll call Bob Edmiston over at M.G.M. and we'll get you in to audition for *Combat*. They need to cast German roles all the time. You do speak German, don't you?"

"Some. I spoke German in 'The Great Escape.'"

"Of course. Leave the next few days open..." he instructed me. The following morning we were off to the studios. We began at Universal in the Valley. Paul literally took me by the hand and walked me from office to office. We began in Casting and worked our way over to the Producer's bungalows. In most cases we struck out but Paul knew how to charm the secretaries and by the end of the day, they would call to say that I had a firm appointment on such and such a day. We spent about two days at Universal, and then we moved out to Fox Hills where we knocked on doors at Twentieth Century Fox. Then it was over to MGM in Culver City and from there to Goldwyn. Back in Hollywood we did Columbia and then we drove out to Studio City where we did CBS Studios. In the matter of one week we had covered almost every studio in town. Those were the days when agents could take an actor in to meet a director or producer. That procedure has long since gone by the wayside. (Today agents read script breakdowns. Then, they send their submissions to the casting director via e-mail over the Internet. The casting director scans his computer until he comes up with a handful of actors he invites in for readings. He boils down his choices to one or two submission that he delivers to the director and producer. From those submissions the director makes his choice, usually someone he has worked with in the past. It's all very impersonal and lacks heart. Speak to actors from the past and you will hear stories about how they met this director or that producer and how, after numerous interviews, they got the part. Their stories are inspiring. Today, I know actors who have signed with agents and after a year or more, they have still to get their first "live" interview at a studio. The system sucks!)

After the first week of doing our dog and pony show at the studios, Paul began to call me with live interviews. I went out to read for one casting director or another, then got callbacks to read for the director or producer. It was a very exciting time and I knew that sooner or later it would all come together and I would begin to work. Paul did not let me get discouraged; he continuously told me how it was just a matter of time before I would be working. If anyone should have been jaded, it should have been Paul Wilkins. In the forties and fifties, Robert Mitchum had been about the biggest star in Hollywood and Paul had been his agent. Then, when Mitchum went to prison for using marijuana, Paul stood by him and when Mitchum came out he was able to pick up right where he left off. But a short time later, when Mitchum was on a roll, the big agencies began to romance him and it wasn't long before one of them managed to convince him that his career would flourish better in their agency. But Mitchum was a special sort of person and knew that what he was doing was morally reprehensible so instead of just walking out (which he had every right to do), he kept Paul on the payroll as an adviser and I believe their relationship continued right up until the time of Paul's death.

Then there was Ernie Borgnine. I had worked with Ernie in Roccarazzo and I was rather disappointed to hear this strory. Paul was his agent and as he told it, "The night Ernie got the Academy Award, he sent two letters; one to the Wilkins Agency and one to his wife. He fired us both!" Had I been in Paul's shoes I would have been nasty-mean when it came to actors but I honestly believed that Paul loved every one of his clients and no one could have tried harder than him to get my career off the ground.

After a couple of weeks of having interviews almost every day, I got a call from Paul. "They want to see you over at MGM for a role in *Combat*. You'll have to speak French and German..." That week I did three days on my first television show in L.A. Thankfully, the dialogue was written out for me so I didn't have to do the translations. And a few days after I finished at MGM, I got a call from Universal for the role of Lieutenant Agostino in the Arthur Heller film, *Tobruk*, in which I spoke only Italian. It starred Rock Hudson and George Peppard. This was fun...and lucrative.

Fate smiled on me when Paul got me an interview at CBS Studios to audition for a charming series called *The Rogues*. It had a great cast that included David Niven, Charles Boyer, Larry Hagman, Gig Young, Robert Coote, and Gladys Cooper. I knew David Niven from Europe a few years before but I didn't impose on him by asking his help to get me this role. It wasn't really much of a part but just to be working with this cast would have been quite a feather in my hat. I auditioned for Hy Averback, the director, and he hired me on the spot. One day on the set, I was sitting around talking with David and we were laughing about the fact that the total ages of the six regular cast members added up to close to five hundred years. (It was actually four hundred years.) He marveled at the thought that this series did not have any young blood to attract the younger audiences. Of course, in my naivety I couldn't imagine a show with that many well-known actors not being a tremendous success. But the ratings were just a bit on the mediocre side and David was concerned about the age thing. So one day after shooting he marched me up to the office and we sat with Hy Averback who was also one of the producers.

"Can't we work Lawrence into the cast in some way?" he asked Hy. "We need some young blood. We're dying on the vine. The kids don't watch the show because we're just a bunch of old fogies that they can't identify with."

I was speechless. David never said a word to me about working me into the show. He just blurted it out and caught me completely off-guard. Hy listened to David's suggestion but was quite up-front and forward when he told us that with six regulars already signed, there really wasn't any room to add another character. It was only a half hour show. But he picked up a handful of scripts from his desk that were on the schedule for that season, and rifling through them, he pulled out two scripts and handed them to me. "Take a look at these. There are a couple of parts you could play without any conflict. One is an East Indian guard and the other is a British chauffeur. I'll keep you in mind when the new scripts come in."

And so it was that I did three *Rogues*, almost one right after the other. And I probably would have become a semi-regular on the show had word not come down a couple of weeks later that the series had been cancelled. I loved that show. It was funny, intriguing, bright, intelligent; that's probably why it only lasted two seasons.

I went on to do a number of other shows for Hy Averback.

The Great Escape opened with great fanfare and Paul's phone was ringing off the hook for my services. I was going from one television role to another playing a variety of roles but I could tell that something was not going according to what I had envisioned. I was a bit player and nothing more and that's not where I had thought this whole thing was leading. When would I be stepping up into more substantial roles? When would I be doing those co-starring or starring roles? I had been working almost steady for six months. I had purchased a new Ford Mustang convertible, put a down payment on a house in Laurel Canyon, and had not slept in months. I kept thinking about what would happen if this rollercoaster suddenly stopped. I spoke to Paul about trying to find me some more substantial roles and he promised he would try but over the next couple of months, nothing changed.

I had been with Paul just over a year and I was working on a movie being made for television called *A Time For Killing*. It starred George C. Scott, one of my all-time favorite actors. I was playing a submarine officer, a small part but one that ran through the entire two hours. It was a good gig as bit parts go.

* * *

Amidst all this activity, my friend Walter Maslow mentioned that he had run into an old friend of ours from Rome, Morgan Jones. Morgan and his wife, Joan, had purchased a Spanish villa on Outpost Drive. I had done photographs of both of them in Rome and we had a casual friendship. Walter said that Morgan and Joan would like to see me, that I should give them a call. First break I had, I called the Joneses. Joan gushed when she heard that I was back in Los Angeles and trying to find work. She and Morgan were managing to pick up a bit of work as actors but they didn't purchase a Spanish villa from the money they made doing bit parts. It was obvious that they were part of that fortunate few that came from wealthy backgrounds. In a matter of minutes, Joan had invited me to their home for dinner.

Their home was spacious and very impressive. It was one of those estates that had been built in the pre-war era when money flowed like wine and the elite of Hollywood inhabited the Outpost area. Joan and Morgan took great pleasure in showing me through their home. Joan had recently had a baby boy and a happier couple couldn't be found. Upstairs was a large room that was being converted into a theatre. It was their dream to have a place where they could put on plays but it never occurred to them that they would eventually do it right in their own home. Now, they were in the process of making their dream come true.

The evening included a sit-down dinner for some dozen people in a dining room that included a table fit for King Arthur's court. All the guests were actors and people who were going to be involved with the theatre project. I had never met Ray Aghian or Bob Mackie before but it was soon apparent that they were principals in the theatre project. Ray was in the process of re-writing two of Lillian Hellman's plays, *Little Foxes* and *Another Part of the Forest*. His plan was to cut the two plays down to an hour each. These two plays were actually a saga of the trials and tribulations of the same family over the period of two generations. Ray planned that in between acts, while the actors were performing the miracle of aging twenty years, the audience would be served a buffet dinner. It was an imaginative and very ambitious idea.

"Are you familiar with *Little Foxes* and *Another Part of the Forrest?*" asked Ray.

"I remember seeing *Little Foxes*, the film with Bette Davis. I'm not sure I remember seeing the sequel."

"Are you thinking what I'm thinking?" Joan asked Ray. "He'd be perfect for the role of Ben, wouldn't he?"

I suddenly got the feeling that my presence at this dinner was anything but accidental. I was being fattened up for the kill.

"Would you like to do a play?" asked Ray. "You'd be perfect for the role of Ben, the brother. It's a very dynamic role. Before you answer, why don't you take the script home and read it over."

At this moment in time, I had not thought about doing anything so ambitious as a play. I felt I was on the verge of having a breakthrough in television and possibly films. Doing a play could very well be an amusing diversion but did I have time for diversions?

"Do you know who Ray Ahgian is?" asked Joan when everyone else had left the party. "He's the hottest thing in costume design in all of Los Angeles. If he directs a play, you can be sure that everyone who is anyone in the film community will be beating down the door for tickets. Do yourself a favor," she confided, "and do this play."

Joan's sincerity was infectious. I promised I would take it under consideration; I wanted to see if I just wasn't planning to bite off more than I could chew.

I ran the idea of doing a play by Walter Maslow and he thought it might be a good way to open some doors. After all, a good showcase in Hollywood was hard to find. (Those were the days when casting people and directors got off their dead asses and went to the theatre, not only for entertainment but to search out new talent. Times have changed. Today, in order to get someone of any import in Hollywood to attend a play at a small theatre, one would have to be a relative.) I also sought out the advice of Paul Wilkins who felt that "activity could only breed activity." It was his favorite expression. And I no sooner called Joan to tell her that I would love to do her production when I got a call from Paul telling me that Columbia casting had called to say that they were interested in me for their upcoming film, *King Rat*. I had read for the casting director, he had recommended me to the director and now it was only a matter of signing the contract. But twixt the cup and the lip, there was a slip. It appeared that the role in *King Rat* didn't amount to very much. Its redeeming feature was that it would be a long running contract, but in truth, I was hoping for something more substantial. That's when Paul called to tell me that I was being pulled from *King Rat* for a better role in *Synanon*, the true story about Chuck Dederick, the founder of the drug rehabilitation center in Santa Monica. It had a star studded cast including Chuck Conners, Edmond O'Brien, Eartha Kitt, Stella Stevens, Alex Cord, BarBara Luna, Bernie Hamilton, and the list went on. The details were worked out and the following week, I began work in Santa Monica. I didn't realize how much of a drive it would be to travel every evening from Santa Monica to the theatre on Outpost for rehearsals. But activity was most definitely breeding activity.

Taking the role of Ben in the Outpost Theatre production of *Little Foxes* and *Another Part of the Forest* was probably the most fortuitous thing that could have happened to me at that time. Joan was right: Ray Ahgian and Bob Mackey had a great deal of juice in the film community and in a matter of days, the entire run had been sold out. Of the numerous casting directors that attended the production, the one from Quinn Martin Productions turned out to be my guardian angel. Her name was Dodie McLean. The day after she attended the show, she called Paul Wilkins and arranged for me to come in for an interview.

Quinn Martin was one of the hottest producers in Hollywood and anyone who was fortunate enough to break in with that company was assured of at least a few jobs each season. *The Fugitive* was probably the most popular show of its time, starring David Janssen. After reading for John Conwell, Quinn's right hand man, Dodie cast me to play a Police Officer. It wasn't a great role but it opened the door for me with QM Productions. In the industry, it was known as "the Quinn Martin stock company." Once an actor was fortunate enough to break into the QM organization, chances were that he or she could count on working all the shows for that company in one season, and sometimes two of each show. In dollars and cents, it amounted to a tidy sum of money and every actor in town wished he could get in. On the other hand...and of course, there is always the other hand...John Conwell might call one day with a guest-starring role on, let's say *The Fugitive*. A few weeks later he might call and offer the same actor a one-day bit on *The Invaders*. An actor knew that there was no turning down the bit part or chances were there would never be a chance to do that guest role at a later date. I would say that over a period of two years, I must have done at least a dozen shows for the QM organization. I did six different episodes of *The F.B.I., Twelve O'clock High, The Invaders, The Fugative, The Streets of San Francisco,* and *Cannon*.

It was like having a small annuity.

* * *

This is the part of my life that I don't cherish retelling but your reading this comes under the heading of entertainment; for me it is more like therapy. We sometimes do things that we regret when we look back on them later in life. My marriages to four women still haunt me, my relationship with my daughter was a disaster; but they don't hold a candle to what I did to a good and cherished friend. While I was going from job to job in television, ("Bicycling from studio to studio," said the Hollywood Reporter) I met a number of agents, some of whom would invite me to lunch with them in what appeared to be an innocent gesture. After all, everyone knew that I was signed with Paul Wilkins and that that relationship was sacrosanct. But one agent, Larry Kubrick, struck up a friendship with me and we began to party at the Candy Store in Beverly Hills a couple of nights a week. In fact, Larry became my mentor and if there was something that stuck in my craw about how much I was being paid to do a certain role or if I was unhappy with the billing I was getting, I would run it by Larry and he would give me his professional advice. He worked for a very well known office, The Robert Raison Agency. They only had a handful of clients, most of whom were in series. The reputation of the Raison Agency was without question one of the finest boutique agencies in Beverly Hills. Besides Larry and Bob Raison, the other agent in the office was Phil Gittleman, and like Larry, a hustler. These guys were good. It appeared that no matter where I worked, they always had a client working in the same show. I knew that if I would ever consider changing agents, I would go with the Raison Agency.

I don't know if it was any one thing or if it was just "the winter of my discontent" that made me take stock of where my career was heading. Other than opening the door at Paramount, my two roles on Star Trek did nothing to advance my career. Star Trek in its time was not a big hit and no one in the industry took it very seriously.

I was going from one bit part to another and periodically I was landing a sizeable co-starring role but never was I getting those meaty roles to which I aspired. It was just before Christmas and I had not worked for quite a few weeks. I was getting antsy. It is usually indigenous of the industry to slow down near holiday time but I took it as an indication that Paul wasn't doing his job and when I had a few drinks under my belt, I could rationalize that I was being slighted and my representation was not of the level I expected. One evening, at the Candy Store, I queried Larry about my moving over to the Raison Agency. He didn't jump at the idea but said "he would have to discuss it with Bob and Phil." And the next time we got together he assured me that the Raison Agency could do for me what Paul could not; get me those guest shots I thought I should be doing.

If there is a God she sure as hell has been paying me back all these years for what I did next. I sent Paul Wilkins a letter dismissing him. I posted it Christmas week so it arrived a day or so before the holiday. Then, Christmas eve I got a call from Paul's wife. She was a woman in her early seventies who always seemed very genteel with a sweet smile on her face but this evening she was drunk out of her bird. She proceeded to rip me a new asshole. "You little, fucking prick," she began. "Do you have any idea what you've done? My husband loved you like a son and you've broken his heart. You are a nothing piece of shit and I hope you rot in hell!" There was nothing I could say as the phone went dead in my hand. I knew I had done a terrible thing but there was no turning back. I had committed to joining the Raison Agency.

I really think that of all my guardian angels, the one who made the greatest impact on my career would have been the director by the name of Murray Golden. Bob Raison called me to audition for a producer by the name of Aaron Spelling who was doing a show, *Amos Burke, Secret Agent*, starring Gene Barry. (This was long before Aaron became an icon in the world of television.)

The role was that of a Swiss gold smuggler and I had to laugh because this was right up my alley; been there, done that. All I had to do was convince Aaron Spelling that I could do a Swiss accent. "But what the hell was a Swiss accent?" I thought. There was German/Swiss and Italian/Swiss and French/Swiss. Pick one. I settled on German and when I arrived at the studio for my interview, there in the waiting room were half a dozen *real* German actors. I was dead in the water. After almost an hour, when all the other actors had gone in and auditioned, I was the last one. This last German actor who I knew, by the name of Hans, came out of the interview office with this great shit-eating grin on his face. "They told me to come back in half an hour," he announced as he confidently walked out the door.

A few moments later, the secretary told me to go in. As I opened the door, I was greeted by this huge German Shepard that came bounding across the room at me. I don't know what possessed me, but in German, I said, "My God, what a beautiful German Shepard," and with that I got down on my hands and knees and began to roughhouse with the dog. He playfully took my head in his mouth and we must have played for a at least three minutes and when I looked up, there were half a dozen people in the room staring at me in disbelief. They must have thought I was out of my mind. And when I got to my feet, I was speaking with this perfect German accent!

"Forgive me, but I have a German Shepard in Germany where my wife and baby still live. You have no idea how much I miss that dog. This one looks almost exactly like mine but mine is not quite so large." I figured that if the owner of the dog had any pride at all, saying that his dog was of good size was the greatest compliment I could pay. He belonged to Aaron Spelling.

"Where are you from in Germany?" asked a tall, lean man with a goatee sitting on the couch. He introduced himself as Murray Golden, the director.

I began to make up this long story about living in Germany and only recently coming to America. I avoided mentioning *The Great Escape* because it was still too fresh in everyone's mind and if I explained that I played the role of a Canadian, I would have blown my cover. But I did mention that I played a German soldier in *Combat* and another in *Blue Light*. After a few minutes, Murray handed me a script and asked me to read with him. It was a very small role, about three pages long with not much meat but I was more concerned that I could sell them on the accent. When I finished reading, no one said anything for what seemed like forever. I just stood there while everyone looked from one to the other.

Murray finally broke the silence. "Aaron, I think he would be very interesting with blond hair, don't you?"

"Oh, yes," agreed Aaron. "Would you mind if we sprayed your hair blond? Nothing permanent. You can wash it out in the evening after work."

"No, no problem," I assured them.

But as I stood there, I could tell that something wasn't kosher. "It appears we have a small problem," said Aaron, almost apologetically. "We've already committed to another actor."

My heart skipped a beat. It was a nothing part so I don't know why I wanted to play it so badly. Maybe it was because Hans, the German actor, was so damn smug when he walked out of the office.

"The young Swiss man who was in here before you," said Murray.

I wanted to scream out, "HE'S NOT SWISS. HE'S A GERMAN!" But who the hell was I to call the kettle black?

"We told him to wait across the street in the bar. Would you mind going over there and telling him to come back. I'll think of something to tell him."

I still hadn't a clue what they wanted to do. "Does that mean you want me to do the role?" I asked, still feigning that German accent.

"Oh, yes," said Aaron Spelling. "Here, take a script with you and give us about half an hour until we can work this out."

With script in hand, I turned and headed for the door. Then I turned and faced the gathered group. "May I ask you a question?"

"What is it?" responded Aaron.

In perfect English, I asked, "Now that you're sure I have the role, may I drop this fucking accent?"

It was Murray who broke the tension when he started laughing and was soon followed by Aaron and everyone else in the room. That was my introduction to Murray Golden. Before shooting began on that segment of *Amos Burke*, Bob Raison called to tell me that the Spelling office sent over a new script. Aaron was so impressed with me that they rewrote the role and upgraded me to co-starring billing. It was the beginning of a beautiful friendship between Murray and myself. Thereafter, whenever he was doing a show he would have the Casting Office call my agent and have me come out to the studio to meet the producer. Sometimes it would be a featured role but more often than not it was a guest-starring role. Sometimes he would just have casting call Bob or Larry, send over a script, ask about my availability and without a reading or interview, they would cut a deal. I did about a dozen really fine roles for Murray. He and his wife, Charlotte, became good friends and invited me to their home on numerous occasions. Murray was originally a musician from New York and I believed that his heart was really back in the Big Apple because one day, he and Charlotte just disappeared from the scene and I never heard from them again.

On one occasion, Murray called me to do a role of a Native American in a the retelling of the tale of General Custer at Little Big Horn for the series, *Time Tunnel*, for Irwin Allen at Twentieth Century Fox. It is funny how one thing leads to another because this role opened up the door for me to work with Irwin Allen Productions at Fox. His films, *Poseidon*

Adventure and *Towering Inferno* were tremendous box office successes. I did two *Time Tunnels*, both very good roles and finally I got a call to do a guest appearance in *Voyage to the Bottom of the Sea*. I had no idea that this was not just another acting job because no one intimated that it could possibly lead to anything bigger.

Shortly after we finished shooting the segment of Man Beast on *Voyage*, Bob Raison called to tell me that Irwin Allen called him to see if I would be interested in doing a series for him. As it turned out, my role in *Voyage* was my screen test although no one said anything about it before we commenced shooting. I guess it worked out pretty well because I probably would have been nervous as hell had I known what was at stake. And by not telling me up front, Irwin kept his options open if he decided that I was not right for the role. Anyhow, Irwin was preparing another science fiction show called *City Beneath the Sea* and was considering me for the part of a human fish, Dr. Aguila. There was no script, only fifteen pages that they referred to as "a presentation." When I got the pages it was obvious that Dr. Spock in Star Trek had influenced Irwin because it was almost the same sterile type of personality that Leonard Nimoy played so well. But instead of wearing pointed ears, I was outfitted with gills that I used to breathe underwater and I could talk to dolphins.

Lawrence as Dr. Aguila in the pilot *City Beneath the Sea* for producer Irwin Allen

The cast of *City* was impressive; James Brolin (who had just come off a long running series with Robert Young where he played the role of Dr. Kiley), Francine York, and Cecile Ozorio. At the time, Irwin had three shows running weekly on television: *Land of the Giants*, *Time Tunnel* and *Voyage to the Bottom of the Sea*. Word around Fox had it that Irwin was going to New York to sell the networks into buying four more shows so he would have one show on television each night of the week. Talk about an ego trip! He was planning a series called *Man From the Twenty-First Century* starring John Crawford, a friend of mine from the Players Ring Theatre back in the fifties and also one of the cast members of *Captain Sindbad* in Germany. Then, there was a series starring Ricardo Montalban called *Joaquin Murrieta*, a sort of Mexican Robin Hood adventure. The forth presentation had already been shot during a previous season so I knew nothing about it, and finally, there was our pyrotechnic extravaganza, *City Beneath the Sea*.

The presentation for *City* included about five minutes of introducing the characters and ten minutes of blowing up everything in sight, with water cascading down on the actors from every nook and cranny on the sound stage. Most of my work and dialogue was done in a tank where they had to anchor me down to the bottom because I kept floating up to the top. They had an air hose that a stunt man held at the ready so I would not have to resurface between takes. At the end of a day of shooting, I could have done a Sunshine Prune commercial. My skin was shriveled and I took on the appearance of crepe paper. As I remember, we shot for about ten day before they called it a wrap. Word around the set was that *City* was a shoo-in for the next season's schedule and the entire cast was on a high. Jim Brolin and I talked about purchasing a racecar so we could go on the circuit during hiatus. He was having marital problems at the time and I guess he would have taken any suggestion to get out of the house.

City Beneath the Sea was not only the highlight of my television career but as fate would have it, it was also my demise as an actor. My contract with Fox was for six months and the Raison Agency was not anxious to find me further employment once we had wrapped *City*. When I would call Robert or Larry about work, they would kid me and say that I was greedy, that I had a series that would commence in the Fall of that year, and that I should enjoy my good fortune. But I, on the other hand, was concerned that if the series did not sell, and I had not worked for the better part of six months, I would be dead in the water. There was a stigma in those days that when an actor did a pilot or presentation for a series and it didn't sell, it was always the actor's fault. Doors that were previously opened were then suddenly closed.

A Vulcan Odyssey

I know I had been out of work for quite a few months when word finally came down that Irwin had returned from New York with disastrous news. Not only was he not able to sell any of the new shows but the network had also cancelled one of the shows that was already running, *Time Tunnel*. Word on the street had it that Irwin had gotten too big for his britches, that the networks did not want to be dictated to and that they were going to show him a thing or two. If that was their intention, they sure got their point across. I do believe that it was this series of events that lead to Irwin's death only a couple of years later. When he died there was nothing on television that bore his name.

(Irwin's last venture was a made-for-television film, *City Beneath the Sea*. For some reason, he got a bug up his ass that the cast of the pilot was responsible for the series not selling so when it came time to cast the film, none of the original cast from the pilot was included.)

While I was cooling my heels waiting to hear about the series, Larry Kubrick and Phil Gittleman had left the Raison Agency. Larry decided to go into production and Phil became a personal manager but he was not interested in handling me. Bob Raison was a great organizer but he was not a legman and that's what the Raison Agency needed at that time. He brought in a nice young man by the name of Robert Bach to service the clientele but the agency began to slide downhill and interviews for me were far and few between. I had been living high on the hog and thought that nothing could alter my rise in the industry. One morning I awoke to the realization that I could not keep up the mortgage on my Laurel Canyon home and the car payments on my new convertible Mustang were eating my lunch. I loved that house on Nash Drive. It was the last house on a *cul de sac* and it was built into the mountain with a view from downtown Los Angeles all the way to Catalina (on a clear day.) I had built a bedroom with thirty-five feet of windows from floor to ceiling, overlooking the city. When my mother came to visit for her birthday in August, she cried when she returned home; such was her attachment to that house. I had bought it for twenty-five thousand dollars and put in about ten thousand dollars in remodeling. And I guess I really would have done everything possible to keep the place were it not for the road leading up the hill. There was a wooden bridge a few yards down the road before one got to my house and it must have been built sometime between the two big wars. Nash Drive was not a paved road and after a rainfall, it was rutted and almost impossible to maneuver. Then, one day, I got a notice from the city declaring that the bridge was unsafe and that the city planned to condemn it. For the next few months I got caught up in a mess of bureaucratic garble. The road was an easement, not a dedicated road and therefore, it was my responsibility to maintain it. That was a load of hogwash because city trucks came up that road all the time to do work on their utilities and after a rainfall, the city sent up a grader to level the ruts in the dirt. Why didn't they demand that I pay for the grader if I was responsible for the maintenance of the road? I had very little money saved and although I could have taken a second mortgage on the house, I was mentally on the skids, mostly because of the failure of the series to sell. With an estimate of ten thousand dollars to replace the bridge, and the fact that there was no prospect for work on the horizon, I sold the house for thirty-three thousand dollars. (I recently spoke with a real estate person who informed me that the house was on the market for five hundred and fifty thousand dollars!)

The Raison Agency was unable to move me. I had a few interviews and a few small jobs that paid the rent and the car payments. At the time I was friendly with a lovely lady, Cathy Potter, who managed a restaurant on the corner of Sunset and Crescent Heights, The Steak and Stein. The restaurant's bar was not a very successful operation and Cathy was able to talk the owner into letting me have the bar on a rental basis. At the same time, I decided to return to school, this time to study law. I enrolled at the University of West Los Angeles in Culver City. Along with an occasional acting job, the bar brought in enough money to sustain me and except for the weekends when business picked up, I used the evenings to study, being interrupted only by an occasional customer.

One day, Cathy had lunch with an acquaintance at Disney Studios. While there she met a producer, Jerry Courtland, with whom I had worked in New York on the sci-fi pilot for Enright and Friendly's production of *The Gillmen*. We had also spent some time together in Rome after his series, *The Vikings*, closed down. And when I had worked on *The Flying Nun*, it was Jerry who gave me the chance to write three projects with him while he was still under contract to Columbia before the studio went into bankruptcy. In the course of conversation, Cathy mentioned my name and Jerry told her that we were friends from way back. He asked that I give him a call. S'funny how casual incidents sometimes open doors. I called Jerry and we made an appointment to have lunch.

Jerry was most cordial and we had many friends in common, the most notable was Walter Barnes. Jerry was now a Producer/Director for Disney Productions in Burbank. As we talked about old times, he mentioned that his job at Disney was hampered by his inability to find suitable material for films to be done at Disney. Over the years I fashioned myself as something of a writer, having written perhaps a half dozen scripts that were gathering dust somewhere in storage. I would write a script and then, after reading it, decided that it wasn't worth the paper it was written on and either junked it or stashed it away in some dark recess. But more recently I had been working on a pilot for a television series in the foreign intrigue genre. It was called *The Silent Wall*. It was the story about an organization in Switzerland called Freedom, Inc. that was privately endowed, and whose job it was to extricate persons from behind the various walls of oppression throughout the world, most notably the Iron and Bamboo Curtains. The four leading cast members would alternate from one show to the other or work in pairs to travel to exotic places to face danger and intrigue while performing acts of daring in the name of personal freedom.

The pilot show was about an emissary from the Catholic Church who went to Freedom, Inc. to ask for their help in getting ten children out of East Germany. The children were wards of the church but were being sent to Russia for indoctrination into Communism. Two of the agents were assigned to the job of getting the children out of the East and into the West. And of course there was the usual chase and all sorts of incidents that hampered the escape to freedom.

On a subsequent visit to the studio for lunch, I sat in Jerry's office and told him the idea I had for a TV pilot or film. I ran the story by him in detail and when I was finished, he was quite candid.

"I like the idea," he said. "But Disney is very careful about not getting into politics or religion. Communism and the Catholic Church are both taboo subjects."

We went to lunch and when we returned to his office I informed him that I had another idea for a film. "The time is the Civil War and there is a group of children from very rich Northern families attending a school in Virginia. A Southern Officer decides to kidnap the children, take them to Atlanta and hold them for ransom to help the Southern cause. While in captivity, the children drive their captors crazy and one day, while on an outing, the children find a runaway, wounded, black, Northern prisoner in the hayloft of a deserted barn. The children nurse him back to health and in payment for their help, they convince him take them with him on his run for the North."

Jerry sat there with a grin on his face. "Why does that story sound familiar?" he asked.

"Because it's the same story I told you before lunch. Only the time and places have been changed to protect the innocent."

"Can you give me a synopsis?"

"Is tomorrow soon enough?"

The following day I returned with a fifteen-page outline of a script that had yet to be written. The wheels of industry move very slowly and it was about two weeks before I heard from Jerry. "Looks like we've got a deal," he informed me. "Who's your agent?"

That was the tricky part. The first rule in Hollywood is never sign anything without an agent. I didn't have a literary agent. I began calling around until I finally found someone who would front for me for this one script. Rather than a commission he agreed to take a flat fee. But he called me back a couple of days later to inform me that Disney was interested in a buy-out of the property. Nothing was said about me writing the script. They were offering some paltry sum for the rights to the story and I would be left out in the cold. I had written three projects for Jerry when he was at Columbia and he had read a number of scripts that I had pulled out of storage. He knew that I could write. I had just assumed that he would go to bat for me when push came to shove. I called Jerry.

"I thought we were talking about me writing the script," I said.

"I tried to sell you but they wouldn't buy it. They said you don't have a track record and they're only interested in the property. I'm sorry."

"Well, that makes two of us. I'm not selling," I informed him, defiantly. End of conversation.

A few days later I got a call from Jerry Paris, head of the Story Department for Disney. "We've been having meetings with Ron Miller, the executive producer for Disney, and we've come up with a deal. You get a shot at writing the script but it's broken down into three phases. You write the original script for which you get paid so much money. If we like what you've done, you go into the second phase, which is the first re-write. For this you get another fee. And if we still like what you've done, we hire you to write the final draft and you get the remainder of the contractual agreement."

"So what you're asking me to do is take a gamble on being retained through to the final draft, is that right?"

"You show us that you can do the job and we'll pick up your options. We've got to protect ourselves."

I called Jerry for a final meeting. I was so close to a deal but there was the smell of me working my ass off and then being dumped and another writer being brought in. I couldn't even get the studio to assure me that I would get sole billing unless I was hired to do the final draft.

"Take the deal," Jerry advised me. "We'll be working together. I can dictate how I visualize the script and when it comes time for them to pick up your option, I'll be in your corner. Trust me on this one."

That's the second no-no in Hollywood; don't trust anyone. I instructed the agent to cut the deal. I went to work for Disney in 1975 and I felt that everything would work out if I just listened to Jerry. "Write it the way you see it," he told me.

"I want to write the dialogue for the kids as regular kids would talk, not like Disney kids talk."

"Do it," he instructed me.

Every few days I would deliver up the pages I had finished and Jerry and I would go over them. I had an office just down the hall in the writer's part of the building where there were a dozen writers working on projects. We all shared one secretary who typed up our work in order of submission. I was not accustomed to working nine to five but those were the rules and each morning I punched in just like I did when I was working on the assembly line at Lockheed. It took a while for me to be able to write on cue but over the period of the next few months, I fell into line and was turning out my quota on a daily basis. It took approximately four months before I came up with a finished "first draft." Jerry was involved with setting up the production for a film he was getting ready to shoot. I took the script to Jerry's office but the secretary informed me that he was in conference with his new director from England, John Hough. She would give him the script when he had some time to look at it. I was just about to leave when Jerry came out of his office and greeted me.

"I want you to meet someone," he informed me. Coming out of the office behind him was a rather short, pleasant looking man with a warm smile. "John, this is the guy I told you about. I think he'd be perfect for the role of Uberman, don't you?"

John Hough shook my hand. "I saw you in *The Great Escape*. It was one of my favorite films of all times," he pleasantly informed me. "Why don't you join us for lunch?"

Just like that. By the time we had finished eating, John told me that there were two roles I could possibly play in the film he was preparing, *Escape to Witch Mountain*. "One part is that of a Sheriff and the other is a driver and gunman by the name of Uberman. The Sheriff is the better role but it only works for about a week. The role of Uberman is a lesser role but it runs for about six weeks on location in Carmel. Why don't you take the script and look it over. Let me know which of the two roles you'd like to play."

That's the way it was done. No reading, no audition. It would be a while before Jerry would get around to going over my first draft and longer until Ron Miller and Jerry Paris decided if they wanted me to do the first re-write. By this time I knew my days as an actor were numbered so I wasn't looking for a "better role." The following day I returned to Disney to tell Jerry and John that I would like to play the role of Uberman. They notified casting and the deal was set. (My dear friend, Walter "Piggy" Barnes eventually played the role of the Sheriff.)

Carmel, California, has to be heaven for anyone who has not been there. The homes along Seventeen Mile Drive were exquisite as only California wealth can dictate. I met a bartender/owner of a place called Sadie's. His name was Benny Enia and he was first generation Italian. When he heard that I spoke Italian, he invited me to his home to meet his mother and we sat around talking about the old country in her native tongue. Benny was into just about everything in Carmel. He owned part of Sadie's and I think he was into some pretty shady stuff. But he treated me like I was kind of a celebrity and I could never pick up a check at his bar. In Carmel, there is sort of a code that if someone owns a bar or restaurant, he is entitled to eat and drink at any other place in town. It's called "reciprocity." So I had plenty of time off from work and spent most of it with Benny at his bar. After all, I met some very foxy women at his place but they were only interested in Benny so I never did score. Benny was a heavy drinker and I thought I could keep up with him. By the time he got off work each evening, we were both six sheets to the wind. But the evening did not stop there; we moved on to one of the better restaurants in the village and gorged ourselves. I remember waking up one morning and in my pocket I found two receipts for dinners at two different restaurants. I was eating and drinking as if the Russians were in Carmel Valley. I had been in Carmel for about three weeks and when I got a call to report on the set for work, John Hough, the director, came over to me and took me aside. "Lawrence, what the hell are you doing?"

"What do you mean?" I asked. I had no idea what he was referring to.

"I can't match the footage we've already shot. You must have put on twenty pounds!" he announced.

He was right. I had not been to a gym for over a month, which was anathema to me. Actually, the weight was not in my face but in my body. I had developed a potbelly and my ass was almost dragging on the ground. Right then and there I resolved to get my act together. I went on what was tantamount to a crash diet, determined to lose the weight and restore my sanity. Before leaving for Carmel, I had broken up with a young lady with whom I was having a very torrid relationship and when I got to Carmel, it just seemed natural to drink and smoke. I had been off cigarettes for five years and I had taken them up again along with the drinking and overeating. I was thankful that John Hough had become a very good friend because by all rights, he could have canned me right then and there.

While working on Witch Mountain I ran into an old acquaintance from The Great Escape, a stuntman by the name of Bud Ekins. He was playing the role of a Motorcycle Policeman. He was an easygoing sort of guy who looked enough like Steve McQueen to be his stunt double when we worked in Germany. Everyone thought that Steve did that spectacular motorcycle jump over the barbed wire fence near the end of the film, but in truth, it was Bud Ekins who did it. The Mirisch Company wasn't stupid enough to take a chance that Steve just might get injured doing that jump and that would have held up production. Besides, it was written in Steve's contract that he was not to do any stunts.

One evening after work, Bud and I were having dinner together and we were well into the sauce, when he told me that he owned a warehouse full of antique motorcycles. Besides doing stunts, he owned a motorcycle dealership out on Ventura Boulevard in the Valley. Bud had been the U.S. motorcycle champion for a number of years and he knew bikes inside and out. The idea of all those old bikes piqued my imagination.

"I sure would like to do a picture with Steve McQueen using my bikes," he said. Bud knew that I had written a script for Disney that was on the back burner. "If you can come up with something, I'd be glad to show it to Steve."

And that got my juices flowing. While waiting to see if Disney was going to renew my option, I had time on my hands to try to develop a script using Bud's motorcycles. A couple of months later I finished writing *Cyclone 25* (the name of a racing bike), a post World War One motorcycle film written especially for Steve McQueen. I called Bud and delivered the script to his home in Nichols Canyon. A few days later he called to say that he really liked the script and he was going to pass it on to Steve. My hopes were soaring. If I could put this together there was an outside chance I could get a shot at directing, a secret passion of mine. Bud got back to me a couple of days later to say that Steve had the script, that he was going down to Mexico for a few weeks and would get in touch when he returned.

* * *

Finally, there was good news. Disney had renewed my option for a first rewrite. I moved from my apartment to one across the street in the same building where my dad lived. It was like a townhouse with two bedrooms upstairs; not very big but comfortable. And shortly after my return, a friend of mine, a girl from Germany, called to say that she wanted me to meet a young lady who was in town from San Francisco.

I don't remember if I mentioned it before, but I have always been very partial to redheads. And this young lady had this marvelous crop of red hair with skin like milk. She was originally from Hungary and came to the U.S. during the uprising in Hungary in 1956, when she was only a child. And ironically, her adoptive parents lived in Carmel Valley. Her name was Margie Stanley and she and I had instant chemistry. So much so that before she returned to San Francisco, I suggested that she move down to Los Angeles and move in with me. It was an impetuous offer on my part and knowing that she was involved with her job and

A Vulcan Odyssey

new apartment in S.F., I hadn't a clue that she would take me up on my offer. We spoke on the phone almost every evening. She would call from work at the hotel where she was working in banquet sales. And before I knew it, she had packed up her things and was on her way down to Los Angeles.

I won't say that Margie was the love of my life and in many ways, she was more like a daughter to me than a lover. She had an innocence about her that was refreshing. She was naïve to a fault but in business she was intelligent and efficient. She wasn't in Los Angeles a week when she interviewed for a job at the Beverly Hills Hotel for the same position she held in San Francisco. Her father, who was the manager of one of the top hotels in Carmel, had made a couple of calls and opened the door for her. But Margie did the closing. She could walk into a room and heads would turn. I believe if one looked up the word "perky" in the dictionary, there would be her picture.

For the longest time I had wanted to get another cat but for one reason or another, I never got around to it. One day, Margie walked into the house with this animal that at first I thought was a raccoon. She had found it on the street and it was the sweetest cat I had ever laid eyes on. We decided to keep it and named it Rocky. Margie and I both loved animals and Rocky was just another way for us to bond.

My father, Robby, who lived two doors away in exactly the same apartment plan as I had, adored Margie. And she knew how to manipulate him with offers to shop or do other chores to help him out. It was Robby who first brought to my attention something about Margie that I was too close to observe. In a very short period of time, she had become a clone of me. She had taken on every thought I had without regard for her own personal side to issues. Whether it was politics or religion or almost any issue in the news of the day, Margie took delight in repeating everything I said, word for word. It was most weird. She wasn't a stupid person and if there was a subject about which I had no opinion, she was capable of organizing her own thought and opinions. But on any subject that I took a stand, she seemed to take a back seat to almost everything I said. At first, when my dad called it to my attention, I pooh-poohed the idea as a harmless trait. I had no idea that there was something much deeper going on inside her.

In the past, there had been many different reasons for my not being able to sustain a relationship but never had a cat been the underlying reason. One evening, when Margie and I were talking about the current headlines of the daily newspaper, I mentioned, "I think the Kennedy assassination was the act of a single person. The FBI would have us think there was some underlying, international conspiracy. Christianity tends to promote paranoia in a diverse society." I did not intend it as an overall indictment but rather as an oversimplification of what precipitated the witch-hunt after Kennedy was killed. A few weeks later, having dinner with friends and talking about a current movie with the assassination of Kennedy as the central theme, Margie said, "I think the Kennedy assassination was the act of a single person. The FBI would have us think there was some underlying international conspiracy. Christianity tends to promote paranoia in a diverse society." She had repeated my thesis, word for word. I was dumbfounded. She was bright enough to remember my words well enough so that she didn't even change any of the text. I felt I had to say something to her. A few nights later, as we were sitting at home with Rocky on her lap, I asked her if she was aware that she had quoted me word for word when she was discussing the Kennedy assassination a few evenings before.

"I don't know what you mean," she replied.

"I was wondering if you were aware how many times you tend to quote me, word for word. I find you an exceptionally bright woman who is able to handle a complicated and responsible position at the hotel. You solve problems, you communicate with people from all walks of life, and you arrange meals and seating for a multitude of guests, but I rarely hear you express your own opinions."

"I never thought about it. I guess I repeat what you say because I concur with your opinions. You're able to put into a few words what would take me volumes to express. Am I doing something wrong?" she asked.

"No, not at all. In a way, it's flattering. It's just that sometimes it's jarring when I hear my own words coming back at me, unedited."

"If it bothers you, I'll try not to repeat anything you say."

I had hurt her feelings and felt that I had better get off the subject before it became a major issue. "I noticed that you let Rocky out of the house again. I wish you wouldn't."

"But he's so pathetic. He stands at the door and screams to be out. He's not used to living in a confined space."

"I know, but we live on a busy street and I'd hate to think that he might get run over."

"He never strays from the patio and I always check on him when he's out," she assured me.

I let that conversation rest. More importantly I had been thinking that Margie might be interested in getting involved with something to do with theatrical representation. She was damn good at sales. She made friends easily, was able to talk to people, and had great business acumen. She loved being involved with my friends who were mostly actors. I had recently moved over to a new agent and was friendly with her and her husband. "I was speaking with my agent, Joan, and she said she was looking to hire a sub-agent. I mentioned that I thought the two of you should get together to see if it might be something you'd like to pursue. Would you like me to set it up?"

She was elated with the idea and a few days later, after her meeting with Joan, she gave notice at the hotel. Two weeks later, Margie began working as a sub-agent, representing a small, but quite select clientele. Her first job was to make the rounds of the studios, introducing herself to the various casting directors. In a matter of days she was getting calls for some of her actors, myself included. She was a natural. In three months, she became a driving force at the agency and one would believe that she would be rewarded for her accomplishments. Joan called her into the office one day and told her that she would have to leave. I never knew that there was any dissention between the two of them and for that matter, neither did Margie. She was terribly hurt and depressed. But I saw it as a chance for Margie to make a stand on her own. I spoke to a friend of mine who owned a small office building in the heart of Hollywood in a fairly good location. He all but gave us a suite of offices that he said were empty, with the stipulation that when she began to make money, she would be expected to sign a rental agreement.

In the beginning, Margie was scared out of her wits. After all, a good agent is one who has her client's well being as the first consideration. She had learned how to draw up contracts, she knew all the rules, she could pick up the phone and shmooze with casting people, but she questioned her ability to successfully accept the responsibility for other people's

ived home each evening filled with self-doubt and
 her that she was doing a great job. The industry is
 and Margie had never been exposed to that aspect of
 is not something that one learns to accept overnight.
 rifted into weeks and the weeks into months, clients
 ɔ pick up a day here and there and the ten percent
commissions were beginning to cover her expenses. But the agency business is a cold and hard aspect of the theatrical world. Margie's first "real world" experience occurred when one of her clients, a young man in his twenties whose picture "came in over the transom" and she signed him to an agency contract. She worked her ass off for that kid. She had taken him by the hand from studio to studio, introducing him to casting directors and a list of producers and directors that she had accumulated along the way. He was a good-looking young man with a lot of potential and Margie and I could both see that in a short period of time, he would be considered for a major role in a series. Then, without warning, he sent her a short message saying that he would be leaving the agency. Obviously, one of the larger agencies had gotten to the kid and romanced him away from Margie and she was thoroughly crushed. After all, her entire clientele was no more than twenty actors, all of whom were getting very special attention. And I could not offer very much sympathy because he had done exactly what I had done when I left Paul Wilkins for the Raison Agency. Shortly thereafter, I could see that Margie's heart wasn't in the agency. She picked up the breakdown sheets each morning and made her submissions but by noon each day, she returned home, checking into the office to see if there were any messages.

By this time, I had finished my second draft for Disney and with Jerry's help, they picked up my option for the final draft. Actually, the script was in pretty good shape and in need of only a few minor revisions. I had over-written it at Jerry's suggestion and now it was time to take out some of the fluff and concentrate on the nuts and bolts. I had visualized only one actor for the lead role: Yaphet Koto. I wanted someone who was physical but at the same time, able to touch the kids with tenderness. I knew Yaphet only slightly but I just assumed that when it came time to do the casting, he would be at the top of the list.

Shortly after the first week of 1977, I turned in the final draft of *The Million-Dollar Dixie Deliverance*. I packed up my things, emptied out my desk and moved off the Disney lot. I had been working on that script the better part of two years and I was anxious to see the film go into production. A few weeks later, not hearing anything, I called Jerry.

"We're putting it on the shelf," he said. "Ron Miller doesn't think it's a good time to be making a Civil War film."

I could feel the air go out of my bubble. It was not a very encouraging time of my life. Margie and I had hit the wall. It all began one day when I returned home to find her in tears. She had not been to the office. She had been spending the past few weeks calling clients and telling them that the office was in the process of closing down and that they had best be looking for other representation. The fire in our relationship was fast diminishing and we both were walking on thin ice. Since we had been living together she had demonstrated periods of depression and I was always able to hold her and assure her that everything would soon be all right. But with my own personal downslide, I couldn't find the peace of mind to reach out to her.

"Rocky is dead!" she informed me through her tears.

I gasped for breath. "What happened?"

"I don't know for sure. I let him out this morning..."

"I thought we agreed that he wasn't to leave the house," I admonished. "How did it happen?"

"One of the neighbors found him. He was in the gutter but by the time I went down to find him, someone must have taken him away."

We sat for what seemed like hours without saying a word. She continued to sob and I was wrought with anger. I finally walked out of the house; I needed to get air; I needed to get away from Margie. For the next few weeks our relationship was strained and almost unbearable. We were strangers living under the same roof. I left the house early each morning for the gym and when I returned, I usually spent time visiting with my father. And Margie took to her bed, spending the better part of the day and night in retreat from the world and her failures. I couldn't find a way to offer her comfort or help.

One day, while reading a copy of the Hollywood Reporter, I ran across an article saying that "Disney was preparing production for a two hour television film entitled, *The Million-Dollar Dixie Deliverance*, written by *Ed Jurist*!" I couldn't believe what I was reading. I almost broke my neck running to the phone.

"Jerry, did you see this morning's Reporter?"

He could hear the panic in my voice. "Don't worry about it," he tried to reassure me. "Just a glitch between the publicity office and the Reporter."

"Who the hell is Ed Jurist? What's he got to do with *The Dixie Deliverance?*"

"Well, Ron Miller felt that some of the language was a bit much…"

"But you told me to write it as I saw it. I even asked if you wanted me to write Disney-ish and you said to write it just like kids would talk. You didn't have to bring in another writer to clean up the dirty words."

"It's just a Disney policy."

"Is it a Disney policy to put someone else's name on a script that I've been working on for two years?"

"Doesn't mean a thing. The Writers Guild has the last say on who gets billing and who doesn't."

What he said was true. Every script made in Hollywood under the jurisdiction of the Writers Guild goes before a committee to determine who gets billing and in what order. But until that time when the script went before that committee, I would be a basket case. And although there was another writer working on my script, the studio had not actually given Jerry a start date for production. In the back of my mind, I had the feeling that there really wasn't anyone in the entire business that I could trust. Jerry and I had been friends for years and for all I knew, he was stroking me while stabbing me in the back. But my paranoia diminished when I finally learned that a Writers Guild Committee had decided that I was the writer of record and that I would get sole screen credit for screenplay and original story.

A few weeks after the Rocky incident, I got a call from Jerry saying that he was prepping a film called *Return to Witch Mountain*. "John Hough is going to direct and he wanted to know if you'd be interested in working with him again."

My heart soared. I would be back at Disney, back with Jerry, back with John and back to acting. "Anything," I said. "Big part, little part, just anything."

"That's the catch," said Jerry. "Because you were in the original film we can't have you back as an actor for this one. You were too prominent in the last film. I discussed it with Ron and he agreed. But John Hough said that he could use you as dialogue coach and I think you'd do a great job. We'll be shooting right here in Los Angeles so there won't be any distant location shooting."

"Dialogue coach? You mean, teaching kids their dialogue?"

"And Bette Davis. She'll be doing one of the leads along with Christopher Lee, Kim and Ike (the two children who starred in the original film.)"

My first reaction was to turn it down cold, but a sudden revelation came over me. Right or wrong, I have always been my own worst enemy. I am quick to make faulty decisions in the heat of anger, decisions I have lived to regret. "When do I have to give you an answer?" I asked.

"The sooner the better," responded Jerry. "You'd be working with John again and he said to say 'hello.'"

"Well, you tell him 'hello' for me and I'll get back to you in a day or two."

The next couple of days I spent in introspection. Was this a good move for me? Why did John ask for me? I hadn't seen or spoken to him since we got back from Carmel, almost a year ago. Was Jerry buttering me up to soften the blow if the Guild decided to put Ed Jurist's name on my script? And just what the hell was I going to do about Margie? Damn, if I wasn't up to my ass in turmoil and confusion.

In the words of my old agent, Paul Wilkins, "activity breeds activity," and sitting around feeling sorry for myself was not very constructive. I called Jerry and said, "I'd like to work again with John in any capacity." The deal was set and the following week I reported for work. Bette Davis was a delight to work with, although at first, she took umbrage with my presence on the assumption that someone thought she couldn't remember her lines. I assured her that such was not the case, that I was actually there for the kids but if she needed to run any dialogue, I was at her disposal. We got along famously. And the children were all bright and required very little tutoring.

One day when we were on the downside of principal photography, Jerry came down to the set and pulled me aside. "I've got good news and bad news for you. How do you want it?"

"The bad news, first."

"You're fired."

I was stunned. "Haven't I been doing a good job?"

"Has nothing to do with it. We only have another week before we wrap so there's no need for you to stay on." He took a long pause while I digested this disturbing news. "Don't you want to know the good news?"

"I'm not sure I can take it."

"How would you like to go to Atlanta?" he asked.

"Atlanta...Georgia?"

"Yeah. I cleared it with Ron Miller and I'm sending you down there to scout locations and do preliminary casting for *Dixie Deliverance*."

At first I thought he was kidding; then I was overcome with emotion and realized that this was no joke.

"I'm sending you down there as my assistant. Normally, the title would be Associate Producer but since Disney has a history of giving that title only to Associates under contract, you'll be acting as my assistant." He mentioned the salary which was very fair and said that I would have all my expenses paid for by the production. The next week was spent in meetings with various members of the production team with their own individual needs. "Anything you can't find down there, we'll bring from the studio. The more actors you can find, the more money we can save on transportation and living expenses. That money can be put back into the production. We'll stay in touch on a daily basis."

When I told Margie, I thought she would be delighted for me. Quite the opposite.

"I won't be here when you get back. I'm going to look for a place of my own."

"You don't have to do this, Margie. Take the time to think this whole thing over and we'll talk when I get back in five weeks."

CHAPTER ELEVEN
GEORGIA ON MY MIND

Two days later I was on a plane to Atlanta. Ed Spivey met me at the airport with a private car. He was the Film Commissioner for the State of Georgia. Accommodations had been made for me at the Omni Hotel, a complex situated in the heart of the city in a very unsavory neighborhood. I could have spent my entire stay in Georgia without ever leaving the Omni, it was that all-encompassing. The Georgia Film Commission was located on the premises in the office part of the complex and within hours I set to work making contact with union reps and actor's agents. A location scout had accompanied me, and Ed Spivey and he set out to explore the state in search of locations for the film while I began preliminary casting. During the first week I auditioned over two hundred actors. I didn't know there were two hundred actors in the state of Georgia but they began to come in from the surrounding areas. I was impressed at the depth of the talent pool. The only roles I was not required to cast were the roles of the children and the black actor who helps them in their escape from the South. I spoke to Jerry every afternoon to keep him posted as to how the preliminary casting and scouting for locations was progressing. He told me to pick a role that I thought I would be right for. The only role I could see that came close to me would have been the Sergeant. As much as I wanted to do a role in my own film I ultimately decided that my production responsibilities took precedence and I cast Ben Jones as the Sergeant. (Ben later went on to play the role of Cooter in *Dukes of Hazard*, after which he was elected to Congress from the State of Georgia for two terms.) I was trying to be as objective as possible. By the third week, I had boiled down the casting to at least two actors for every role not being cast in California. The location manager, with the help of Ed Spivey, had located two distant locations, one in South Georgia and the other at the northernmost part of the state.

Lumpkin is a small town seventeen miles south of Columbus, Georgia. One of the town's founding fathers, Sam Singer, who owned one of the county feed and seed general stores, also was responsible for raising the money for an antebellum town known as Westville. It consisted of some twenty restored homes of the Civil War era. Numerous artisans were living in the village and they earned their livings creating crafts in much the same way as the people did over a hundred and fifty years ago. There was no electricity, running water or sewer so life was very primitive. The town was a perfect location for our little film and for a small donation to the museum, we cut a deal to film in Westville with access to all the antebellum houses. The people of the town of Lumpkin set to work making their own costumes as they were promised work as extras when the company began shooting. It was a big event in a small southern town. I met with members of the local Teamsters Union and hired drivers and grips. Along about the fifth week, Jerry arrived with the director, Russ Mayberry. I was disappointed in Jerry's choice of directors because last time we conversed, he was considering Lou Antonio who I thought was one of the finest television directors of the day. Mayberry had refused my choice of Yaphet Koto to play the lead and opted instead for Brock Peters. In fact, no matter what I suggested, Mayberry chose to ignore me. I guess he was trying to show that he was the director and that his was the final word. As far as I was concerned, he was nothing better than a hack and when I look back, his direction was barely adequate. He chose the most unimaginative way to film the story and in the final cut, I was terribly disappointed.

When the final casting was completed and the production was ready, we moved the company down to Lumpkin, Georgia, where we would spend the next two weeks in the antebellum town of Westville.

I met Sam Singer who owned most of the land in and around Lumpkin and was active in community politics, much like Willy Stark in Robert Penn Warren's *All the King's Men*. Any time I had a problem in that area, I went right to Sam and he solved it. I also met a woman by the name of Henri Carter who was the picture of old Southern gentility. She was related by marriage to Jimmy Carter, her deceased husband's cousin. Henri and I became very good friends and she opened her home to me when I needed it.

Dixie Deliverance moved up to the Northern part of the state for the battle scenes where we recruited the services of a group of men who made a hobby of recreating battles of the Civil War, complete with uniforms and weapons. Again, this was a big money saver for the production. The final scenes of the film were shot on the Chattahoochee River with some very exciting escape scenes on the raging waters.

While working on the final scenes, I got a call from my father informing me that Margie had killed herself! She had moved out of the apartment, taken a small pad in the Valley, began to see a young man and when that didn't turn out, she took sleeping pills and washed them down with whiskey. She went into cardiac arrest and died before they could revive her. I don't think I was ever so angry with anyone in my entire life. I wanted to cry but I couldn't. I walked around in a state of pissed and confusion trying to figure out why she would do such a thing. I knew that she had tried suicide before when she was living in San Francisco but I never imagined that she would ever attempt it again. If it was her intention to get even with me, she did an admirable job.

The entire shoot took less than six weeks and before I knew it, I was on a plane heading back to Los Angeles. But I had made some interesting contacts while involved with the three months of pre-production. Lloyd Adams, a heavy-drinking Southerner who owned a film company known as TIPS, The International Picture Show Company, suggested that I might want to consider moving to Georgia because there was a film renaissance happening in the state. Burt Reynolds was in the process of shooting *Smokey and the Bandit* and Tim Conway and Don Knotts were doing a comedy for The International Picture Show Company. There was talk that no less than half a dozen films were preparing to come into the state. Ed Spivey, the Film Commissioner, expressed his hopes that Georgia was on the verge of implementing its own viable film industry capable of competing with Hollywood. The Fairgrounds on the south side of Atlanta had numerous building that could serve as sound stages and some had already been converted. I could see untold opportunities and I began to formulate a plan to return to Georgia to get in on the ground floor. Since my career as an actor was fast declining, I could see untold opportunities for me in the production and writing end of the business. Lloyd Adams was looking for an in-house production manager and if I was interested, there was an offer on the table.

The apartment on Laurel Avenue was filled with ghosts of Margie so it was not too difficult to vacate the premises and point my car east. My father was disappointed that I was leaving but I think he understood that I had to make the move.

CHAPTER TWELVE
WHAT GOES UP USUALLY COMES DOWN...
WITH A BUMP

Shortly after I had returned to the States I wrote to Monika to see how she and the baby were getting on. I had a few dollars in the bank and I had intended to send some to her but she never responded to my letters. I hadn't a clue how to get in touch with her except through Walter Barnes but he and Britta had already left Germany for points unknown. Then, one day I got a subpoena from the District Attorney's Office in Los Angeles summoning me for a hearing for "non-payment of child support." Monika had managed to find her way to California with Jessica and they were living only a short distance away. But the D.A.'s office would not give me any information regarding my right to see the baby; they were only interested that I pay Monika who had applied for public assistance. I hired an attorney to represent me and he was finally able to cut a deal where I would pay child support and in return, I would get to see Jessica once a week. It was a fair trade-off. I was able to pick up the baby, who was three by now, and take her with me to visit with friends. She had only been in the country for a few months so I had to converse with her in German. Everyone thought it was so cute, the two of us talking in baby-German, she dressed in a *dirndl*, a kind of Tyrolean outfit.

Cecile Ozorio had been my leading lady in the series, *City Beneath the Sea,* and although she had since married the producer, Robert Wynn, we stayed in touch and I often visited their lovely home in Hidden Hills out by Calabasas. On a number of visits I took Jessica up to the Wynn place where they had horses corralled down behind the house. The first time I put Jessica up on a horse I thought she would panic but she took to it like a duck to water and it was difficult to get her to leave the Wynn's place at the end of the day. Those were precious times we spent together but they were short lived because one day I went to pick up the baby only to learn that Monika had packed up and left town. There was no forwarding address and no paper trail. I paid a detective agency to try to find them but after a while money was running out and they hadn't a clue as to the whereabouts of Monika and the baby. It wasn't until some ten years later that I heard that they had returned to Los Angeles and were living in Malibu Beach.

* * *

When I returned to Los Angeles, my first call was to Bud Ekins. I had sent him the revised script some time before but had not heard back from him. I was hoping he had some good news.

"I guess you haven't read the papers" he said with no small amount of emotion. "Steve is sick."

"How bad?" I asked.

"I don't know for sure but he's been going down to a clinic in Juarez, Mexico for treatments. They say he has mesothelioma, some kind of lung cancer. He's been taking peach pit extract or some such crap that's supposed to be a new cure."

We were both utterly destroyed. Not because it looked like our deal with Steve was off but because we were both concerned for his health. I told Bud that I would just put the script on the back burner and when Steve was back on his feet, we'd pick up where we left off.

With Margie's death, I never tried to find another agent. I was adrift at sea with my sights set on Georgia.

* * *

I took my time driving across country in my Chevy pickup truck and I made it from L.A. to Atlanta in three days. I had acquired another cat, Squidge, that I left with a friend who promised that she would send him to me once I got settled. I was unencumbered and ready to begin a new adventure. When I first met Lloyd Adams I had no idea that he was an alcoholic. He could dish out the bullshit faster than a cleanup squad at a rodeo. He had more damn plans for film production than I could follow and I just went along with the flow. The International Picture Show Company was situated in the Omni Complex, an area with which I was already familiar. I found a small apartment minutes away in Buckhead just off of Peachtree in the heart of Atlanta. I had an office with a secretary, and Lloyd put me to work reading scripts that had piled up in his office over the past year. I had learned years before that if a writer didn't grab your interest within the first ten pages, pass. I went through scripts like a bunny through clover. Then, one day Lloyd came into my office and handed me a book.

"Ever hear of it?" he asked.

I looked at the title. *Murder in Coweta County* by Margaret Anne Barnes. "Good title," I offered.

"I want you to read it and give me your opinion. I took an option on it."

Now, when I initially negotiated with Lloyd to come to work for him he assured me that he would not make any professional decisions before he ran them by me first. As his production manager he was depending on my expertise and good taste in selecting material for filming. In a matter of a few weeks, he had already broken that rule. I read the Margaret Anne Barnes book and found it intriguing. I told Lloyd that I thought it could be turned into a powerful film if we could find a good screenwriter.

"Way ahead of you, boy. I just signed two writers from Hollywood," he said with no small amount of pride. He threw out their names and neither of them meant a thing to me. Without Lloyd's knowledge, I called Len Chapman, the executive director of the Writer's Guild in Los Angeles and a friend of mine. I asked Len to do a background check on the two writers. He came back with zilch. Of course, that didn't mean the two writers weren't good; it only meant that they weren't registered writers with the Guild. And I could easily figure out how Lloyd came to choose these two writers. Lloyd had a compulsion to fly out to Los Angeles every now and again to hobnob with some of the motion picture industry hotshots. Once Lloyd got a few drinks under his belt, anyone could sell him just about anything.

I was living a very frugal existence in Atlanta and managing to pick up some voiceover work through Cathy Hardagree who owned Atlanta Models and Talent Agency. When I was casting Dixie Deliverance, most of the talent I used came out of Cathy's stable. She was beholden to me and when I arrived in Atlanta, if there was a voiceover job or a narration to do and I could get away from the office, she threw it my way. I had managed to save up quite a nest egg and I got an idea to go into a side business. I bought a cargo truck to rent out to film companies. I found a second hand Ford truck that needed some work and I was able to purchase it for almost nothing. I put it in a shop and had the necessary work done and then I told Cathy that if she heard of any film companies coming into town, I had a production truck for rent (and she would be in for ten percent.) It didn't take long to get the truck rolling and as the money began to come in, I purchased a second truck, and so on down the line until I had bought and borrowed enough money to run six trucks and my Chevy pickup. I never told Lloyd about the trucks because I had set up a dummy company and if TIPS ever got into production, I planned to rent my own trucks back to the company. I believe it's called "conflict of interest" but they had to catch me first. Lloyd Adams had been correct when he said there was going to be a film renaissance in Georgia. I got one of the I.A. union drivers, a guy by the name of Duke, to keep an eye on the trucks and I gave him a few extra dollars each month to manage my interests since he was also a hiring boss for the union. I didn't want any drunks driving my trucks because I was paying through the nose for insurance and the last thing I needed was an accident. I was playing a long shot.

I was spending an inordinate amount of time by myself. I had almost no social life away from the office. I placed a call to Los Angeles and had my friend crate up my cat, Squidge, and send him to me. A couple of days later I went to the airport and picked up the kitty. He was really pissed because he hated the carrier and he hadn't had anything to eat all day at the vet's suggestion. So when I got him home to my second floor apartment, I opened the kitty carrier to let him roam while I got him something to eat. Last I saw of him, he had walked out onto the balcony two floors above ground and by the time I placed the food down on the kitchen floor, he was gone. He had jumped two floors to the ground, thankfully landing in a plush bush beneath my window. I searched for him for hours. I called him by name and roamed the neighborhood putting up signs, but I never found him. Animals and women: I just didn't have much luck with either of them.

I had been working for Lloyd three months when he came into the office one morning looking as if he'd been run over by an eighteen-wheeler. He wasn't hung over so I knew it had to be something really serious. He put an envelope on my desk and just stood there as I opened it. Inside was a final draft of *Murder in Coweta County.* Just from the look on Lloyd's face I could tell it was crap. But he made me promise to read it that night and we'd have a meeting the following morning. I don't know who sold Lloyd on those two writers but they surely did not have a clue on how to write a script. They didn't know the first thing about formatting, something a first term college student learns when studying screen writing. The whole thing was a hodge-podge of jumbled dialogue and exposition. I could barely make sense of it and I dreaded my meeting with Lloyd the next morning. What could I say? "I told you so?" Oh, yeah, that would have gone over great. But the next morning, before I even opened my mouth, Lloyd said, "I want you to do the re-write."

"What re-write?" I asked. "There's nothing to re-write. It's not a script; it's a bunch of unintelligible notes. You've got to find yourself a writer and I mean a reputable one this time."

"I want you to write it," he insisted. "I'm paying you and I expect you to write it."

"Hold on a minute," I cut in. "You are not paying me to write a screenplay. You are paying me to be a production manager and that's it. I don't do dishes, I don't do laundry, and I don't write scripts. I'm your production manager."

He sat down heavily in the chair across from my desk. "I'm in the shit," he said. "I paid these guy in advance; big bucks. You gotta help me out."

"You paid a couple of yahoos big bucks to fuck up a perfectly good book and now you expect me to clean up their mess? No way, Mr. Adams." I took a moment to think it over. "Okay, I'll make you a deal. I'll write your screenplay but I want at least union scale for the script in conjunction with my salary as P.M."

I could tell that Lloyd was hurting but he had gone behind my back, made a deal without my knowledge, and I wasn't about to pull his coals out of the fire. I never signed a service contract with TIPS so I was free to walk at any time. If Lloyd thought I was going to write that script and it would be part of my weekly salary, he had another guess coming. I think the going rate for a script from another source at that time was about fifteen thousand dollars and if Lloyd wanted to pay me fifteen thousand dollars, I'd write his script...but I wanted a Writer's Guild contract! He agreed and the following week I packed up, moved out of the office and headed down to Lumpkin, Georgia, where we had shot the first two weeks of Dixie Deliverance. I called Sam Singer, the peanut farmer who owned most of the land in the area, and he told me to come on down. He said that he had a cabin on a lake and it would be a perfect place for me to write. I could stay there as long as I wanted.

Sam was leaving town on business but he gave me directions to go to the feed store that he owned in Lumpkin and ask for Patty. She would give me the keys and directions on how to get to the cabin. It was the dead of winter and I had to drive my pickup down a dirt road that was covered with red clay that had frozen over. It was all I could do to keep the truck on the road but I finally found the turnoff and half a mile beyond the barbed wire fence I came out into a clearing. I was sure I had gone to the wrong place. The "cabin" Sam Singer talked about was a three thousand square foot chalet set back in a cluster of tall pines and situated right on the edge of a private lake. This wasn't privacy; it was heaven. There was no one around for miles. I could write my little heart out until I came up with a viable script. There was electricity, a working phone and a ton of cut firewood, and I was off and running. I had brought a few provisions with me from town but only enough to last me a couple of days. Sam Singer had put out the word that I had returned to Lumpkin and by the second day, Henri Carter, one of the town locals, came calling with bags of groceries and a bucket full of her very special home-fried chicken. Henri had decided to adopt me.

"I was one of the extras on the film you made in Westville. Patty, over at Sam's store, told me you were staying here and I thought I would come by and see if there was anything you might need."

"That's very nice of you, Mrs. Carter…"

"You can call me Henri."

"Okay, Henri. I shopped yesterday and I'm pretty well stocked for the moment. But it's very kind of you to make the offer. Can I offer you a cup of coffee?"

I made the worst coffee in the entire world but it was really all I had to offer her. Actually, I was happy for the break. I had been sitting at the typewriter for a prolonged period of time and my arms and back were beginning to bother me.

"Sam's father built this place some years back," she shared with me. "Each member of the Singer family has a house on this lake. It's private and no outsiders can build here. The Singer family pretty well owns Lumpkin. I guess I'm the only competition for miles around. I own the other feed and grain store so you might say that Sam and I are competitors. My husband, Billy, was a Carter. He passed a couple of years ago. He was a cousin to the President, you know." No, I didn't know. I soon learned that that was a Southern way of talking. They'd make a statement and tag it with "you know." I found it rather charming.

Henri turned out to be a true Southern belle, in the true tradition of a Tennessee Williams' play. Henri could have been Blanche DuBois in *Streetcar*. In the couple of hours break I took from my work, she filled me in on everyone in Lumpkin, living and dead. I was mesmerized by her wealth of knowledge regarding the history of the area. Sam Singer had built Westville. He had traveled all over the south hunting down rumors of decaying houses that might have been built around the time of the Civil War. He was on a mission to purchase the houses, pay for their transport to Westville and their restoration. There were some twenty antebellum homes in Westville all dating back to pre-Civil War times. But Westville was more than a museum for dead houses. There were people, craftsmen and women, living in the town. They dressed in clothes made by hand and they devoted their days to creating crafts to sell to tourists that flocked to the town, mostly on weekends. There were no modern conveniences in Westville and the people who lived there had to make do with very primitive conditions. I didn't know Sam all that well but my first impression of him was that he was something of a wheeler-dealer. That he created something as noble as Westville made me think of him in a very different and positive light.

The forth day of my stay, Henri returned with a pot of stew, a dish of mixed vegetables, a bowl of salad, hot baked biscuits, peach cobbler and a six-pack of beer.

"You can't work on an empty stomach," she informed me. "My Billy and I were married for forty-two years before he took ill. I nursed him from the first day he took ill until the day he passed, two years ago. I miss him."

There was nothing maudlin about her talking about her dead husband. It was very matter-of-fact, as if we were talking about the weather. Billy Carter (not the President's brother, but Cousin Billy) owned the local bank. They also had a modest brick home on an acre of land along with two hundred wooded acres just on the outside of town. Some years before his death, Billy had arranged with the Corps of Engineers to come in and build a dam to create a ten-acre lake on the property. He and Henri were going to build their dream home in the fantasyland setting but he didn't live long enough to realize his dream. There was a small cabin (not a Sam Singer cabin) down by the lake where a black family lived as caretakers of the property. Blacks outnumbered whites two to one in Lumpkin and the surrounding area. Henry spoke of the local blacks in a most maternal way. I had the impression that she felt responsible for every black man, woman and child in the community with whom she came in contact. She was a slight woman and from photographs I later viewed, she was a beauty in her day. I guess the only real word to describe her was "genteel."

Henri came to the Singer cabin every day. Sometimes she would not even knock on the door but would walk around to the back of the house to find a place at the foot of a tree to bask in the warmth of the winter sun. She respected the fact that I had work in progress and she didn't want to disturb me. It was comforting to know that when I wanted to take a break, there was Henri to keep me company. Sometimes, if I tarried too long, she would say, "Don't you have work to do? I don't want to keep you."

By the end of the second week I had finished the first draft of the screenplay. I tried to be as true to the book as was humanly possible. The characters in the book seemed to come right off the page and I didn't want to violate the author's intent. Each day Henri came to the cabin she would pick up the new pages and quietly read through them. The screenplay format is not easy to read and it took her some time before she was able to follow the maze of camera directions and descriptions of the action going down in a particular scene. Sometimes she would question me on a particular incident because she couldn't figure out what was happening. In re-reading the text I could see that my intent wasn't clear and I would re-write a particular scene to clarify it. I liked having Henri there while I was working. In only a few days that she was there, we had become quite good friends. She was a lonely, elderly woman that needed someone to communicate with and I was on a mission and needed someone there when my creative fire was reduced to mere embers. It was a good trade-off.

I was slaving away at the first re-write and after some hours at the typewriter, I decided to take a break. I took a fishing pole from the utility room and walked down to the pier. The late afternoon sun was warm and it felt good to be out in the fresh air and the pristine environment. As I sat at the end of the pier with my line in the water, I heard the sound of a car approaching and just assumed that it was Henri coming down to the cabin with her daily offering of Southern hospitality. But as I looked up, here came Sam Singer carrying a six-pack.

"Hey, boy," he greeted me. "Fish biting?"

"Sort of."

"Whatcha usin' fer bait?"

"Bait?"

"Yeah. You know, that stuff ya put on the hook to catch fish. Worms. Bread. Anything to attract the fish."

I was too embarrassed to answer.

"Whyn't you reel in and let me see if I can give you some pointers. Impossible not to catch fish in this here lake. We stocked it some ten years ago and I doubt if we take more than a hundred fish a year out of it."

I just sat there wishing Sam hadn't show up at quite this moment. He reached down and took the rod from me and began reeling in the line.

"You lost your hook, boy."

"Did I?"

He looked at me for a moment, then popped the top of a beer can and handed it to me. "Did you have a hook on this line when you cast it into the lake?"

"Guess I didn't check."

"You been fishing without a hook, boy? Can't catch anything without a hook."

"I guess I wasn't aiming to catch anything."

"Then why you fishing?"

"I like to fish; I just don't like killing anything."

Sam took a swig from his beer and looked at me intently. "You're very strange, boy."

Sam had a way with words in the true Southern tradition. He had a story for just about everything on the planet. His face lit up as he told me about how he and a doctor friend of his over in Eufala, Alabama, stole an election for a friend of theirs who was running for a State post. They literally stuffed the ballot boxes with names of voters they got from the County Recorder's Office of persons who were deceased.

Sam took great pride in his friendship with one of the Saudi billionaires, Prince Faisal, who had bought a magnificent Georgian mansion in a very fashionable section of Atlanta. During production of *Dixie Deliverance*, Sam had invited me to join a dinner party that Faisal was having at the Omni Hotel in Atlanta. I thought it a bit unusual that we were to meet at eleven at night but Sam assured me that the food would be good and everything was on the Prince. A group of some twenty friends and hangers-on met in the lobby of the hotel and when we made our way to the restaurant in question, the management was just closing down for the night. Faisal walked over to the maitre d', shook his hand and like magic, we were seated with half a dozen waiters attending to our every need. I can imagine how sizeable a tip the Prince must have passed to the maitre d' to keep the entire restaurant open for the next few hours.

Sam loved telling family stories. "Did I ever tell you about the time I took my wife to Germany? I was determined to trace my roots so we arrived in Munich where my Daddy had told me our family had lived for generations. Well, me and the wife checks into the Four Seasons and I take this huge suite of rooms and I hired me this translator cause I don't speak a word of German. We take the phone book and begin looking up "Singer" and there must have been at least a hundred of 'em. So I rent the dining hall of the hotel cause I know that out of all these Singers there has to be some that were related to me. My wife and me gets all dressed up and I'm as nervous as a virgin on prom night and we go down to the dining room where all these Singers and their families have gathered for this dinner I am throwing. Well, we walk into the dining room and it doesn't take me but a minute to figure out that I ain't related to any of 'em. My gawd, they was all Jews!"

By the end of the third week I completed my rewrites, packed my clothes, closed up the house and headed back to Atlanta. I stopped by Henri's to say goodbye and she informed me that she would be in Atlanta in a week on business and would I care to have lunch with her. We made a date and I returned to the city.

Lloyd Adams didn't have time to read the script but threw it into a bag and was off for New York. I was a bit apprehensive because a lot was riding on whether or not he would be able to get financing. But a few days later I got a call from an elated boss informing me that the bank was going to put up the money for the making of the film. Now, I hadn't been in that end of the business for very long so I had no idea that banks financed films but I just assumed that Lloyd had been sober long enough to cut a legitimate deal and I was elated. After all, there was still the matter of payment for my writing the script.

A week after his departure, Lloyd returned to Atlanta bloated with his eyes resembling a Georgia road map. He'd been on a toot and I couldn't rightly blame him celebrating his good fortune. I waited a few days before I brought up the subject of payment for writing the screenplay. He blanched.

"When you joined TIPS I hired you for your services. That included any writing you're required to do."

"I don't think that according to the Writers Guild that would wash. You hired me as a production manager. That doesn't include writing a screenplay."

"Well, that may be the way you do it in Hollywood but here, in Georgia, it doesn't work that way."

I could see that I was pissing up a rope with this drunk and I wasn't going to get into it with him. "I don't think you're very happy with my employment, Mr. Adams. Perhaps it's time for me to move on."

He didn't blink. I think he was hoping I would quit and he was waiting for me to make the move. There were no goodbyes or words of appreciation for work well done. I returned to my office, collected my things, told the secretary to forward what was owed to me, and left.

Shortly thereafter, I contacted Len Chasman at the Writers Guild in Hollywood and explained my situation. He assured me that TIPS did indeed owe me for the writing of the screenplay. Over the next year we went into litigation. I made two trips to California, as did Lloyd Adams, for hearings. He agreed to abide by the Guilds decision. After the first hearing a decision was handed down in my favor. Lloyd reneged and refused to pay what was owed to me. A few months later we returned to California for another arbitration where I was again awarded the price of the script plus interest accrued since the last award. Over the next few months I waited patiently but no check was forthcoming. Then I received some legal papers informing me that Lloyd Adams was declaring bankruptcy and I was only one of many creditors. My heart sank. I knew what was happening. He had transferred all his assets into his wife's name so he could avoid paying what was owed. I thought the Guild was protecting my interests but as it turned out, Lloyd managed to get another writer to rewrite the script and with Johnny Cash in the lead, they went into production. I never saw the finished product but I heard that it was awful. Somewhere along the way, I got a call from one of Lloyd's attorneys offering me ten cents on the dollar for the money he owed to me but I told them to shove it. I cut off my nose to spite my face but I wasn't going to make it easy for him. I never received one cent for my work on that film. I became terribly disheartened with the whole industry, both in California and Georgia.

After I left TIPS, I still had my trucks, which were doing quite nicely and bringing in enough money to more than sustain me. Every once in a while I would have a breakdown when I least expected it and I'd have to dip into the kitty to pay for a new hydraulic system for the lift or a new transmission. (Speaking of kitties, along about this time I found another black cat that I adopted and named him Shah. I guess I needed someone to talk to.) There was always something going wrong but I managed to keep my head above water. Then, late one evening I got a call from Duke, the union rep who was looking out for my trucks, saying that he wanted to meet with me at the Raffles, an all-night hangout in Atlanta. It was close to eleven when we met and I knew it had to be something important for him to drag me out at that hour. He was a rather large, burley man with a red face and little hair. He greeted me with a smile and a vice-like handshake as we sat across from each other. I owed Duke a lot because he had been keeping the trucks rolling and kept the drivers in line. On the other hand, he was being paid handsomely. He had been going from one job to another and now he had a bit of security, something almost unheard of in and around Georgia. But I knew that Duke had not called me to pass the time of day. I smelled a rat.

"I been talking to some of the drivers and we come to the conclusion that it ain't fair that we're doing all the work and you're making all the money…"

"Whoa," I stopped him. "Before you get into this, I've been offering jobs to union drivers when I could be hiring drivers off the street. This is 'a right to work state' as I recall. But I've always been a supporter of the union and being in Georgia hasn't changed that."

"Because you know you can trust union drivers. You're not hiring us out of any kind of allegiance to the union so don't be blowing smoke up my ass."

"Well, if that's where you're going, why don't we cut to the chase."

"We want twenty percent of your take!"

"Is this union sanctioned?"

"This is Duke sanctioned."

"Well, let me ask you something. Where the hell was Duke a year ago when I had to beg to borrow enough money to purchase my first truck? And if my memory serves me, you were sitting on your dead ass collecting unemployment insurance when I hired you."

"That was yesterday. Today you've got six trucks rolling and we feel that we're entitled to a share of the take."

As I looked across the table I realized that I was dealing with a certified gorilla that was about to put the squeeze on me. I pushed my chair back and got up from the table. "I don't think we've got anything more to discuss. And I don't think I want you driving for me any more. Not you and not any of your drivers. You tell them that for me."

"I think you're making a big mistake," he said menacingly.

"You're not threatening me, are you Duke?"

"You fire me and my men and there's a good chance they'll be floating your ass down the Chattahoochee along with all your trucks!"

I had the impression I'd seen this film years ago with Bogart or Cagney. This guy was right out of a thirties film and he thought I was going to be scared off. But I had an ace in the hole: I had been thinking that I had overstayed my welcome in Georgia. It was definitely time to move on.

I'll admit that I had raised something of a sweat being confronted by Duke and the thought of physical violence to my person. I couldn't control the racing rhythm of my heart and the throbbing of the blood in my temples. It was the middle of the week and I had to figure out a way to move six trucks before Duke and his goons decided to firebomb my entire stock. That night I lay awake with visions of my trucks going up in smoke.

The trucks were vulnerable and I had to do something and fast. At first light I placed a call to Henri down in Lumpkin.

"I've got to get the trucks out of Atlanta, Henri. You know anyone who can sell them for me? I'll take ten cents on the dollar if I have to but I've got to get them out of here."

I don't know how she did it, but by lunchtime on Saturday of that week a truck with six black drivers pulled up to my unit. "Miss Henri said you need help moving some trucks. She's got a cousin in the used car business down in Columbus. She told us to bring the trucks down to his place..."

And just like that, I was out of the trucking business. I loaded up my few belongings and Shah and followed in the pickup. A couple of hours later in Columbus I paid off the drivers and thanked them. Then, I drove on down to Lumpkin to spend some time with Henri.

I was at the end of the road. I had no idea what I was going to do. I knew that sooner or later I would have to leave Atlanta but I hadn't formulated a plan for my next move. The thought of heading back to Los Angeles did not set well with me. I had burned too many bridges and I wasn't ready to return. And there was the ghost of Margie still hovering over me. Had I not left Los Angeles would she still be alive? Could I have prevented her from taking her own life? The thought of that beautiful child lying lifeless in her grave haunted me and I couldn't get her out of my head. No, I was not ready to return to the coast.

"Let's take a trip over to Dallas," suggested Henri. "I'm due for my yearly pilgrimage to see Billy's sister, Katherine. You'll adore her. And it will do you good to get away for a while..."

I didn't need too much convincing and driving cross-country with Henri would be a pleasant diversion. She arranged for her housekeeper to come over every day and take care of my cat. Henri was very laid back and as I drove for hours, she would sit silently giving me all the thinking room I needed. I had never been to Dallas but I had a friend down there and was looking forward to making contact with him.

Chet Norris and I had been photographers together when we worked for a guy by the name of Marv Lincoln. We were hired by the day to take still photos on the set of porn films being made in and around Los Angeles. The thought of shooting stills on porn films was, at first, very titillating but after the first hour passed and the novelty of the nudity wore off, the daily chore of photographing naked bodies in the position of simulated sex soon became a bore. Most of the girls were rather seedy and I could not imagine taking any of them home to meet my mother. But the pay was good, Marv covered all our expenses and he kept a woman on salary who did all the lab work. Marv's "thing" was publishing. He turned out magazines that publicized the particular film and he must have done quite well because Marv lived high on the hog. Sometimes, if it was an expensive shoot, Chet and I would work on the same film. He had a rather dry sense of humor and everything was a joke to him. I never knew there were so many jokes one could make about a woman's private parts but Chet managed to keep me laughing from morning till night. And then one day he packed up and decided to move to Dallas.

Henri's sister-in law was a formidable hostess. She opened her home to me and waited on me hand and foot. She and Henri treated me as if I was royalty and for a while, I was beginning to think I was. Katherine's home was modest but comfortable. And within days she assured me that if I planned to move to Dallas, there was a room waiting for me for as long as I wanted it.

I met with Chet after the first few days and he filled me in on the local market and whether or not there might be an opportunity for me to make a living in Dallas. In fact, he went one step further; he set up an appointment for me to meet with his agent, Sarah Norton. I don't think I was in the office ten minutes when Sarah pulled out a contract and said that she was ready to sign me on the spot.

Dallas was cooking when it came to commercial and industrial filming and if I could get my foot in the door, it was as good a place as any to throw out my anchor. I told Henri and Katherine of my plans. Henri was not very pleased that I had committed to returning to Texas but Katherine had already offered me the hospitality of her home. It was settled; my next stop would be Dallas.

CHAPTER THIRTEEN
CLOSING THE CIRCLE

Just as I was getting ready to leave Georgia I learned of the death of Steve McQueen. He was only fifty years old when he passed away and although we were only casual friends, I felt a great sympathy for him. He was riding a comet when his life came to an untimely end and my heart ached with his passing. I took the script of Cyclone 25 and buried it deep down at the bottom of my possessions. It would never be a motion picture. On Oct. 10, 2007, I learned that Bud Ekins died four days previously. He was the motorcycle stuntman extraordinaire who doubled for Steve McQueen in The Great Escape. He was one of the invincible acquaintances who I thought would live forever. If you're a believer, I guess you could say that Bud and McQueen are somewhere out there riding thier motorcycles together off into the horizon. That's the way I'd like to think of his passing.

It didn't take long to pack up my few belongings and head west. The Chevy Pickup was loaded to the roof of the camper shell so I had Shah, my black cat, in the cab with me. Shah did not like traveling. We left at six in the morning and we were no sooner out of the parking lot of the complex than the cat began to howl. I don't mean cry like a cat; I mean howl like a wolf calling for his mate in the frozen tundra. I turned up the radio trying to drown him out but vocally he was far superior to some little old car radio. And then he began to climb and before I knew it, he was hanging upside down from the headliner of the cab, screaming at the top of his lungs. I tried to talk to him, to soothe his angst, but to no avail. I don't know how long we traveled like this before I pulled into a rest stop outside a town called Lawrence, Mississippi. (I swear, Lawrence, Mississippi!) I had purchased a harness type leash that I fastened to Shah before we had left Atlanta. I wanted him to get accustomed to wearing it in case of an emergency when I might have to get him out of the car in a hurry for some reason. Now, I figured he needed to do "cat things" because he hadn't used the litter box. Holding onto the end of the leash,

I opened the door and Shah made a beeline for freedom. He hit the end of that leash like a marlin breaking loose from a fishing line and the last thing I saw was his little butt disappearing into the woods. He had slipped that harness like a greased pig and never stopped to look back. I spent hours in the woods looking for that crazy animal. My god, I thought, he could have chosen a better place than Lawrence, Mississippi! There was nothing there but a few dilapidated shacks inhabited by a few black families and I'm sure that from the looks of things, a cat would have been better for dinner than as a pet. I had shlepped that animal from Los Angeles to Atlanta and I was sure that after he had a chance to look around at how meager were the pickings, he would make his way back to the pickup. But after an interminable wait, it was evident that Shah had preferred the wild from whence he had never come. His possibilities of surviving were slim to none. With a heavy heart I headed the Chevy west.

Henri's sister-in-law greeted me warmly. "Where's the cat?" she inquired. I related the saga of how my cat was now living off the land somewhere in the outback of Mississippi. Just the thought of it brought tears to my eyes. I took a few days to recover from the trip and finally called Sarah Norton.

"When can you begin to work?" she asked.

I thought she was kidding. I delivered to her office some head shots and voice tapes, and within a matter of days the jobs were beginning to come in. At first just a few radio spots for some local companies, and then an industrial here and there. But I had been there before and I was not about to think that this was going to last. My career had always started on a high and then fallen into the toilet over a period of time. But Sarah was very supportive and tried to assure me that Dallas was where it was happening.

After a few weeks I decided that I had overstayed my welcome at Katherine Forest's house and decided to move closer into the center of the city. She seemed disappointed. I am sure she enjoyed my company what with her two grown girls already out of the house and on their own. But I felt I needed a bit of privacy and access to my work. Sometimes the trip in from Garland was painfully slow with the Dallas traffic and I had to allow plenty of time to make it to a session without being late.

This is where things get a bit cloudy because it appears that I am losing the time line and I can't figure out how everything got all squished together. So to the best of my recollection, I was at a party one evening when this guy came over to me and asked if I ever knew a woman by the name of Monique Montaigne. Now, this was way off the wall by some fifteen hundred miles from where I had last heard of Monika, who it appeared had now changed her name to Monique. I didn't want to scare this guy off so I casually asked how "Monique" was doing and if this guy knew anything about Jessica.

"Oh, yeah," he said. "Jessica's a real sharp kid," he reported. "They're both very good friends of mine..."

"No kidding. And they're still living..." I stalled, fishing for information.

"In Malibu. I saw them just a few weeks ago."

"I've been traveling so I haven't spoken to them in quite a while. You wouldn't happen to have their phone number, would you?"

He knew it right off the top of his head and I immediately wrote it down on a cocktail napkin. The following day I called Malibu.

I won't say that Monika was ecstatic to hear from me but she was as cordial as she could possibly be under the circumstances. She extolled the virtues of our daughter, telling me how smart she was and how great she was doing in school, how she was very popular with her classmates, and how well behaved she was. We made small talk and I finally broached the subject of seeing Jessica. Surprisingly, she wasn't unreasonable about my request and I said that I would come into L.A. first chance that I could break away. A few weeks later I flew to California, made plans to stay with a friend, rented a car and drove down to Malibu for a "family" reunion. I learned that Monika had moved to San Francisco the time she disappeared from L.A. She had been seeing some guy whom she had intended to marry but plans didn't work out and it took her all this time to get back to Southern California. I wanted to tell her how angry I had been when she just took off with my daughter without leaving a forwarding address, but getting into a pissing contest with Monika would only alienate her so I bit the bullet and let it ride.

Jessica was now a lovely young lady of fourteen. I got permission from Monika to take the kid for lunch. We found a little café along Pacific Coast Highway and we spent the next couple of hours getting acquainted. She had very little recollection of the times we had spent together when she first came to the States. I was disappointed that she didn't remember the Wynns and the times she spent riding the horses at their home. As we talked, I realized that Jessica was trying to impress me with stories of her life in Malibu. She related how she and Sammy Davis's kid were best of friends, and how she knew this celebrity's kid or that one; she sounded very impressionable. I guess that's the way kids who lived in Malibu talked in those days. I asked her if she worked.

"I have to work," she said. "I'm into smoking dope and my mom won't give me any money so I hook on the side!"

I couldn't believe what I was hearing. Dope? Hooking? This was outside my venue and I tried to be stoic and show enough sophistication not to sound like a doting father. But I guess I wasn't a very good actor because I could tell that she was not very pleased with my reaction to her choice of professions. Again, I bit the bullet to avoid confrontation. If I was ever going to have a relationship with this kid, the last thing I wanted to do was alienate her from the get-go. Later, back at her house, I told Monika what Jessica had told me but she sloughed it off as the fantasy of an adolescent and told me not to pay her any mind. Before I returned to Dallas I managed to elicit from Monika a promise to let Jessica come to visit me over school break although I wasn't really sure what I would do to entertain a teenage doper who hooked for money to purchase drugs. I'd figure it out.

Chet Norris lived in a complex with a number of actors and I found a vacancy in the same building. I moved into a small two bedroom townhouse. The rent was reasonable and I was within walking distance to most of the trendy shops and restaurants in Oak Lawn. But after a few weeks I was not so sure I was going to last in Dallas for very long. The weather was stifling. It was the summer of 1980 and we had something like 61 days of temperatures over 100 degrees. But most of my days were spent inside air-conditioned studios, which made my life somewhat bearable. By fall the weather began to break and Dallas was a city of opportunity.

Just before the Thanksgiving holidays, I was doing a commercial for some department store advertising a special for the season sale. Another actor was working at the same recording studio and during a break we got to talking. His name was Bob Magruder and I was soon to learn that he was the top voice talent in Dallas. Over lunch we talked about the commercial business and he gave me some invaluable information. He knew Chet and some other friends I had made over the past few months so we hit it off famously. He invited me to have dinner with him and his wife, Patsy. It was the beginning of a long friendship. The Magruders invited me to their home for Thanksgiving dinner and their place was filled with family and friends, most of whom were actors from the local market. One man in particular, a tall, good-looking Irishman from Boston, struck up a conversation.

"You ever run across a guy in Los Angeles by the name of Jerry Courtland?" he asked.

What were the odds? "Sure. He and I have been friends for years," I said. I went on to tell how Jerry and I went back to the early fifties when we did a science fiction pilot and how I had worked with Jerry at Columbia when we tried to get some properties off the ground in the face of a bankrupt studio. And then of course, how Jerry was my producer at Disney and how, in a roundabout way, he was responsible for my being in Dallas. Small world. But Lo Jordan was able to do me one better. He knew Jerry in Japan when they served in the Army of Occupation at the end of the war. On one particular occasion, a group of soldiers were on a train traveling from one part of the country to another. Lo and Jerry were on the train's outside platform with some other men and as young soldiers do, they were screwing around, pushing and joking. The door to the train was open and as the train was passing over a large concrete abutment, someone pushed Jerry and he lost his balance and fell from the moving train some fifty feet down to the ground below. Lo immediately pulled the emergency cord and when the train came to a halt, he and some of the other men climbed down to where Jerry had landed. It was obvious that he had a broken leg and possibly some other injuries. They were in a rural area with not much in the way of civilization but it was clear that Jerry needed immediate medical attention. Lo managed to find a house from which he commandeered a door to use as a stretcher. He and the men tied Jerry onto the door and carefully hauled him back up to the train and eventually got him to a hospital and medical attention. That was 1945 and here we were in 1980, sitting around talking about a mutual friend that we had both known for ages. It was indeed a small world.

Lo and his wife, Collette, invited me to their home on Lake Dallas. He had designed and built the home and it was very modern and modular. It was built in a woodsy setting only a few meters from the lakeside. I soon learned that Lo was the owner of the oldest film company in the Dallas area, Tecfilms. Most of their work was military related to contracts with Boeing, Lockheed and E Systems. Lo suggested that I apply for secret clearance from the government, which I got, in order to work for his company. Meanwhile, he hired me as on-camera spokesperson for a number of commercials in the Dallas market. But aside from being a talented filmmaker, Lo was an accomplished sculptor. I have a brochure of his artwork and the following is a reproduction of an excerpt from that resume:

"A graduate of Columbia University, School of Painting and Sculpture, two years of graduate work, followed by the award of a Fulbright Fellowship to study in France. He studied with Maldarelli, Zorach and Hale. Attended the Sorbonne: Ecole de Beaux Arts; Universite d'Aix-en-Provence, and worked in Vence with Henri Matisse duplicating some of his designs in ceramics for the Chapelle de la Rasaire."

His sculpture work adorned his home and I was soon captivated with one piece that I was determined to buy just as soon as I could raise the money.

It was New Years 1980, and the Jordans and I were invited to the Magruders for the holiday festivities. I was not feeling very well, having just recovered from my yearly bout with the flu. The plan was for me to drive down to the Jordan's home and from there they would drive me to the party in Dallas. But as the time to meet them grew close, I was not feeling well enough to make the trek down to their place. Collette decided that we would all go together and they insisted on driving up to my place with the promise to return me home after the party. They had to go some thirty miles out of their way but they were determined so I agreed to join them. I put on my tux with my cowboy hat and my camelhair coat and off we went to Dallas. It was a great party with tons of food and interesting company. Towards the end of the evening, everyone began to declare his or her resolutions for the New Year. When it came to me, I said that I had been smoking three packs of cigarettes for the past

A Vulcan Odyssey

thirty-five years and that it was time for me to give them up. That got a rise out of the party. How many times had they heard that resolution? But I was feeling so bad and the cigarettes tasted so lousy that I had no doubt it was time to kiss my nicotine habit goodbye.

On the way home, and just a few blocks from my house was a Seven Eleven Store. I asked Lo to stop the car while I went in to make a purchase. When I came out I showed them that I had bought a carton of cigarettes.

"That's got to be a record for breaking a New Year's resolution," said Lo.

"Listen, if I say I am going to give up smoking, I mean it. But if I ever wake up in the middle of the night craving a cigarette, I'll be damned if I'm gonna drive all the way down here in the freezing cold for a lousy pack of cigarettes…"

That carton of cigarettes stayed unopened on the top of my refrigerator for two years until I finally threw them away. I haven't smoked for over twenty-five years but I still consider myself an addict and I wouldn't light up a cigarette if my life depended on it. (I went to dealers school when I first moved to Las Vegas and by the time I had finished the course, I realized that I was allergic to cigarette smoke so how the hell could I deal cards in a smoking environment? The human mind is a marvelous thing.)

Chet called to tell me that the Dallas Repertory Theatre was holding auditions for the Jean Anouilh play, *The Lark*. I had not done theatre for quite a few years and the thought of getting back on stage was both terrifying and exciting. I got a copy of the play and realized that the only role I could do was that of the Inquisitor, a stone-faced cleric who tries Saint Joan and eventually condemns her to death. It was a strangely written role because the character is on stage for the entire first act without saying a word. Then, in the second act, he rants and raves for a full fifteen minutes without let-up. It was the kind of role any actor would give his right arm to play. I went to the audition well prepared. I had familiarized myself with the role to where I could almost do it in my sleep. And my tenacity and resolve paid off because I got a call from the theatre informing me that I got the role. My only concern was that I was a member of the Actors Equity Association and I could not do a play unless there was Equity contract and pay. But as it turned out, the producer/director of the theatre, Ed DeLatte, had arranged for me to be paid through the union.

The Inquisitor in the Dallas Repertory Theatre production of
The Lark 1980

A Vulcan Odyssey

I had no idea how important this play would be to me. Ed DeLatte was a Drama professor at North Texas State University in Denton. Opening night of the play was a gala affair and everyone turned out. In the audience was a small army of professors from the university, among which was Dr. Don Staples, chairman of the Department of Radio, Television and Film. At a cast party after the opening night show, Don introduced himself and we struck up a friendship. He asked me about my education, how far I had gone in school, had I ever thought about teaching on the university level? I told him I never got a degree but that I must have had close to 200 hours of classes. We made an appointment for me to come up to Denton so he could go over my credentials with me to see what I might need to acquire a degree with the thought of eventually teaching at NTSU. I queried some half dozen universities that I had attended asking for transcripts of my work while in residence.

After an hour or so of going over my credentials, Don shook his head. "This is a mess," he informed me. "According to your transcripts, you've got enough credits for a Masters Degree. But I doubt if you've got enough core requirements for an Associate Degree." It was all foreign to me. He would have to turn all my credentials over to the administration office and let them evaluate where I stood. From what I could surmise, most of the sciences I had taken at NYU in the fifties were obsolete. The teaching of science on the university level had drastically changed; especially Chemistry and Biology. When I went to school there was no such thing as DNA. New discoveries had changed the course structure of the sciences drastically. Then, there was Math. In order to qualify for admittance to fulfill the core requirements at the university, I would have to take an entrance level exam in English and Math. Hell, I couldn't remember high school math if my life depended on it. Not once since I graduated from high school had I found a need to use Calculus or Trigonometry. And Algebra? It wasn't part of my vocabulary.

But for some reason, and perhaps it was just the challenge, I could see myself teaching at NTSU and the idea excited me. In the final analysis, I would have to enroll at a Junior College and pick up my core requirements. I actually had enough upper level courses without having to go over them again. Don assured me that if I were serious about it, I could get my Bachelor's degree within a year and if I agreed to pursue my Masters, he would hire me while I was working towards it. I went up to Richland College in North Dallas and got their applications and catalogue. I was on a mission. I could do the acting and voice work around my schooling. I had visions of how it would work out and there was nothing that could deter me from my goal. Well, almost nothing.

About this time I got a letter from Jessica saying that she would like to come to Dallas for a visit. We had kept in touch by mail since our last meeting and I looked forward to spending some quality time with her. I had no illusion that we could ever be father and daughter, but if we could just be friends, that would suffice. She came for a short three day visit. I no sooner picked her up at the airport than I realized that our spending time together was a big mistake. Our relationship was strained, we really had nothing to say to each other, and by the end of her stay we were both relieved to be saying goodbye. I did learn that she was into bodybuilding, which I attributed to her grandfather's influence. She had begun a telephone relationship with him and saw him on occasion when she could get a ride into Hollywood.

I had been bed hopping for almost five years; at least most of the time since Margie's death. I had no desire to get involved in a serious relationship and for the time being, it was working quite well for me. But I hadn't been a week at Richland College when I fell head over heels for a professor in the Language Department. Her name was Linda Rae Smith. She was blond, petite, with a great sense of humor and a delicious sensuality that near bowled me over. I was taking Spanish from her and it was all I could do to keep my mind on my class assignments. And it didn't take me all that long before I was sniffing around her office after school on some pretext while trying to get to know her.

Meanwhile, I had become friends with two girls living in the building, Patti and Samantha. Patti was an actress and Sam was working during the day as a sub-agent while at night she was a bartender. The three of us became close friends and many a night with nothing to do, I would stop by the bar where Sam was working to have a drink and pass the evening. It took me quite a while to figure out that Sam and I were hitting on the same women and more often than not, Sam was winning! Over a period of time I decided I wanted Sam to represent me and I moved from the Norton Agency to the stable where Sam was working. And Patti had loaded me up with a couple of needy cats to round out my life.

After a few weeks at Richland College, I finally cracked the door of Dr. Smith's office. She was most receptive. We began with dinner that eventually turned into marathon sex, much to my delight. But we no sooner got our relationship off the ground than she informed me that she was off on a tour of the world on a sailing ship. She would be gone for some three weeks and much to my advantage, she engaged me to care for her five cats. Now, any woman with five cats had a future in my life. Her one cat, Blackie, was trained to use the toilet and flush, which blew me away. And Linda Rae was the proud owner of a sizeable townhouse situated just across the street from the college. I was invited to stay there if it would be convenient for me so I split my time between my apartment in Oak Lawn and the town house across from the college. But the days Linda Rae was gone seemed like years and I got to counting the minutes until her return. By the end of the three weeks, I spent every minute of my waking day contemplating her return. But by this time my own cats were being neglected. I depended upon Sam and Patti to feed them and clean their litter box but I was getting really screwed up in the head.

Linda Rae did not want me to pick her up at the airport since she had parked her car in long-term parking and it was more convenient for her to drive directly home. I decided to decorate the apartment with balloons, each with a note attached. The first balloon said, "ENTER" and was attached to the front door. The second balloon said "GO TO KITCHEN" where I had made a floral arrangement on the counter. The third balloon said "GO UPSTAIRS" where I had salted the stairway with stuffed animals and streamers saying "WELCOME HOME." The final balloon said "I LOVE YOU." As I lay on the bed in the buff. I could hear her laughing with glee all the way up the stairs and within moments she had divested herself of all clothing and we made love late into the night. The following morning, over breakfast, she suggested that I move in with her. But there have never been any free rides in my life and the stipulation that accompanied the invitation was that I could not bring my newly acquired cats. I was not without sympathy to her request since five cats were about as many as any one household could bear but I told her I had to think it over. I had only had the cats for a couple of months and I learned a long time ago that cats do not bond. It is the caregiver who bonds and there was no way in the world I was going to put the cats down to satisfy my convenience. One evening I invited Linda Rae for dinner at my apartment and I included Chet, Patti and Sam. The three of them immediately adored Linda Rae and when I announced that she had invited me to move into her town house, they were all for it. So Patti and Sam went on a mission to find a suitable home for my animals while I informed Linda Rae that if her invitation was still good, I would like to try it. In a few days the cats were well placed in a loving home and I was packed and ready to make the move. We had known each other for only six weeks but already the word "marriage" had been bantered around more than a few times. I don't think either of us got out of bed long enough to realize the ramifications of a long-term relationship. But we discussed eventually making a move to Florida where she had purchased some land that she wanted to develop. The prospect of working on her project together only secured the bond between us.

I got a letter from Jessica saying that she was contemplating enrolling into college. I thought this was an admirable goal and I told her so in a subsequent letter. Then she wrote asking that I subsidize her schooling to the tune of six hundred dollars a month. As usual, money was very tight. I was giving Linda Rae money towards her mortgage, I was helping with house expenses and I was paying tuition for my own schooling. But I suggested that if she was sincerely interested in getting her education, she could come to Dallas where she could live with Linda Rae and me, that the college was just across the street so she wouldn't have to travel, and if she wanted, she could get a part-time job on weekends for spending money. This idea went over like a lead balloon and after she sent me a curt letter, I didn't hear from her for a number of years.

But true to form, the dew was off the rose in a mere three months. If I could isolate the reason for the diminution of our feelings I probably would have arrived at a milestone in my life. Feelings just ceased to be on both our parts. Even the sexual enjoyment had ceased and although we tried to go through the motions, we both knew that the party was over and it was time for me to move on. I moved into a complex a short distance away from school and although we were no longer lovers and roommates, we could not help but see each other. I was still in her Spanish class and until the end of the semester we were bonded together as student and teacher. I was finishing my core courses and in a matter of a couple of months I would have enough required credits to move up to Denton and get into the university. Bob Magruder and his wife, Patsy, had introduced me to a German lady who was teaching at one of the local schools. She and I began to keep company, which took some of the pain off my recently failed relationship with Linda Rae. To put it mildly, my plate was full. But I was soon to learn that there is always room for a bit more.

My new apartment was situated on the ground floor and the small, enclosed patio gave me enough privacy so that I could leave the sliding glass door open to get some fresh air. One day, I looked around and there was this ghastly looking cat sniffing around the patio. I tried to get near him but before I could take a step, he bolted. For the next few days he kept coming around so I bought some cat food and put it on the patio for him and he managed to eat and run before I could make physical contact. Each day I put out the food I placed the dish closer and closer to the patio door hoping to lure him into the apartment. If I said that he was the dirtiest looking cat in creation, that would be an understatement. One day, as I was leaving for an appointment, the cat ran out from the patio and just to satisfy my curiosity, I followed him to see exactly where he hung out. To my surprise, he jumped into the open dumpster into which I threw my garbage every few days. And on one occasion, when I came upon the dumpster, there was this cat eating what looked like the remains of a pizza. So I decided to name him "Trash." It was apropos because he looked like something that had lived in a dumpster the better part of his life. But even after a month of casual contact with him I still couldn't get near enough to pet him. Then, one day, while I was in the bathroom, in walks Trash. There wasn't much I could do from my position so I just talked softly to him as he walked past the bathroom on his discovery of the interior of my apartment. He appeared to be on a mission as if to say, "Just looking around to see if this place is good enough for me to call home." By the time I had regained my composure Trash was out the door. But for the next few days, he braved my presence and brazenly walked into the apartment, sniffing at every piece of furniture and occasionally marking a wall. I was determined that Trash was going to be my pet. There was something about him that spelled "special." So one day, when he was making his daily inspection, I closed the sliding door! Once he became aware that he was not free to leave, he began pacing the apartment looking for a way out. But I was prepared with a kitty carrier and once I had him cornered in the bedroom, his sex life was on the line. I was able to grab him by the nape of the neck and I gently placed him in the carrier and off we went to the vets. The following day I retrieved him and my newly acquired, neutered cat and I began to bond.

Shortly after acquiring Trash, I finished my studies at Richland. Linda Rae was seeing another man but the pain in the pit of my stomach was subsiding and Sylvia, my new lady of choice, helped me through the pain. I found a small two-bedroom apartment near the university in Denton and Sylvia and I loaded all my worldly goods into a rental van and off we went. I still came up short for a bachelor's degree so I enrolled for a final semester at NTSU.

Fortunately, I had found the Dallas market very generous and I was doing voice-overs almost on a daily basis. I picked up a couple of sizeable accounts that would mean recurring work. I got a Foley's Department Store radio spot that renewed each week or whenever they had to advertise a sale. I became the spokesperson for the Dallas Morning News. One day each week I went into Dallas and did an on-camera spot along with some five or six radio spots. It was a great gig for as long as it lasted. But it was not a very productive campaign and after some six weeks the Dallas Morning News decided they wanted out of the nineteen-week contract. They sent me a notice saying that they were cancelling my contract while invoking…a morals clause. I was being accused of drinking and being drunk while on the set. I was in shock.

Herein lies the truth according to Montaigne. While we were shooting at a very exclusive bar/restaurant overlooking the city, my agent at that time, Sylvia Gill, dropped by to see how the shoot was progressing. During a break, I invited her to have a drink with me at the bar. One lousy drink was all we had. But The Dallas Morning News was looking to get out of a contract, and on legal advice, they could do it on the basis of a morals clause in my contract. There was close to twenty thousand dollars due me and I was determined to be paid, whether we finished the contract or not.

I turned to Kim Dawson, the owner of the agency, for help and advice. It was her agency that negotiated that contract as my representative. I assumed that Kim would stand behind me but she had another agenda. She represented a stable of actors and every ad agency with whom she dealt was a potential job for one or more of her talent. By taking the side of a single actor she could very well jeopardize her relationship with the ad agency in question and The Dallas Morning News. Was it ethical to assume that the welfare of a single actor was worth jeopardizing the potential employment of many actors? I put myself in her shoes and realized that she and I had come to the parting of the ways. I hired a lawyer and left the Dawson Agency.

My contract dispute was eventually resolved in my favor but I felt as if I had not really won. The Dallas Morning News agreed to pay what was due on the remainder of my contract. I wanted to carry it one step further and sue them for breach of contact, emotional distress and anything else I could think of, but my lawyer was reluctant to get into a pissing contest with some of the most powerful attorneys in the city that represented the newspaper giant. He was going to get his thirty percent for passing on a few letters and he was perfectly content to let it go at that. So after a number of tedious meetings between us, I agreed to settle just to get on with my life.

All in all, I figure it took me about thirty-five years to get my Bachelor Degree. Don Staples kept his word and hired me on as an adjunct professor teaching part time on the contingency that I continued with my schooling and get my Masters.

That year, NTSU hosted a film convention that was attended by a number of Hollywood dignitaries. One was Nate Monaster, a writer with whom I worked when we were involved in a Writer's Guild program to teach minority students film writing. When Nate had finished his speech, Dr. Joe Barnhart, a tenured professor, approached him and asked whether Nate would have the time to teach him screenwriting if Joe came to Los Angeles. Nate was charmed with Joe's desire to learn but he suggested that Joe get in touch with me and save himself the trip and the expense of going to Los Angeles. I was attending the convention and Joe sought me out and we talked.

"Do you have time to teach me how to write a screenplay?" he asked. "Nate Monaster recommended you and said that you're a competent teacher. I'd be glad to pay you."

I had met Joe Barnhart a couple of times through mutual friends but we never really got together to talk. In fact, I had to laugh when I first met him because he spoke with this Tennessee twang that belied his brilliant mind. Now he was asking for my help to write a screenplay. But just about this same time, I had been trying to work out a class schedule for my marathon run at my Masters Degree. I was planning on fulfilling my requirement for a course in Philosophy when here was this philosophy professor offering me a deal to teach him screenwriting.

"What kind of philosophy do you teach?" I asked.

"This semester I'll be teaching Philosophy of Religion and Philosophy of Literature. What are you looking for?"

"I'm thinking that maybe Philosophy of Literature might fulfill my degree requirement. How about I take your class and in return, I'll tutor you in screenwriting." So a deal was made.

The first day of the semester, I showed up in an auditorium that must have seated two hundred students. Dr. Barnhart did his opening day introduction to the course and dismissed the class with instructions for us to read The Brothers Karamazov by Dostoyevsky. We would all be required to turn in a comprehensive report on that book as part of our final grade. Then, as he dismissed the class he called out for me to meet him at the class exit.

"I'll see you at the end of the semester. Don't forget the book report," he reminded me.

"What do you mean, the end of the semester? I'll be here next week," I assured him.

"I don't think so," he said. "Most of these students are undergraduates and I've got all I can do to stay in control of this class. Now, you and I would just be getting into long, drawn out discussions about the underlying philosophy behind the author's intent and that would detract from my teaching. Why don't you just plan to come back for the final exam and we'll be even. And if you have a compulsion to discuss the philosophy behind Dostoyovsky's work, give me a call."

Dr. Joe and I spent many a night discussing and arguing about philosophy and religion until the wee hours of the morning. He and his wife, Mary Ann, a social psychologist in private practice, were both mentally stimulating and when I wasn't down at the lake with the Jordans, I was with the Barnharts and their family. Joe and I were to become very good friends and we still are to this very day.

I had one major obstacle to overcome in getting my Masters Degree. I was required to write a thesis. I mulled the obstacle over in my mind until I finally came up with a solution. I met with the department chairman, Dr. Staples, and presented him with my idea.

"Since this is a film department, how about I write a screenplay to satisfy my requirement for a thesis?"

To his knowledge it had never been done before but he liked the idea and said he would run it by the dean. A few days later he asked me to give him a short synopsis of what I had in mind. Out from under all my clutter came Cyclone 25. I wrote a one-page outline and delivered it to Dr. Staples' office. A few weeks later I got word that a screenplay would be acceptable to satisfy the department requirement of a thesis. It was a great load off of my mind because I was pushing the envelope between classes and my work obligations in Dallas. I brushed off Cyclone 25, did a cursory rewrite, put it between new covers and at the proscribed date, I delivered it to the committee for evaluation.

There is a process in education called "defending the thesis." It's not enough for one to deliver a finished manuscript; the writer must be ready to go before a committee and defend what he has written. The committee was made up of faculty members who familiarized themselves with the work and were prepared to challenge the writer in order to ascertain whether the candidate was indeed the writer as claimed. A few days before I was to defend my thesis, Don Staples called me. He wanted to discuss the process of thesis defense and we made an appointment to meet at his office. But on the day of our appointment, I got a call from Dallas to do some voiceover work and I called the office to tell Don that I would not be able to keep our appointment. He was disappointed because he told me that I would have to be prepared to defend my work because the committee might attack my veracity. I assured him that I could handle anything they might throw at me but I was not prepared for what happened at that meeting.

There were three faculty members assembled: Dr. Staples, Dan Viamonte, Dr. Donna Klevenger. Everyone had familiarized himself or herself with Cyclone 25 and they were prepared to question how I came to write this particular script. I did not go into the previous background of the script because it was supposed to be written specifically for this course work. I addressed questions regarding the characters, the development of the characters, how I developed the conflicts and how I resolved those conflicts. I had to be on my toes to respond to their questions. Then, Dan

Viamonte, a good friend as well as a fellow professor, hit me with one out of left field.

"I enjoyed reading this script," he began, "but by the time I was halfway though, I realized that I had seen this film before. Isn't it possible that you lifted much of the material in your script from a film you had previously seen?"

Everyone in the room just froze. I looked from face to face as they waited in anticipation of my response. I couldn't very well say that I had written this script five years ago and that Dan's allegations were false. If he claimed that he had seen this film on the screen, then someone had either stolen my script or he was blowing smoke up my ass.

"Are you accusing me of stealing the material I used for this story?" I defended.

"I'm only saying that it's very reminiscent of a film I saw a couple of years ago and that I don't see how two stories could be so closely aligned."

There was a long pause while I gathered up my defense. I was being accused of stealing the material for my original screenplay. I could understand it if Dan accused me of previously writing the screenplay but to say that I had stolen it...that got my juices flowing. I could feel the sweat forming around my collar and running down my back. I was being accused of thievery! This piss ant schoolteacher who didn't know a film script from a roll of toilet paper was accusing me of cheating. Where was Dr. Staples in my defense? Why didn't he intercede? I looked over at Donna Clevenger, a professor from the Drama Department whom I had dated from time to time. She was staring at me as if she had never seen me before. That's when the shit hit the fan.

I looked Dan right in the eye. "Who the fuck are you to accuse me of stealing?" I spat. "Who the hell are any of you to sit in judgment on me? You're only a bunch of teachers whose collective experience comes out of books. Not one of you has ever done a professional day's work in your life." I stared Dan in the eye. "How fucking dare you?" By now, the faculty was frozen in place by my outburst as I grabbed up my scripts, jumped to my feet and stormed out of the room. I was so pissed that I did not hear Don calling me to come back and settle down.

When I got home I took a stiff tumbler of whiskey to calm myself. Fuck the faculty and the school. They could all go to hell. I didn't have to take their shit, I told myself. I didn't need a Masters Degree in some bullshit subject like Communications. I was still fuming when the phone rang. It was Don Staples.

"Well, you really did it this time, didn't you?" he said. He wasn't angry and I could hear a bit of irony in his voice. "That's why I wanted you to meet me prior to facing the committee. I wanted to prepare you for what was going to happen."

"Hold on," I said. "You mean that this whole thing was scripted?"

"Exactly."

"Dan knew I didn't steal the material for the script?"

"He knew."

"And you let him attack me like that?"

"It's called 'defense of thesis'," he said.

"Oh, shit," was all I could muster. Neither of us said a word. Finally, I meekly asked, "What now?"

"Well, to begin with, I think you need to apologize to Dan and Donna."

"Oh, my god. I don't know if I can do it. I've made such an ass of myself."

"Yes, you did. But if you want to get that degree that you worked so hard for, I suggest you swallow that over-inflated pride of yours, make an appointment to meet with both of them, and do what you have to do. Also, I might mention that your tenure here at the University is hanging in the balance. No degree, no job."

It was all I could do to place a call to Dan Viamonte but I did it. In his usual jovial manner, he laughed at the whole situation. He wasn't the least bit offended and told me that he and his wife had been laughing for days at my outburst. It was the most entertaining defense of thesis he had ever experienced.

On the other hand, Dr. Klevinger was not so gracious. She accused me of being immature, of being crude and insulting. I agreed with everything she said. By the time she hung up, she had not forgiven my outburst and was determined to recommend to the dean that I had not successfully defended my thesis. She felt that I was not prepared to teach on the University level. My ass was grass. Don let me stew for a couple of weeks before he got back to me. He had spoken to the other two members of the committee and they unanimously agreed that I had indeed defended my thesis. I guess he must have put some pressure on Dr. Klevinger because I was really doing a yeoman job in my teaching duties. But for the remainder of my tenure at the University, whenever I saw Dr. Klevinger, she chose to ignore me. It was a shame because we never did consummate our relationship.

Once I had that Masters, Don Staples was true to his word and hired me as a full time Associate. I taught two classes in WRITING FOR MEDIA and one class in PRODUCTION MANAGEMENT. The writing classes were entry-level courses and a requirement was that each student had to complete a screenplay by the end of the second semester. When I laid it on the kids, there was a lot of moaning and groaning but I was pleasantly surprised at the caliber of work they turned in. As for the course in Production Management, I had to write the syllabus because I couldn't find a text from which to teach the course. When I took Production Management at Cal State, the professor winged it because his background was immeasurable and he knew the business inside and out. And my tenure with The International Picture Show Company in Atlanta gave me enough hands-on experience to teach a comprehensive course.

I stayed on at NTSU for five very productive years, all the while working in the commercial and industrial field in Dallas. I purchased a great little brick house just up the road from Texas Women's University. The street on which I lived was lined with trees and all the neighbors were friendly. There was a park with tennis courts about four blocks from my house and each morning when I went to play tennis, Trash would heel and walk with me all the way to the courts. Then he would find refuge under a large bush because there was a mockingbird that attacked him every time we came to the park. And when I was finished playing, he would heel all the way back home. I loved that cat. I had friends, a home, a cat, and job security. What more could a person want out of life? I settled in for the long haul.

* * *

But all was not well in Paradise. I had not worked in Dallas for over a month. I called my agent who assured me that it was just hiatus and that work would soon pick up again. I called Lo who was in a transitional period with his company and there was no work for me on the horizon.

Then, I got the word that Don Staples was stepping down as Chairman of the department! This was a crushing blow because Don was my mentor and if there was ever any question as to what was or was not permissible in the scope of my teaching, his door was always open to me. Now he would be stepping down and there was an uncertainty as to who would take his place. My worse fears were realized when it was announced that Dr. Ed Glick would be taking over. Here was a man with a Doctorate degree whose only professional experience was his role as moderator on a Sunday morning talk show on a local television station. He disliked me with a passion. He wasn't in the Chairman position for five minutes before he called me to say that my tenure with the department would be terminated at the end of the current semester. The bottom line was that all eight professors in the department had Ph.D's but none of them had practical experience in the real world. On the other hand, I only had a Masters but I was loaded with experience. In academia, the degree counted and experience meant little. And to compound things, if one was to read the papers on a regular basis, it wouldn't come as a surprise when the school system throughout the state began to feel the financial pinch brought on by the dwindling supply of Texas oil and the import of foreign oil. The school system in Texas was dependent upon taxes generated by in-state oil and by the middle eighties, independent oil wells were producing a fraction of their yield of the previous years.

While I still had a few dollars in the bank, I should have picked up and headed back to Los Angeles. Most of the work I did in Dallas came under the jurisdiction of the actor's union, the American Federation of Television and Radio Artists (AFTRA). During the ten years I had been absent from Los Angeles I had built up a credit under the AFTRA jurisdiction towards a retirement plan. I had nine years vested and I only needed one more year to qualify for a small pension under that jurisdiction. I had a feeling that I might not be able to get work in L.A. for quite a while and if that were the case, and I couldn't get in another year, I would have forfeited nine years towards my retirement under AFTRA. If I could just hold out one more year in Dallas and make enough money for full vesting, it would be worth the investment of my time. And it would give me enough time to decide how to unload my house. After all, I wasn't destitute; I could still make the house payments,

I could still afford to eat three squares a day, and I could still afford to buy cat food for Trash. What more could I want out of life?

I was just beginning my last semester at the University when I got a call from Don Staples. He was directing a play at the Denton Community Theatre and was wondering if I might consider doing the lead. I explained that I had a full plate and that there just weren't enough hours in the day to undertake such a responsibility. But he was directing *To Kill a Mockingbird* and he wanted me to play the role of Atticus Finch. My God but I loved that play. But I was reluctant to make a commitment because I was going through a crisis in my life. I had noticed over the past few months that I was having trouble remembering things, like committing lines to memory. For the past ten years I had been doing voice work in the studio or television spots where I read the copy off a teleprompter. I had not been forced to actually sit down and remember lines and on one occasion, while working for Lo Jordan, I had four lines to memorize and I couldn't for the life of me commit them to memory. We had to shoot each line separately and I was thoroughly embarrassed. There is an adage, "If you don't use it, you lose it." I hadn't been required to learn lines for years and now I was convinced that I could no longer do it. I owed it to Don to consider working on his play but before I would commit, I wanted to test the waters. I asked when I would have to audition and he said that if I wanted to do the role, it was mine. But I insisted that I wanted to audition and we set up a date. I got a copy of the script, picked out the longest monologue in the script and settled down to learn the lines. It was about three pages long and I worked night and day trying to commit it to memory. I lived on only a couple of hours sleep a night when I would awaken trying to remember the lines. The day of the audition, I walked into the theatre and Don assumed that I would be reading from the script. I did the monologue cold turkey without a glitch. I was going to do the role of Atticus Finch.

Okay, so it was only amateur theatre, I wasn't being paid and we were only able to rehearse at night and on weekends, but I put my heart into that production. I couldn't remember when I ever worked so hard over a role and Don and I worked well together. He was open to my ideas and together we were determined to create one of the finest productions ever seen in Denton.

The week before opening I arrived home late one night to be greeted by the daughter of one of my neighbors. I could tell by the look on her face that something was drastically wrong.

"It's Trash," she said. "He's over at the pet hospital. He was hit by a car!"

Robinwood Lane was one of those streets where everyone knew everyone else. The residents drove with extreme caution because everyone owned at least one animal and there was a common respect for a neighbor's pet. Trash had the habit of lying in the middle of the street, especially on cool nights when he enjoyed the residual warmth of the asphalt. No one who lived in the neighborhood would have run over a cat. It had to be someone from outside the area who was either speeding or driving with reckless abandon. I was almost in shock to think that my invincible Trash had been run over and was now in a hospital.

The doctor met me with rather grim news. "His back leg is shattered. I'm afraid we'll have to amputate his leg."

"But is he going to be all right?" I asked.

"If we amputate it's going to run into quite a bit of money. I want you to carefully consider the alternative..."

"You're not suggesting I have him put to sleep, are you?"

"As a vet, I've got to give you every option."

"Well, that's not an option. You do what you have to do but I want that cat taken care of, no matter what the cost. I'll cover it."

The vet took me into the back of the clinic where Trash was in a cage. He was filthy but that was perfectly normal for him. But he was swathed in bandages and his eyes were glazed over from the medication. The doctor insisted that I go home, assuring me that there was nothing anyone could do until the following morning. I stayed up half that night until I was overcome with exhaustion and fell asleep on the living room couch. I sometimes wonder how it is that anyone can get so attached to an animal, can treat it as if it were almost human. I found it perfectly normal to carry on a conversation with Trash, knowing full well that he was a cat and hadn't the slightest idea what I was saying. But it gave me comfort in talking to a living thing, in being able to express myself to something other than a plaster- covered wall. And late at night I would derive comfort from his closeness as he pressed up against my body and although we could not communicate on human terms, there was that unconditional love that existed between man and beast and I was the better for it.

The following day, they amputated Trash's hind leg at the hip. I sat in the clinic all day and was there when he came out of surgery. He was the most sorry looking thing I had ever seen. I kept thinking that perhaps the doctor was right in suggesting that I put him to sleep. He was a natural predator that took pleasure in chasing squirrels and birds, in climbing trees and rummaging through the neighborhood dumpsters. As I looked at him in the cage, I could see where the bandages covered the hind part of him where once a leg had been. I was heartbroken. How would he ever adjust to the loss of a leg? How would he ever again find pleasure in the hunt, in clawing his way to the top branch of one of the black oak trees in the backyard, in making that one graceful, perfect leap to the edge of the five foot dumpster in search of the treasures that lie within?

But when the sun went down, I was at the theatre and ready to rehearse. All the worries and anxieties about Trash were put on the back burner. He would survive this; I was sure. But would I?

On the fourth or fifth day, I brought Trash home. He was still groggy from the ordeal and I was instructed to give him medication to prevent infection. It appears that animals can take pain better than humans but I'm wondering how anyone came to this conclusion. Looking at the bewilderment on Trash's face and the low groan that he emitted as he tried to stand but obviously could not, I could not conclude that he was in any less pain than I would have been had I gone through the same ordeal. The next few days were a constant succession of dashes from home to the theatre and back in preparation for opening night. Trash was now wearing a large plastic collar to prevent him from reaching back to try to remove the bandage. I was not in any hurry to see the results of the operation but when the day finally came for the doctor to remove the dressing, it was all I could do to hold my lunch. The wound was a ghastly, discolored scar that ran from the middle of his body almost to his tail. And no sooner was the bandage removed and the collar discarded, he made his first attempt to stand. I guess animals don't understand the ramifications of an amputation because he immediately fell over on his side. It was obvious that he had no understanding that he was short one leg and that he would have to learn to compensate. As he lay there looking up at me, I wondered if he would ever understand what had happened to him. He had been a lean, strong, muscular animal and now he was an invalid with his coat turned rough from weeks of convalescing. But each day, he seemed to grow a bit stronger and aside from the few humorous incidents when he would get up on his three good legs and attempt to take a step, only to fall over on his scarred, vacated hip, it was obvious that he was almost aware that he would have to adjust to this new configuration. He was like a human child attempting to take that first step. And the first time he managed to take that small step forward without falling over on his side, it was a feat that I thought I would never witness.

The play opened to a full house with perhaps three hundred people in the audience. I was confident with the lines and managed to turn in an adequate performance. I was one of those actors who was never content with the outcome of his performance. And each time I played the role, I managed to make small adjustments, looking for that perfect moment when I would be pleased with what I had done. I was aware that the role carried the actor; that's how formidable was Atticus. And over the eight weeks we were together, I grew comfortable with our relationship as I melded my own personality into his. I began to see myself as this caring, warm, intelligent, Don Quixote as he charged the windmills of injustice in a time of turbulence in our society. By closing night I knew I would miss Atticus.

The house had been on the market for a couple of months and with the softness in the Texas economy, it was apparent that I was not going to be able to unload it within my time frame. I was a collector of bric-a-brac and books. The small workshop attached to the garage had tools hanging from nails above the workbench and there was no way in the world that I was going to divest myself of my precious tools. Over the last few years I had hauled furniture and junk from Los Angeles to Atlanta to Denton. There was a time, when I left Los Angeles, that I had put most of my belongings in storage to the tune of some hundred plus dollars a month. Over a period of five years I had spent nearly seven thousand dollars in storage fees. For some reason it never dawned on me that for seven thousand dollars, I could buy most of the stuff I had in that storage space ten times over. The expression, "penny wise and pound foolish", surely applied to me.

I finally got an offer on the house. It was disappointing and true to form, I would be losing money in real estate. I held a few garage sales and parted with a number of antique pieces and various items I had acquired over the years. The sales were quite successful as I netted some twelve hundred dollars. Of course, I parted with some things that were dear to me and with the sale of each item went a small memory that was irreplaceable. I was selling off, piece by piece, the one place I thought I would spend my remaining years. It was a painful experience.

A friend of mine, "Big" Mike Caldwell, was looking to sell a fourteen-foot trailer and he cut me a very nice deal. Loading that trailer became something of an engineering feat but I started with my motorcycle and working back from there, I roped down boxes and pieces of furniture that I could not part with. (I had an armoire that my father purchased at auction some years before. I was working the day of the auction so I gave him a price I wanted to pay for this particular item and told him to bid up to that price. Little did I know he would get "auction fever" and he got into a bidding contest and ended up paying twice what I had intended to pay. Realizing what he had done, he made up the difference. I still have that armoire here in my apartment in Henderson).

As I've intimated before, I have never been a very good saver. I like to spend money. Oh, not on material things but on eating at nice places and entertaining friends and going to the theatre and concerts. So in a pinch, I am one of those people destined for the soup kitchen and nearest local mission. I guess I've been fortunate that it's never come to that but I've always followed a simple rule in the face of adversity: pack up and get the hell out of town! I waned philosophic; I had been in Texas for ten years, made a number of lifetime friends, and it was time to move on.

I had called my dad and told him I was thinking of returning to Los Angeles. He was ecstatic at the prospect and said I could stay with him for as long as I wanted. Then I called Stuart Sobel, a friend of mine from law school. (Stuart and I had attended the University of West Los Angeles in Culver City for three years and neither of us was able to pass the state bar. I took the bar one time and walked away but Stuart took it three times before he gave up. It was during the period when I had the bar up on Sunset Strip and in the evenings, when business was slow, we'd study together. I made a drink called a Negroni and by the end of an evening's studying, he and I were feeling no pain. Stuart finally philosophized that we had spent too much time in the bar to pass the bar. He may have been right but he went on to be a very successful businessman without selling out to the legal profession. We later learned that he was dyslexic which probably accounted for his inability to pass the state bar exam. Me? I was just not cut out for the law.) Stuart now owned a storage warehouse near Glendale and he offered me storage space in which to keep my stuff until I could get settled. I hadn't a clue what I was going to do when I got back to L.A.

The last bit of business was to take Trash to the vet's clinic for his last visit. I was concerned that the trip was going to be an ordeal for him considering his most recent accident. But I felt it was too much of an imposition to ask friends to care for the animal until I was ready to have him shipped to the coast. He was still on medication and needed lots of attention.

"I'm not so sure this trip is a good move for him," said the doctor. "You'll have to keep him tranquilized most of the time..."

"I don't have much of a choice, Doctor. I seem to be in one of those Catch-22 situations. I'm damned if I do and damned if I don't."

The doctor checked the scar that now was almost covered over with hair. "I've never taken an animal home from the clinic since I've been in practice. It's a decision my wife and I decided on some years ago in order to keep our home separate from the clinic. To be honest, we've all grown quite attached to Trash; the staff, the attendants, and I. Perhaps we could keep him here for a while until you get settled. He could come home with me on weekends and during the week he could stay here at the clinic. There's lots of room and the girls would give him plenty of attention..."

If I was in the habit of praying, this would be considered a miracle. I knew that shlepping Trash across country could be harmful to him and here the doctor was offering me an alternative. "Could I take a day or two to think about it?"

"As much time as you want."

There was nothing to think about. I could not take a chance of jeopardizing Trash's life with a trip across the country. When you bond with an animal, you assume a certain responsibility for the well being of that animal. It would have been easy to put Trash down, to wash my hands of him and chalk it up to bad luck for the cat.

I knew a woman whose daughter had a cat for half a dozen years. In casual conversations with her, one would think that her cat was absolutely human. Then, I heard that the daughter was going to marry a man who claimed that he was allergic to cats...so she had the animal destroyed. When I heard about it, I lost all respect for the daughter. I was angry beyond words. I, too, am allergic to cats; have been for most of my adult life. Over the years my allergy has dissipated. I figure that I must have sneezed the damn thing out of my system. Yet, if I were to take an allergy test, it would show that I am indeed allergic to cats. But I would never in a million years give up an animal just for some minor inconvenience on my part.

Early one morning I got on the I-35 and headed south to where I picked up the I-10 just outside of Ft. Worth, and it was a straight shot to L.A.

CHAPTER FOURTEEN
STAR TREK REVISITED

I didn't have much of a plan. By the time I arrived in L.A. I was no clearer about what I was going to do than when I departed Denton. It was my friend, Stuart Sobel, who had been my study partner in law school, who put me on the road to a new career. When I arrived in L.A. after the grueling trip, I went immediately to the warehouse owned by Stuart. He and some of his workers helped me unload the trailer into a storage bin. Then he suggested that I leave the trailer at his facility and in a matter of days, he had it sold.

My absence from Los Angeles for a period of some twelve years proved to be something of an eye-opener. Most of the people I knew years before were nowhere to be found. It was apparent that finding an agent was more difficult than finding a job. I sent out a hundred photos, resumes and voice tapes to agents and production houses: I did not get one reply! It did not take long for me to realize that my dream of getting back into "the business" was going to be something of a fantasy. After a couple of months of not being able to open a single door, I had to look for other options. It was Stuart who came up with a plan.

"You've always been knowledgeable with tools and how to build things. How about you try finding work as a handyman. You'd be working for yourself and working on your own terms and later, if the acting door opens, you'd be free to jump in. I know that I could use you here at the warehouse for a starter..."

And so it was that I began working for my friend, Stuart. Admittedly, I didn't know half of what I needed to know to do all the work he expected of me at the warehouse so I purchased some books on building and construction and read myself to sleep each evening in preparation for the next day's work. When I had completed the warehouse chores, Stuart sent me over to a condo that his father had recently purchased. And when I finished working for his father, Stuart sent me over to his sister's condo to work there for a few weeks. I was getting pretty proficient doing handiwork and Stuart, his father and his sister, began to put out the word that I was a fast worker, I could handle most residential chores, and I charged reasonable rates. The work began to roll in as I was going from one job to another.

I finally broke down and called Jessica to see how she was getting along. She and her mother were now estranged and Jessica was living in a small bungalow down in Venice. I invited her for lunch and I picked her up at her place. I learned that she was working as a personal trainer at Gold's Gym. Instead of going to college, she decided to study for her certification as a trainer and was apparently doing quite well. She was also into competing in bodybuilding and had taken first place in the Iron Maiden competition. She was quite buff and lean, which she attributed to her competing in long distance running. She ran in the New York marathon as well as the one in Los Angeles, and competed in a number of triathlons. I told her that I was working as a handyman and if she needed any work done around her place, I would be glad to help out. When I had time, I traveled down to the beach and constructed some shelving and bookcases for her. I was hoping that we were getting closer but shortly thereafter, I got a letter from her:

Dad,
I know it seems like I've been avoiding you for the past few weeks; the fact is I have. This is why; as you know I've been in Psychotherapy for a few months now. I initially started therapy as a result of problems I'd been having with my relationship to John (or so I thought.) During the course of my therapy other issues concerning my childhood have been coming up for me. These issues are very sensitive and confronting. I'm not sure yet where this stuff comes from or how to deal with it so I feel comfortable. Your presence in my life right now as my "father" is confusing and the confusion is irritating. This irritation makes it difficult to be around you right now. I can't just push it all aside and be friends because we have little in common on a social level. Therefore my irritation consumes my ability to be around you and enjoy it. I'm writing to tell you this because I imagine in your shoes my behavior may seem unsubstantiated. And I can certainly appreciate your need to have a "relationship" with your daughter. I'm working on that possibility. I just need the space to do it. I hope you can understand and not take it too personally. I'm concerned about Robby and you and I'd like to

see you both occasionally to keep up. I just need to take care of me. Please understand.
Love, Jessica

Her letter really hit a nerve. I discussed it with Robby and he told me to back off and be patient, that she would come around in her own time. I was really pissed at her and it would be almost twenty years before we would be in contact again.

After a few months, it was apparent that construction was a viable line of work for me but being a handyman was only a means to an end. My friend of many years, Phil Posner, was making big money working as a carpenter at 20th Century Fox. He tried to get me into the studio but the union was too hard to crack and although I was able to pick up a few days here and there, I could never quite get in enough hours to qualify for my union card. I finally decided that the only way to go was to take the California State Contractor's License exam. Phil and I decided to enroll in night school and for the next three months, I spent all my free time studying for the exam. Finally, Phil and I drove out to Pasadena and along with a thousand other applicants, we took the state exam. Two weeks later I got word that I had passed and was now a licensed building contractor.

One of the first calls I got was from a Beverly Hills realtor by the name of Sue Casey. She was in the process of putting a house on the market and the owner needed to bring it up to code. Would I come out and give her a bid? We made an appointment and at the given time, I was still driving around the streets of West Los Angeles trying to find the address. I arrived at the house some fifteen minutes late and as I drove up, there was this stunning, tall, blond lady standing in front of the house tapping her foot. It was rare for me to be late for an appointment and as I walked up the path to the house, she asked, "Are you looking for me?"

I was quick as a blink of the eye, I responded, "All of my life."

I did a thorough inspection of the house and instead of giving her an estimate, I suggested that we retire to a local eatery while I did the calculations. She agreed and over coffee I got to know a little about this lovely woman. She had been a dancer and in the forties she was a Goldwyn girl, in a very famous group that appeared in numerous musical films of that era. She had also appeared in an aquatic ballet swimming with Esther Williams, a star at MGM Studios. Coincidentally, I had worked on that same film doing a stunt where I went down a long slide standing up and holding onto streamers that trailed behind me. We talked about working at the same studio at the same time and all the people we knew in common and by the time I had calculated the cost of doing the reparations on the house, she and I were making personal plans. I invited her for dinner that evening and half a dozen subsequent evenings until it was apparent that we were both very attracted to each other. She had just terminated a relationship so my timing was perfect and within a few weeks, she invited me to move into her very fashionable Beverly Hills condo. I was hooked. It wasn't long before that "m" word was heard throughout the nights of passion.

All was moving along quite well in Paradise until one evening, she invited her three adult children over to meet me. The two older boys were fine but the daughter took an immediate dislike to me and told her mother in no uncertain terms that I was nothing more that an opportunist looking to take advantage of her. Sue let her daughter's remarks slide but the seed had been planted.

Over the next few months I found myself working extremely long hours and by the time I returned to the condo at the end of a day, it was all I could do to stay awake through dinner. My birthday rolled around in February and as a gift, Sue bought me a beautiful, longhaired cat that we named Missy. I guess on numerous occasions I must have mentioned how much I had missed having a pet. The kennel where Sue got the cat assured her that Missy had been fixed. When she brought the cat home, it was just recovering from a slight cold and she was all skin and bones. We fed her morning and night and as she appeared to be gaining weight, we just assumed it was nothing more than her response to our loving care. But five weeks later, in the middle of the night, I was awakened by strange sounds and when I looked under the bed, Missy had delivered a litter of three kittens! How was that possible? We were instant parents. Sue managed to find homes for two of the kittens but we were having a problem placing the runt of the litter, a small black cat that we named E.T.

My schedule was wearing me down and it was beginning to affect our relationship. When Sue wanted to make plans for an evening out, I was too tired. I would fall asleep in the cinema or during a concert at the Hollywood Bowl. There was nothing I could do short of giving up my business that would ameliorate our problem. The relationship worsened by the day and with the daughter adding fuel to the fire it wasn't long before Sue asked me to pack up and leave. Hey, we had a good run. It was time to move on. I found a small apartment over in Hollywood, packed up my few personal possessions, loaded up the cats, and moved.

I had intended to put E.T. up for adoption but I got a job working as construction foreman on a film that was shooting fifty miles north of the city. Each morning I had to leave the house at five a.m. in order to be to work on time and I often didn't get home until late at night. I didn't want to leave Missy alone all day so my intentions were to keep E.T. until I finished work on the film, and then I would find him a good home. I guess I never learned. By the time I finished the film, E.T. had wormed his way into my heart and there was no way I could ever give him up.

Stuart had a young man working for him down at the warehouse doing odd jobs. His name was Ricardo and he came from El Salvador. I hired Ricardo to work with me, explaining to him that the job was only as secure as my ability to find work but he agreed to throw in with me. We worked together steadily for three years. Ricardo made enough money to return to El Salvador and build a home for his mother. He returned a few weeks before the big earthquake of 1993 in Los Angeles. As unfortunate as it was for the devastated homeowners, it turned out to be a windfall for me. I was running three crews in the Valley, all at the same time. The earthquake had produced a plethora of work for anyone who could wield a hammer or knew which end of a shovel was used for moving debris. I was still running three crews two years after the quake had struck. It was too good to be true; I knew that sooner or later, something would rain on my parade. As the work in the Valley began to diminish, I laid off my crews and headed into West Hollywood. I bid on a restoration and an add-on to an old stucco, single family dwelling. I had been doing mostly interior remodeling and here was a chance to actually get into the heavy framing and construction. My bid on the West Hollywood job was competitive and I won the contract. It was one of those jobs that required sub-contractors to bid on the roofing, plastering, electric and plumbing. I had estimated the job down to the penny and although I didn't anticipate making a lot of money, it could have been a lucrative job if everything went off as planned.

Within a week I knew that I had a problem. Behind the walls I found so much wood rot and termite infestation that it actually was compromising the foundation of the building. It was one of those discoveries that I could have just closed my eyes to and said nothing, or I could have called it to the attention of the owners and renegotiated the contract. The problem was major and because it was a defect that was hidden behind the walls at the time of my original inspection, there was no way that I could have anticipated a problem of such enormity. I guess my understanding of human nature was still somewhat naïve because as soon as I mentioned to the owners that we would have to renegotiate the contract, their lawyer materialized like a jinni from a bottle. There was a contract, both parties agreed to it, both parties signed it, and both parties would be expected to abide by it. I had a couple of options that would have saved me from losing a great deal of money. I mistakenly thought I could weather this storm without too much damage if I minimized my use of sub-contractors and did most of the work myself. I could have just walked away from the job, left it where it stood, and had them take action against me…if they could find me. Of course, that would mean the forfeiture of my contractor's license and I wasn't that desperate, yet.

My first real setback was when I developed a kidney stone on the job and had to be rushed to the hospital. It was not one of those stones that one passes and that's the end of it. I had to be one of those people that had a lodged stone and the doctor had to go in and get it. I get very nervous when strangers play around with my penis, especially on the inside. I was off the job for three days during which time I was paying for a crew of Hispanics to sit around on their dead asses. Had I let them go, there was a chance I wouldn't get them back again and these guys had been working for me, on and off, for the past two years. Ricardo was a good foreman but he didn't know squat when it came to reading blueprints and determining what had to be done next.

I returned to the construction site in the middle of a rainstorm. The new roof, which had been sub-contracted out to a Vietnamese roofer was leaking like an old shower. Nothing could be done until the problems with the roof were resolved. Then, the roofing contractor wanted to be paid again for work he didn't do right in the first place. When I refused to pay up, a couple of his "friends" paid me a visit. I had no intentions of being blackmailed and I guess they just figured it was more trouble than the whole thing was worth. I never heard from them again. And so it went, just one damn thing after another.

The completed job ran over by more than two months and ripped my saving's account to shreds. Then, as the job was closing down, Ricardo disappeared. A few days later I got notice from the State Disability Insurance Board saying that he had filed a claim for disability. He stated that while on the job, he had hit himself in the toe with a hammer, which in turn caused him to have severe lower back trauma. The bill was astronomical and although I was covered by insurance, my premiums suddenly jumped two hundred percent. I appealed to the SDI Board, telling them that I had not been given any notice that an employee had been hurt on my job site but they said that they were shorthanded and could not investigate every claim that came into their office. Ricardo had learned how to scam the system and it was going to pay off, at my expense. I philosophized that he may be getting a chunk of money in front, but in the final analysis, he had lost out on a pretty good job. I doubted that anyone would be paying him the wages he had earned with me.

I took a financial bath on the West Hollywood job but I had the satisfaction in knowing that the house turned out beautifully. I guess, for me that just about sized up my whole life. Financially, I was back to zero, but as I looked at the house that I had put my heart and sweat into, I was more than satisfied that I had done a damn good job.

* * *

Walter and Lois Maslow had retired down to a little town in the desert halfway between L.A. and San Diego. Murrieta was a sleepy little town that has since exploded into a thriving community. Walter and I had known each other since our years together in Rome so on a visit down to see the Maslows, I was impressed with the community and the cheap cost of housing; a truly great place to retire. It was only two hours out of Los Angeles so I could travel in on weekends to visit with my dad. I managed to find a small mobile home with a swimming pool and the modest rent included membership in the recreation center that had two pools, a workout room and a poolroom. Barely a five-minute walk down the hill was a tennis club with a dozen beautifully appointed courts and across the main road was the front side of a regulation, twenty-seven hole, championship golf course. I had died and gone to heaven. I had visions of living forever in the land of outdoor recreation and the very first time I visited the pool, I met this lovely lady with whom I struck up a very close and personal relationship. I basked daily at poolside in the hot desert sun and baked my body into a golden tan. For three months I lived like a man without a care in the world, enjoying the best that retirement had to offer. And then, one day, my desert romance came to a screeching halt. My romantic interest got drunk as a skunk over dinner, called me some names I had never heard before, and told me she never wanted to see me again. And sitting alone that night, it came to me in a flash that I had not had a constructive thought in my head for the better part of three months. My mind was slowly turning to mush. My retirement had come to a screeching end!

While working in the construction business, I had an electrical subcontractor by the name of Harvey. Whenever I needed to have electrical work done on a job, I called Harvey. We became good friends and when I moved down to Murietta, he and his wife, Jane, would come down to visit and be my guest. Jane was a teacher's assistant and she was determined that I should be working as a substitute teacher. It was a position I had not explored because one had to take a very complex exam to satisfy the California State CBEST exam. I had been out of school for too long to try to pass an academic exam but Jane was determined to see me back in the classroom and to get her off my back, I promised that I would go down to San Diego and take the exam. I bought a book to prepare me for the CBEST but I knew in my heart that there was no way in hell I was going to pass. A couple of weeks after taking the exam, I got word from the state that I had passed and was qualified to work as a substitute teacher in any community in the state. Harvey and Jane pushed me into registering with the Temecula Valley School District for substitute teaching and before I knew it, I was back in the classroom. The district was in dire need of computer teachers and I began to work almost every day. I enjoyed the teaching but I sometimes had to work with high school kids that didn't want to be in the classroom and more often than not, I found myself more involved in discipline than teaching. But I stuck with it for two years until I realized that my dad was not getting any younger and it was time for me to return to Los Angeles to be near him. With my credential I could teach anywhere in the state so I made application to the Glendale Unified School District and no sooner had I found an apartment in Glendale than I was back in the classroom.

* * *

I found a great two-story apartment that was adjacent to the back of Glendale College. Almost every morning I could look out my back window and see deer grazing on the hill just a few feet from my patio. I adopted a squirrel and named her Stanley. Every morning she came down and hung on my screen door waiting to be fed and Missy and E.T. knew better than to try to test her. I often saw E.T. nose to nose with Stanley but he never made an aggressive move towards her. I loved that apartment and the wildlife that proliferated on the hill behind my patio.

It was at this time that I began to notice that something was not physically right with me. I began to suffer dizzy spells and one day, while taking a shower, I began to get lightheaded and in anticipation of passing out, I sat down in the bathtub as the hot water cascaded over me. There was something going on in my body that was disturbing so I went to see my doctor at the Screen Actors Guild clinic. I went through a series of tests before it was determined that I had a disability called *spinal stenosis*. For the short time I had done stunts at the beginning of my career, I had suffered whiplash on at least a dozen occasions, either riding horses or crashing cars. Over a period of time the healing process created calcium buildup in my cervical spine and the spinal column was beginning to close. I was not getting spinal fluid to my extremities and on a number of occasions I found myself losing my balance. I went to see a specialist who did a series of MRI's on my spine. Finally, he told me in no uncertain terms that I had about two months before I would be completely paralyzed from the waist down. I laughed at his evaluation and moved on to another doctor for a second opinion. He gave me one month. This was beginning to sound serious but I continued to ignore the prospect until one day, I lost my balance and fell through a glass-top coffee table! Fortunately, I wasn't badly cut but it scared the hell out of me and at the suggestion of the union doctor, I saw another specialist who evaluated the x-rays I had obtained from the previous specialists. There was no doubt about it; I needed immediate surgery.

September 15th, 1999, Robert Wynn, a friend of longstanding came all the way in from the North Valley to drive me to the West Hills

Hospital where I was to undergo a procedure intended to ward off the inevitable paralysis. The six hour operation was harrowing and when I awoke, my throat had been cut across, my esophagus pushed to one side, two vertebrae were removed, a bone was harvested from my hip and placed in my spine, and the whole thing was screwed together with a three inch titanium plate. I spent two weeks in recovery, returned home where I underwent physical therapy for another week and then returned to the hospital to have the whole procedure done again because I had picked up a staff infection while in the hospital. It was a total nightmare and if it wasn't for friends, I would have bailed out then and there. But I had a great support network of people who cared and with their help and attention, I was soon on the road to recovery.

I have never been a good patient. I can stay in bed for a day or two but after that I start to get antsy and strain at the bit. It was a long, slow process that took a couple of months before I could contemplate a teaching job. I had become friendly with the woman responsible for placing subs in various schools in the district. Her name was Nancy Waters and knowing my background with computers she had previously sent me out on some very challenging jobs. Nancy was on the verge of marrying her fiancé, Ron McNair, a real estate broker and developer. They were a fun couple and we had spent a number of evenings dining out together. When they finally decided to tie the knot, I was invited to the wedding.

Nancy kept in touch with me during my ordeal with the surgery and one day she called to ask me if I would call Marie Azizzi over at Wilson Middle School. It was just down the street from my apartment and I liked working there because they had some of the nicest people in the district in their employ. I called Marie, the school secretary, and she asked if I would come into the office for an interview with the principal, Mr. Lucas. I had worked at Wilson as a long-term sub for a while teaching Ancient History. I just assumed that the interview had something to do with my teaching during that period. Did I fail to return a book or did I disseminate faulty information regarding the Roman Empire or Greek civilization? All sorts of thoughts raced through my mind. But why would the principal want to see me? Send me a bill and I'll pay for the lousy book.

Mr. Lucas greeted me warmly, inquired about my health, and informed me that they wanted to open up a teaching position for me on a full-time basis. I was shocked. I also knew that I could not put in a full day of teaching while I was still in the recovery mode.

"I can offer you a full time position teaching English. You'd be out of school by three in the afternoon," he said.

It was a very attractive offer but I knew I could never handle it. "Thank you for the consideration but I don't think I would be up to it. I'm still weak from my operation and it would be too much of a responsibility to undertake at this time."

"What would be comfortable for you?" he enquired.

"I've been subbing half days and that's about all I can handle." Nancy Waters had been kind enough to look for half-day assignments for me while I was regaining my strength.

"Could you handle three classes a day? Say from eight to twelve?" he asked.

"Three classes would be eight to eleven," I corrected.

"Yes, but there would be a prep period which would make it four hours plus twenty minutes for break."

I mulled it over in my mind. I could tell that I was getting in way over my head. "I hate to turn this down, Mr. Lucas, but I'm going to have to pass. It's just too many hours on my feet and I don't think I'm up to it."

I could see from the expression on his face that he was very disappointed. He didn't say anything for quite a few seconds as he peered down at his desk as if there were some great words written there. When he looked up he smiled. "How about three hours with twenty minutes for a break. You'd be out by eleven-twenty each day?"

It was an offer I couldn't refuse. In February of the year 2000, I entered the classroom as a full time, part time teacher at Wilson Middle School. I was only receiving partial pay but it was more than I was making as a sub and I could get full benefits if I wanted them. I figured that either they had come to the bottom of the barrel or I was the only teacher in the district who would take on a part time teaching post. I stayed with Wilson for that one semester when the district decided to cut that class from the curriculum and I was terminated.

Shortly thereafter, I got a call to substitute for a teacher up at Clark Magnet High School in La Crescenta. I had worked there on numerous occasions and as far as I was concerned, it was one of the finest schools in the district. I knew the teacher for whom I was to substitute. Roger Smith taught Cisco Systems, a very complex computer networking system. I hadn't the slightest clue what Cisco was all about but Roger had left me a comprehensive lesson plan that I followed to the tee. But at the end of that day, Barbara Melone, the school secretary, told me that Roger would probably be out for the remainder of the week on medical leave and asked if I would cover for him. I called Roger at home to ask just what he wanted me to cover in his absence and I confessed to him that I knew nothing about Cisco. Actually, aside from Roger, I doubt that there was anyone else in the entire district who could teach Cisco. I went over to Roger's house and he walked me through what I had to do from day to day until he could return. He was too optimistic. Roger was not to return to Clark for the remainder of that semester. He was very ill, underwent surgery, and was confined to his home for a prolonged period of convalescence. When he was able to meet with me, I went to his house where he spent hours trying to keep me one step ahead of the classes and each evening I would spend as many as four hour reading the text to familiarize myself with what I was expected to teach the following day. I had never worked so hard in my life.

On the faculty of Clark Magnet was another computer teacher I had subbed for in the past. His name was Bill Reyna and when I had a question or when I needed help, Bill was an invaluable source of information. He was also a very accomplished guitarist and since I have always been an *aficionado* of the guitar, he and I became friends. One day, after I had been on the job for a couple of weeks, Bill asked if we had met before. He recognized me from someplace but he couldn't remember from where. As it turned out, he and his wife, Barb, were Trekies, followers of Star Trek. When I recounted that I had created two roles in the original series, he was delighted. He asked if I had plans to appear at the Pasadena Star Trek Convention. I hadn't a clue what he was talking about.

"You don't know about Star Trek conventions?" he asked in amazement.

"Haven't a clue," I confessed.

"They're conventions all over the country where thousands of Star Trek fans get together over a period of three or four days to meet with past members of the cast, get autographs, listen to lectures, and get a chance to collect Star Trek memorabilia. You've never heard of it?"

"Nope. But twenty years ago someone called and invited me to a Star Trek thing down by the airport and when I got there, they nailed me for twenty-five dollars at the door. Is that what you're talking about?"

"They didn't," he said in disbelief. "Oh, my God, I wonder who that could have possibly been. Listen, there's a Grand Slam convention coming up next month in Pasadena. It's the biggest event of the year. Why don't you join Barb and me? I'll bet the promoters would love to see you."

I had sworn that Star Trek was a thing of the past. I got nailed for twenty-five dollars on my last invitation and I wasn't curious to see how much they would get me for this time. "Let me think about it," I said and dropped the subject.

A few weeks later Bill called to say that the convention was just weeks away and would I be interested in joining him and his wife as their guest. Again, I managed to avoid the subject and gave him some feeble excuse about having lots of lesson plans to write and papers to grade and not being able to get away that weekend. But shades of my early experience, he called again only a few days before the big weekend. He was wearing me down with kindness and pleasantries. He and his wife would be honored if I would be their guest. And true to form, I could not refuse a kindness and agreed to meet them at the Convention Center in Pasadena on Saturday morning. We set the time and place but something went wrong and when I got there I couldn't find them. I had entered the Convention Center through the garage where someone had left the door ajar and I made my way up into the cavernous convention area, all the while bypassing security and personnel. But once inside there was no way I could work my way back out to the box office. I knew it would be easy to spot Bill and his wife, Barb. He told me that his wife stood six feet, six inches tall and would be a definite standout in any crowd. The main showroom was jam-packed and I walked back and forth through the convention center without sighting either of them. Finally, in a state of *deja vu*, I left the center and returned home. It was not meant to be.

Later that evening I got a call from Bill. He wanted to know where I was, why I didn't pick up my ticket at the box office and why I couldn't find them when they had waited for me at the main entrance. What could I say? They wanted me to return the following day and I told them it wasn't a good idea but Bill said that he had spoken to some of the people who were responsible for putting on the convention and they wanted to meet me. This time I assured him that I would meet them at the front entrance. Bill wasn't exaggerating; his wife was at least six-six. The plate in my neck hurt as I tried to look up at her. But they were both pleased to see me and they ushered me into the convention center. It was Sunday and it was a madhouse. Why weren't all these people in church? We walked from stall to stall where vendors were selling everything from photos of actors to plates to plastic models of the starship Enterprise. Thankfully, Barb ran interference for us or we would never have gotten through the mob. Finally, we came to a room where the actors did "signings." I had never heard of this. Actors who were invited to the convention brought their photos and sold them with their autographs. It was a large room and it was jam-packed with fans waiting to get autographs of their favorite Star Trek actors. I immediately recognized Arlene Martel who played T'Pring in the episode in which I played Stonn. She looked right at me and I could tell that there was no recognition. There on the table in front of her was a color photo of her and me.

"Who's that good-looking guy?" I asked playfully.

No response. She was sitting next to another woman, Carol Martin, whom I assumed was her agent. I later found out that she had a service on the Internet that sold photos of the stars. Bill had said that she wanted to meet me but standing in front of her, she made no indication that she had anything to say to me.

"Just in case you're wondering, that good-looking guy is me." I thought that would shake them up but neither of them flinched. "Nice talking to you," I said and moved along.

I turned the corner and suddenly stopped in my tracks. There was Roy Jensen, stuntman/actor with whom I had worked on *The Great Escape* in Germany. In fact, when I got married to Monika, my mother-in-law gave us a classic Mercedes convertible, but it was too costly to run in Munich because petrol was so costly. I put out the word that I was looking to sell the car and Roy ended up buying it. While in Munich, Roy had met a girl from Yugoslavia, Marina, who was a friend of my wife. Standing there looking down at him, I thought that he had not really changed all that much over the years. I spoke his name and he looked up at me with a quizzical look on his face. "Do I know you?" he asked.

I was really disappointed. I had lost track of almost everyone I had ever worked with in the business and it never occurred to me that I had grown so old that no one would recognize me. This was not turning out to be a pleasurable experience. "We worked on *The Great Escape* together in Germany. You bought my car."

"Oh, yeah. It was a piece of crap. It drove like a truck."

Boy, were we bonding! Thirty-seven years since we had last seen each other and all he could say was that my wedding present was a piece of crap. How the hell would he know how it drove? He got drunk one night and drove it off the edge of Mulholland Drive after he brought it back from Europe. We finished bonding for about eight seconds because I was standing in front of his table blocking the way for people who might possibly want to buy pictures from him. I moved along.

Almost at the end of the row of tables I saw another familiar face but by now I was gun-shy so I just walked up and stood in front of the table. Michael Forest and I knew each other in Europe and we had been in touch with each other off and on when I came back to the States. He was always a pleasant guy but I was afraid to say anything because my last two encounters with actors from the past were disasters. He looked up and squinted. "Larry? My god, how the hell are you?" He held out his hand. He looked great. He hadn't aged at all over the years but he had always been physically in good shape, worked out all the time and he took good care of himself. We talked for a few minutes about conventions. "Hey, I make more money doing conventions than I ever did as an actor."

I was curious so I came right to the point. "Okay, so what can you make signing pictures?" It was crass to come right out and ask but here were actors that I knew over the years and they were signing autographs for money.

"Well, on a good day I can pull down two thousand dollars but I never make less than five or six hundred."

I was astonished. I had never imagined such a thing. "Good god, how much do you get for a photo?"

"I charge twenty dollars a pop. You don't have to sell too many photos before it adds up."

Already the wheels were churning in my head. Mike had done a segment of Star Trek that had high visibility where he played Apollo, the Greek god. Sure, I rationalized, everyone remembers him from the role he played in that Star Trek episode. And the same for Roy Jensen. He also played a memorable role on Star Trek but he was really remembered for the part he played in Chinatown with Jack Nickelson where he stuck the knife in Jack's nose and cut him. Man, I could never forget that scene. Okay, so these guys played roles that had high visibility but what the hell was Arlene Martel doing here? Did people remember her from *Amok Time*? And if they did, they surely remembered me; I was the guy who ended up with her when Spock and Kirk pulled up stakes and went back to the Enterprise. I had played Stonn!

I spent a few more minutes with Mike as he clued me in on some of the logistics and as the people began to converge on his table, I thanked him and moved away. My head was swimming with all kinds of information. Was it possible that there were people out there who would pay for *my* autograph? Did anyone on planet Earth remember Stonn and Decius? And if they did, what the hell would they think if they saw me thirty years after the fact, a shriveled up prune of my former self? "G'wan, you kidding me? You played Stonn? And Decius? What happened to your hair?"

Was I ready to expose my ego to the masses? I was almost to the door when I looked over and recognized another familiar face. She was as beautiful as I remember her from years before. I checked the photos on her table just to be sure I wasn't mistaken. It was BarBara Luna. I knew her before she spelled her name like that. I was in New York doing *Shinbone Alley* with Eartha Kitt and BarBara was doing *South Pacific*. But we both lived uptown on the west side and coincidentally, our shows let out at about the same time and we took the same train home. Her mother was with her when we met and we made small talk about how our shows were going. I think I must have been about twenty-five and BarBara was about fifteen or sixteen and as beautiful and exotic looking as a fine Oriental picture. By the time we reached Ninety-sixth Street, I had promised her mother that I would pick BarBara up from the theater each evening and bring her home. So I became her baby-sitter. Unfortunately, Shinbone Alley closed after ten weeks and it was many years until I saw BarBara again.

"Where is BarBara Luna?" I asked.

"Right here, Larry," she responded without missing a beat. (I hate being called Larry.)

I will admit that she was one of the most beautiful women in Hollywood but the thing that stood out most in my mind was the fact that she had a sense of humor that was like a fine honed blade. I used to love to banter with her; nothing was sacred. I learned that she had married, divorced, remarried, divorced. Who was I to cast stones? I wanted to stand there and talk to her but she was telling me with her eyes that it was time to open the store and if I wasn't buying, would I please move along. She gave me her e-mail address and I drifted off into the crowd feeling almost young again.

This time it was easy to spot Barb Reyna as she towered above the crowd. She and Bill ushered me along to a prearranged destination.

"There's someone wants to see you," said Bill. "He spoke to you on the phone some years ago. Richard Arnold. You remember him?"

The name did sound familiar. It was all coming back to me. He had called regarding the rights to some photos or the use of some film of a character I had played. It had been years ago but the reason I remembered him was because it was after my falling out with Gene Roddenberry and everything the studio asked me to do…releases or whatever…I refused.

I had been living in Texas when Richard had called me just after an incident when my agent had gotten a call from Paramount casting asking about my availability. Could I do one day on a Star Trek film they were shooting in Hollywood? They would pay me two hundred and fifty dollars for the day but I would have to pay for my own transportation to Hollywood! I had been accustomed to being insulted over the years but nothing like this. This Texas agent who had signed me on the strength of my Hollywood credits looked at me as if I had been lying to him about my background. I finally got a copy of one of the Star Trek shows I had done and showed it to him so he wouldn't think I was blowing smoke up his ass.

So after this incident, here comes Richard Arnold, calling from Hollywood to ask if I would sign a release for some *Star Trek* event and I turned him down cold. Now I was standing across from him at the vendor's table and he was smiling and holding out his hand. Before he could say a word I apologized for my rudeness of years before. He smiled and assured me he had run into worse experiences while working at Paramount.

We had a chance to chat and he assured me that he thought I could make some money doing the convention circuit. I could hear Mike Forest saying that he could make two thousand dollars on a weekend signing photographs but I still wasn't convinced. After all, where would I get pictures of myself as Stonn? As Decius?

"I've got pictures of you as both characters," Richard assured me.

This was really getting bizarre. A few days later I had a meeting with Richard at his apartment/office around the corner from where my dad lived. When I arrived he had already gone through his photo archives and pulled out six shots of me from the two *Star Treks* I had done. They were half frames taken from the actual film but I could use them to have negatives made and from the negatives I could get photo enlargements. He gave me the name of a Trek fan, Richard Barnett, who worked in a lab in Burbank. I called him and made an appointment to meet for lunch. He went over the negatives and said he would be able to make prints for me within a few days. The following week I went by the lab and picked up my shots. They came out great! I took them back to Richard Arnold and he picked out two that he thought I should use for signing. At this point I still did not have a commitment from any of the conventions that they would give me signing space.

I went on a campaign sending out packets of photos with a cover letter telling convention promoters that I was currently available to appear in their signing rooms. The response was <u>under whelming</u>. I got a few responses saying that they were booked for their upcoming shows but that they would consider me for something next year or some such rhetoric. I could tell that this was not going to be an easy gig. Richard Arnold had suggested that I get in touch with Stewart Moss, an actor of long standing who had done a number of these conventions. Stewart returned my call and we rapped for a good hour while he gave me a crash course in conventions. He had been doing them for about four years and felt that he had reached the saturation point and it was time for him to phase out. But he gave me much valuable information that helped to launch me onto the convention scene.

Richard Arnold called to say that he had given my name to a woman in Baltimore who was preparing a convention in July of the following year.

Her name was Kett Kettering. Richard gave me a quick rundown on the Shore Leave 22 convention. He said that it drew about two thousand fans, which immediately gave me the impression that it would not be worth my while to travel clear across country. Since I was not an "established name," convention promoters weren't going to shell out money to cover my expenses so getting to the convention would be my responsibility. I had an old airline ticket that I bought a couple of years before and for a nominal fee I could update it and use it to fly anywhere in the U.S. So getting to where I was going was not a financial obstacle. Kett called me within a couple of days to tell me how much she would like to have me as a guest at Shore Leave. When I asked if she could help with some of the expenses she explained that they had already used up most of their budget on other guests but that she could pick up my hotel for one night. Okay, I could live with that. I was trying to budget this thing out so that I wouldn't get burned too badly if I showed up and had to eat all those photos I had brought with me. I went to the airline office and explained that I wanted to fly out of Burbank, not LAX. I lived ten minutes from Burbank Airport, which would make it easy to get one of my neighbors to take me to and pick me up from the airport. But I couldn't get a flight for the Friday of the convention and had to take a Thursday flight that meant another hundred dollars out of my pocket for hotel.

Here was my budget:

Airline ticket round trip	$100
Hotel	$200
Photos	$200
Meals, misc.	$200
TOTAL	$700

Was I getting in way over my head? What the hell; I had pissed away over twenty thousand dollars in the stock market in the past two years and had nothing to show for it so perhaps I owed it to myself to consider this as a vacation and if it didn't materialize...well, so be it.

Shore Leave was a total delight. On the first day I had covered all my expenses and by the time I left Baltimore I had made enough money to inspire me to do other conventions. That year I traveled to Orlando, Raleigh, Long Island, Toronto, Dallas, Denver, Seattle, and Vancouver. I had no idea there were people out there who remembered me from Star Trek. And I also had photos made from when I did The Great Escape.

As it turned out, these photos were in as much demand as were the Star Trek pictures. "You were in The Great Escape? That was my favorite war movie of all times." I heard the same phrase over and over. Some people who bought photos from me stood by my table and were able to rattle off a list of shows I had appeared in during my entire career. I was extremely flattered. I decided that if I did only one convention a month, it would bring in enough money to cover all my monthly expenses and if I continued to sub, I could live quite comfortably. It was a viable plan... until September 11, 2001.

As the world changed and our country was reeling from the disasters wrought by the terrorist attacks, I pulled back from the convention business. Almost overnight, airline travel became a nightmare. Security was beefed up at checkpoints and the thought of arriving at the airport two hours before flight time was incomprehensible to me. A trip to Dallas or Chicago turned into an all day affair where before, I could leave the house at eight in the morning and be at my destination by noon. Physically, I could not endure the long lines and the waiting. There were repercussions from my operation of two years before. Although the prognosis of paralysis had been averted, I was left with a slow progression of neuropathy in my legs. It's difficult to explain exactly what it is because it's not quite paralysis but it's a constant tingling sensation and numbness in the lower legs and feet. And if I stood for a prolonged period of time, I suffered excruciating pain in my lower extremities. My convention activities were now limited to local events but after a few appearances, fans had already acquired photos and autographs and my appearances were no longer financially viable.

On one of my last appearances at the Pasadena convention, I met a woman, a Star Trek fan who had brought her grandson with her from Arizona. Her name was Donna (not her real name.) We talked across the table for quite a while, and I offered her a seat alongside me at my table. That evening I invited her and her grandson for dinner. If timing is everything in life, this was a perfect example. Since my relationship with Sue Casey a few years before, I had not had a sustained relationship with a woman. I had crossed over the line between middle age and old age and felt I had nothing to offer. I had many women friends with whom I could get together for dinner or a movie but nothing on the sexual level. Either I just wasn't interested or I just wasn't turned on. But Donna piqued my interest and I found her sexually stimulating. We began a friendship during which I drove to Arizona on a number of occasions to visit and she came to Glendale to reciprocate. Then, I invited her to join me in Las Vegas for a convention at the Hilton Hotel. It was going to be like a vacation for the both of us and she accepted. She flew into Glendale and then we drove up to Vegas. I had a friend, Jeremy, with the Las Vegas Police Department, and he took time after work to show us around some of the sights off the tourist trail. By this time, Donna and I had been seeing each other for almost a year. While I was in the Convention Hall making a few dollars selling photos, Donna was in the casino playing the slots. The first night she picked me up after work and told me she had won over two thousand dollars! When we got up to the room, I took off all my clothes and she covered me with the money and we took photographs. We were having a ball.

We decided to stay in Vegas for a few days after the convention had shut down. We went downtown to see the Freemont Experience and just a few blocks away was City Hall. On the pretext that we were going to meet my friend Jeremy in the courthouse, we entered the building and stopped in front of the office that said "Licenses."

"I guess Jeremy is going to be late," I said. "Since we're here, how about we take out a license and get married," I suggested.

Donna just stared at me as if I had lost my mind. When the fog lifted, she gave me a big hug and agreed to by my wife. I had already told Jeremy that this might well be the plan and for him to meet us outside the courthouse and the three of us would find a Justice of the Peace to perform the ceremony. As we exited the courthouse with license in hand, Jeremy was waiting for us at curbside with a black and white and dressed in his uniform. As we approached, he took Donna by the arm and put her in the back seat as if she was a perpetrator and I climbed into the front seat. We drove over to a JP he knew and Donna and I tied the knot. It was one of those off-the-wall marriages that would stay with us for the rest of our lives. Yeah, sure.

When we arrived back in Los Angeles, I began to make plans. It was decided that I would pick up stakes and move to Chandler, Arizona. In the process of making plans to leave California, I spoke to my father and Irma, his lady friend, about making the move with us. Donna helped to make my case and before long, we had convinced both of them to join us.

There was a retirement home just a mile or so down the road where they would be comfortable until my plans to build a new house that would accommodate all of us, came to fruition.

Donna lived in Chandler, Arizona, and worked in a chiropractic office. Well, almost. She was part owner of the business that employed her ex-boyfriend and her son, both chiropractors. Donna owned a small house next to the office where she worked and another modular house on the adjacent lot that she used as a rental. All in all, there were three acres of land that backed up to a wash that ran behind the property. There was a corral for horses behind her house where she kept two horses. The place was loaded with animals. She had a goat by the name of Molly. She had a Jack Russell by the name of Mickey and a Golden Retriever by the name of Kelly. The cat was Bobbi because he was a Manx cat with a bobbed tail. And there were chickens running wild all over the place. They weren't for eating but every once in while, a truckload of Mexicans would stop and ask if they could buy a chicken. Donna told them if they could catch one, they were welcome to it but the chickens were too wily to end up in a stew pot. The house was post WWII with an enclosed backyard and a pool. The place needed plenty of work. The area outside the pool fence had been used as a dump for old building materials and kitchen appliances.

It took almost a month to make the move from Los Angeles to Chandler. My father and Irma decided to abandon most of their household effects; just walk away and leave them. The place where they would temporarily be staying had furnished units and aside from their personal effects, there was really nothing they needed to take with them. I rented a truck from my friend Stuart, and we loaded up some of my effects that we planned to put into storage for the time being. It was time to head east.

I no sooner got the truck unloaded than I set to work on Donna's house cleaning up the property. I rented a dumpster from the city, hired a couple of workers to help, and within a week we had cleaned up all the junk from the rear of the property. Twice a month, the city flooded the property for two hours with the water from the wash so there was plenty of grass that managed to proliferate and needed cutting. Whatever Molly didn't eat, I cut and bagged for the garbage man. Meanwhile, I began to make plans for our new house.

A Vulcan Odyssey

I got in touch with my friend Lo, in Dallas, and asked if he had the plans that he designed for his house in Highland Village. He sent me the full set of architecture plans and I set to work designing a house for Donna, my parents and me. But after a while it became apparent that there were a number of logistical problems that would be too costly to make a house feasible at that location. We were in close proximity to a flowing waterway that periodically crested its banks, which meant that the foundation of the house would have to be raised or we would be inundated with water during the winter months. I had hoped that we could continue to live in the house while we were working on the new structure but it soon became evident that that plan would not be practical.

About a half mile down the road and across the street, a developer was in the process of putting in a new community and one day Donna and I went by the sales office to see what they had to offer. There was a sizeable lot on a cul-de-sac that was still on the market at a premium price, and the lot was adjacent to the same wash that ran through Donna's property. But the developer had already made contingency plans for the cresting of the water by building up the banks of the wash to a safe height. We went through the plan book and found a two-story house that would serve our needs. We would not be able to bring Molly, the horses and all the chickens with us, but we would be able to work that out when the time came. Donna had a friend, a real estate broker, and she negotiated the deal for us with very favorable results. Construction on the new 3,500-foot house would begin in a month, after the rainy season.

I don't know if Donna and I were ever really in love but we managed to have our share of fun together. We took a week and drove down to Rocky Point in Mexico where we basked in the sun by day and exhausted ourselves with long sexual bouts at night. I learned that she had a slight drinking problem but it soon diminshed to one glass of wine with dinner. While she spent her days at the office, I went over to the construction site to observe the progress on our new home. More than once I found that the builder was taking a shortcut that was not in keeping with the specifications and I called it to his attention. It was immediately rectified. I didn't care that he thought I was a pain in the ass; I was paying for it and I wanted it done right.

* * *

The retirement home called to say that my father had been taken to the hospital. He was ninety-four years old and I knew that it was just a matter of time but I had hoped that he could hold out long enough to spend his remaining time in the comfort of our new home. He had spent his whole life supporting my insane antics and now it was my turn to give him comfort on his final journey. On December 7, 2002, he left us but not before I sat by his bedside and told him how much I loved him and how grateful I was for all he had done for me. I held his hand as he closed his eyes and passed from this life. He was cremated and according to his wishes, his ashes were scattered in the Pacific Ocean.

* * *

Irma continued to live a lonely existence in the retirement home. We visited with her regularly but it was obvious that she was slipping and there were days when she barely remembered who we were. But she was of strong stock and on weekends we would bring her over to the house to pass the time with the animals that she loved so much.

The house was finished in the spring of the following year and shortly thereafter we moved in. Molly remained tethered outside the old house and every day I went by to love on her and clean up her droppings. The chickens continued to proliferate but the horses were sent to an equestrian center where they were cared for as we contracted to pay their board. Kelly, the love of my life, the ten-year-old Golden Retriever, got cancer and within months I had to put her down. I cried until there just weren't any more tears.

Donna and I spent our weekends shopping for new furniture to fill the huge house. There were four bedrooms and my spacious study that needed filling, along with the living room, the sitting room and the dining room.

Robby had left me some money that we used with abandon and Donna chipped in when I needed help. Whenever I needed to make a trip to the bank for cash, she would go to her purse and pull out a roll of bills that she offered. After a while I asked her where she was getting all this extra money and she soon confessed to me that she was dipping into the petty cash box in the office. If someone paid in cash for services, she would merely not enter it into the daily accounting. And whenever she needed cash money, she would just take it out of the cash drawer. I knew that what she was doing was not legal. She was not only stealing from her ex-boyfriend, but her son as well. But I said nothing and in effect, I was an accessory to a crime.

We weren't in the house for six month when the wheels began to come off the wagon. It wasn't anything overt; just long lapses between talks or little things that got on the other person's nerves. We ceased to communicate and after a while, I moved out of our bedroom and into one of the guest rooms. Donna would sometimes leave the house early in the morning and not return until late at night. I just assumed that she was putting in long hours at the office but after a while, she revealed to me that she was seeing a psychologist and she decided that we needed to get counseling. I agreed but her psychologist said he would not see me and recommended I see an associate. I didn't understand how he could help us if he didn't see us together but he set the rules and off I went to see another psychologist.

After my first session, the woman psychologist said that she could not help me if Donna and I did not take family counseling together. When I passed on the word to Donna, she became irritated saying that her psychologist knew what he was doing and that I should seek another doctor. I could see that we were not connecting. I refused to shell out perfectly good money when the original idea was to reunited Donna and myself. How could we do that if we were both in separate camps?

One day when she came home late, I was in a pissy mood and confronted her. She refused to talk to me, locked herself in her bedroom and would not come out. In frustration, I went to the computer and typed a very threatening letter to her. In it I said that I had a dream in which she locked me out of the bedroom, so I got my gun and when she came out, I killed her. It was one of those stupid things one does in the heat of passion. In all the time we had been together, I had never raised a hand to her or threatened her. I finally suggested that if she didn't want to continue, we should seek legal assistance and dissolve the marriage. A few days later, I was served with papers from her attorney. I was also served with notice from the police department; a restraining order to keep me away from Donna. I had threatened her, in writing, of my intentions to do her bodily harm. How stupid was I?

I got in my truck and drove up to Las Vegas to visit with Jeremy. After a few days, I found a small house in Henderson, in a community called Sun City Anthem. Then I returned to Phoenix by plane, rented a van, drove to the house in Chandler, and loaded up my possessions. In a couple of days I was on the road to Vegas. My marriage had lasted all of eleven months and it was obvious that I was just going to have to find another hobby!

* * *

When Donna and I had gotten Robby and Irma all settled in, we decided to set up the money accounts that would make it easy to pay all the various bills that were accumulating in their interests. I closed out their accounts in California and reopened them in Chandler. I set up a joint account in Robby's and my name so I could write checks to cover his expenses. I thought it would be expeditious to set up a joint account for Irma with Donna. One doesn't think that sometime in the future, such an act of benevolence might come back to bite one in the ass. Irma had over three hundred and fifteen thousand dollars in her account and Donna held the checkbook. Some years before, when Irma made her will, my father was her sole beneficiary. In the event of his death, I would be next in line. When I knew I would be leaving Chandler, I went to the retirement home and had lunch with Irma. I told her I would be leaving and asked her if she would like to go with me. By this time she was almost incoherent but she understood enough to say that she preferred to stay in Chandler, that she would feel more comfortable with Donna to look after her. What could I say? I couldn't bind her hand and foot and drag her off to Las Vegas. And I no sooner pulled out of the driveway than Donna went to the attorney and had Irma's will changed, making her sole beneficiary. Within a month, Donna put the house on the market and made a handsome profit of seventy-five thousand dollars. Three months later, Irma died. And two months after that, Donna remarried.

Many of my friends asked me over the years why I didn't fight Donna for the money from Irma's estate and why I didn't retain ownership of the house. It's difficult for me to come up with some rational reasoning that doesn't make me look like a total ass but this is the best I can do. When Robby was still alive, he grew to worship Donna. On numerous occasions he told me how lucky I was to have found her. She waited on him hand

and foot, helped Irma and him pack their belongings for the move to Arizona, and traveled with them on the plane. She attended to all their needs, their registration into the senior facility, their insurance papers, and their visits to the doctors. I was busy overseeing the construction of the new house and she was their guardian angel throughout this period of time. I couldn't forget how she attended to their every need. But was it worth almost four hundred thousand dollars? Probably not but I was caught between a rock and a hard place. I was now living in Nevada. In order to fight her for the money, I would have to hire an attorney in Henderson and another one in Chandler. Then, I would have to travel back to Arizona to testify in court. I sat down and tried to figure out a ballpark figure of what it would cost. My mother and her brother fought over my grandfather's sizeable estate and by the time it was settled, the attorneys had eaten up most of the assets. I didn't want to follow in their footsteps. I tried to imagine what a prolonged legal action would do to me physically and emotionally. I could very well stand up in court and testify that I knew Donna was stealing money from her partner and son, and that she coerced Irma into changing her will when the poor woman was unable to make a mental decision, that even her own children had been estranged from her for most of their adult lives. I could get into a character assassination diatribe that would probably do more damage to me than to Donna. In the final analysis, and for the sake of my own sanity, I decided to walk away. I figured that I was never meant to have money, and at my age it wasn't going to make all that much difference in my life. And in the final analysis, I concluded that Donna had orchestrated this whole thing right from the very beginning. This may sound like an oversimplification but I did not want to get into an action that was predicated on revenge against Donna. That had been my m.o. in the past and it was turning out to be an expensive lesson in my life. Besides, I was not destitute. There was my social security and two retirement plans from the actor's unions and a few dollars that I had stashed away in stocks for a rainy day. It was now pouring like hell!

* * *

In three years, I had moved into three different houses in Anthem. It is a community of some eight thousand residents, complete with a large

Community Center that includes two gyms, two pools, a restaurant, a theatre, a pool hall, a computer lab and numerous other activity rooms.

I registered with the Clark County school district to substitute teach but I guess I was burned out with teaching because the traffic to and from school was getting on my nerves. I took a job at Nevada State College in an experimental program teaching college English to high school students in which they would get college credit and the promise of a scholarship if they stayed with the program for two years. It was intended to get students interested in teaching. But the school to which I had been assigned was way on the ass end of town and it took me an hour each way. I was promised a school closer to where I lived if I stayed with the program for a semester but promises are cheap, they never produced and I dropped out of the program after one semester. I took a short-term job teaching at UNLV in the Drama Department, filling in for one of the teachers going in for back surgery. I thought it might lead to a permanent position but after he returned, I never heard from UNLV again.

With nothing on my agenda I decided to look into real estate school. A friend of long standing, Elsa, an English lady, was living in Vegas and she was a retired realtor and suggested that I might want to try it. I found a school quite close to where I lived and began attending classes every day. Within a couple of months I was ready to take my exam. I didn't pass. I was very frustrated and determined that I was not going to do like I did with law school; I was going to take it again. I buckled down to studying every day and a few weeks later I took the exam again. This time I passed. Elsa introduced me to a friend of hers, Sandi Curtis, another English lady who took me under her wing and brought me into her office, General Realty. I was raring to go and with Sandi's guidance, I was off and running. Within a month I realized that I was not cut out for real estate. People lied to me right to my face. They would have me spend an inordinate amount of time showing them properties and when it came time to close, I would find out that they had decided to use another realtor. I was spending time sitting on houses on weekends with little or no results and I was getting very negative about the whole business. The only thing good to come out of my real estates experience was that I tied a lasting bond between Sandi Curtis and her husband, Howard, an airline pilot. We still hang out together.

My next fantasy was into the world of casino gambling. I enrolled in dealer's school and for the first few weeks of learning to deal blackjack, I had visions of me making a ton of money as a dealer. I had to learn to deal with my right hand, which was anathema to me because, for some reason, I dealt left handed all my life. But by the end of the second month, I was disenchanted with the thought of spending my life in a smoke-filled environment with a bunch of nasty gambling addicts. I dropped out of dealer's school.

I heard that Anthem was looking for monitors to work the desk at the health center. I applied and when the supervisor asked if I got along well with people, I told her I hated people.

"Perfect," she said and hired me on the spot.

The job was great. It paid less than minimum wage but it was only two minutes from where I lived and I only worked twenty hours a week. Such a deal. I worked nights and I was responsible for checking residents into the club and closing out the register at the end of the evening. It was an easy job and the residents at Anthem were friendly and very cooperative when I asked them to present their membership cards. Sometimes, when the desk got busy, the members would line up and gripe that I was too slow but I was at the mercy of the computer into which I had to scan each and every membership card. I would make light of my ineptness and by and large, everyone was patient and considerate.

One evening, a man and woman entered the club dressed in street clothes. The rules said that no one in street clothes was allowed inside the workout area.

The man presented his membership card and I scanned him in. When I asked for the woman's card, the man said that she was his wife and that she did not have to present a membership card. I apologized and said that I could not let her inside the club but that if she would sign in as a guest, I could permit her entry. The man became belligerent and said that she did not have to sign in and with that, they bypassed the desk and walked into the gym. I came out from behind the desk and intercepted them at the entrance.

"I'm going to have to ask you to leave," I said in my most charming tone.

He ignored me and tried to walk around but I stood my ground.

"Get out of my way," he said, threateningly.

"I can't let you into the club. First off, you're not dressed accordingly, and second, your wife has not registered."

"Screw you," he said, and again made a move to go around me.

One of the members, a woman, came over and got between us. I guess she was trying to mediate but she was barely five feet tall and not making much of an impression. "Call security," she said.

I backed off, returned to the desk and called the number posted for security. I got a recorded message: "This is not a working number." Oh, shit, I thought. Now what?

By this time the man and his "wife" were making the grand tour of the facility, she in high heels. I went back and got in his face. "You've got to leave the club," I said with authority.

"Fuck you," he retorted. "You want me out of here, you make me leave."

Now, I wasn't going to get into a pissing contest with this asshole. The woman who had tried to intercede got between us again and was trying to explain to the man that he was in violation of the club rules, but he ignored her and continued to ignore my demands. By now I was getting a bit hot under the collar and I had an out-of-body experience as I threw a right cross, clearing the head of the woman and catching the guy on the cheek. He backed away in shock and began yelling how he was going to call the police. As the woman stepped aside, the man's testicles attacked my right foot and he doubled over in pain. I was about to nail him again when the little woman grabbed my arm, invoking me to keep my cool. Then, the man turned and herded his woman out the door as he continued raging at me. Within ten minutes two police officers entered the club. The Sergeant came up to the desk. He was big, really big. Behind him and being detained at the door by the other officer, was the guy I had hit. "That's him! That's the guy," he was yelling. By now, everyone in the club had stopped working out and set their attention on the commotion at the desk.

"This man says you attacked him," said the officer. "He said you hit him."

"He was trespassing on private property and when I asked him to leave, he became abusive."

"He says he's a member. Is that right?"

"Yes, sir. But he's not dressed in proper attire, he had a guest with him whom he refused to register, and he entered the gym area against my warning. When I asked him to leave, he threatened me."

"Wait here," said the Sergeant. He turned and he and the other policemen led the man out the door. I waited. About five minutes passed when the Sergeant returned.

"He's filing charges against you for assault. I'm going to have to take you in to the station."

"May I close out my register and call someone to cover for me?"

"No problem."

I began to close out the register. I had to reconcile my cash and credit card receipts, a process that took about fifteen minutes. Finally, the Sergeant returned to the desk.

"He says he'll drop the charges if you'll apologize to him."

"Sergeant, it will be one cold day in hell when I apologize to that asshole."

Again, the Sergeant hauled his bulk back out the door and within minutes he returned to the desk. "He's dropping all charges." He had a shit-eating grin on his face and I knew he must have said something to this guy to make him change his mind. I thanked the officer and in minutes, everything had returned to normal.

The following day I got a call to report to the main office of Anthem. Without a trial or asking for my side of the story, I was fired. I had to laugh. I was being fired from a job that paid less than minimum wage. How low could I get? Word spread about how I started a fight with one of the residents of Anthem, how I beat him up unmercifully, and that only the intervention of the police prevented me from killing him. Rumors proliferated as the membership chose up sides. I was not overwhelmingly supported by the membership. If this guy had brought charges, he was in his right to sue since, as an employee, I was acting as an agent of Anthem. And if he was able to prove his case, the membership could be liable for any monetary award due. I was considered a loose cannon and had to go. On the other hand, there was a small group that came to my defense. I can only imagine that this jerk backed down because the woman with him was not his wife and there is a good chance that his actual wife would not be too happy to learn of his misadventure.

The following day, after I had been drummed out of the corps, I got a call from Bobbye Sansing. She had been a student of mine when I did a ten-week Acting Class for some of the seniors at Anthem. Her husband, Robert, sat on the Board of Directors so I assumed that my troubles were not yet over. Bobbye asked if I would come over to their house; her husband would like to talk to me.

The Sansings greeted me most cordially and I immediately relaxed knowing that this was not a continuation of my recent altercation. Robert and Bobbye had a small business that they ran out of their home. It was called Worldwide Translations. They contracted with major medical companies that were releasing new product and needed translations of their manuals that accompanied their hardware. The Sansings used translators that worked in some dozen languages to do the translations, usually from English to any number of other languages. These translators were certified in their language of expertise but upon completion of a document, their work had to be proofed for errors and/or omissions. Bobbye had been doing the proofing work over the years but she was now contemplating returning to school and hoped to have more time for other personal pursuits. The bottom line: would I be interested in working for Worldwide Translations?

They explained what my duties would consist of, how much they were willing to pay, and that once I proved that I could handle the job, I could work out of my own house. I explained that I would be interested in their proposition if they would give me a few weeks because I had just learned that my lease had expired and that it would not be renewed because the owners were looking to sell.

"We have a house you might be interested in renting," said Robert.

That day Bobbye and I drove over to the house in question. It was larger than the last two places in which I had lived but the rent was also higher. I explained that I couldn't afford what they were asking, so Robert made an offer that I couldn't refuse, and we made a lease.

It was time to pack up and move again. But I had a problem with E.T. For some reason, he had decided to stop using the litter box and he was leaving dropping wherever he decided to squat. That included my bed and my computer keyboard. For a while I tried leaving him in the garage with his own litter box but he ignored it and pooped on the floor or on stacked boxes of personal effects. Then, there came a time when it was almost impossible to touch him. He'd cower from me as if I meant him harm and on a number of occasions, when I tried to pick him up he scratched and bit me. I took him to the vet but they could not find anything wrong with him. He had been a part of my life since he was born under my bed sixteen years before and now, with the move to the new house, I had to make a decision. With a heavy heart I returned to the vet and had him put to sleep. I was angry. I loved that cat from the day I decided to keep him and I was angry that for whatever reason, he turned on me. Sometimes there is no accounting for animal behavior; they live in their own little world and answer to no one. I keep Missy who is in her eighteenth year and is as deaf as a stone. Every day I expect her to tell me that it is time to say goodbye so I give her an inordinate amount of love and touching until that day arrives.

I moved into the Sansing rental, only a short distance from their home where I would be working. Almost a year after I began working for them, they informed me that Worldwide was on the market. During my tenure they had increased my pay by double and on occasion, there was enough money from Worldwide to offset my rent. If I was interested, they would suggest to any prospective buyer that I would be available to continue on with the company.

Bobbye and I became good friends. Her husband was often occupied with his business interests and when Bobbye needed an escort to the theatre or a movie, she called to see if I was available. I kidded Robert that I was his wife's babysitter.

What I find most interesting is that when I returned to the United States from my last foray in Europe, my ability to speak a number of languages served me as an actor in that I could play roles that required the ability to speak in foreign tongues. That talent has since waned and although I would never starve to death in most European countries, the adage, "Use it or lose it," is apropos. I now stumble over words and phrases I once spoke "trippingly on the tongue" but it was the language background that brought me to Worldwide Translations. Again, it appears that if we hang around long enough, nothing in life goes to waste.

CHAPTER FIFTEEN
WHAT GOES AROUND...

Three months ago I got an e-mail from a person by the name of Sky. I hadn't a clue how he got my number or from where I knew him. He informed me that he had introduced himself to me at last year's Star Trek Convention in Las Vegas. He was now in production on a new Star Trek film, *Of Gods and Men*. Would I be interested in reprising the roll of Stonn in the new movie? I responded asking for more information. There was a timely response in which he said that I would only be shooting for one day, he gave me a price, said that the company would cover all my expenses, and if I was interested, he would send me a script via e-mail. Shortly thereafter, I got the script. He was right; it was only a small role but it had an interesting twist and I decided to do it. Then, I realized that Sky was actually Doug Conway. I remembered that he contacted me when he put on the Jimmy Doohan tribute, "Beam Me Up Scotty...One Last Time." I had a conflict at the time and couldn't make it.

A week or so later I attended the Las Vegas Star Trek Convention at the Hilton Hotel. I asked Richard Arnold, the guy who had gotten me into the convention business some years before, if he knew anything about this new movie. He warned me that the film had not been sanctioned by Paramount and that I should be careful or I could end up not getting paid. I heeded his words but I figured that the worst that could happen is I would get stiffed for the work. Sky had said that he was sending me a ticket and that my room would be paid for at the hotel. Then, I didn't hear from Sky for another two months. I did hear from his production assistant who assured me that they would be shooting my scene the last weekend of September and that she would get in touch with me just as soon as they had a definite date. I settled down with the script.

I previously mentioned that I had been having problems learning lines. In the new script, I only had five lines to learn. What could be easier? "They are easily manageable if obtained in their infancy." That was one of the lines; easy. But it took me almost a month to commit it to memory. During that month I beat up on myself until I was almost inclined to call Sky and make up some excuse to back out of the film. I must have repeated that one line five thousand times until I was sure I could do it in my sleep. One day I could do it and on other days it just went out of my head and I broke out in a cold sweat. I decided that if I got stuck, I could always request that the production make me cue cards. What could they say? They would have already had an investment in me and I doubted they would deny my request.

On August 23rd, I was going through some pictures of my mother. It would have been her birthday. A few months before, I got a call from my daughter, Jessica. I heard from a family friend that she was looking to call me so it was no surprise. She was in the process of applying to adopt a baby from China and needed some family information. We exchanged amenities, I supplied the required information and that was the end of our conversation. We had not spoken in almost twenty years. Now, on my mother's birthday I got this sudden surge of guilt and emotion and decided to call her…just to see how the adoption process was going. Damn, I was just looking to open up a door for a dialogue with her but we were both so reserved that by the time we hung up, there hadn't really been any emotional bonding. Now, I was contemplating doing a film in L.A., about thirty miles from Venice where she lived. I e-mailed her saying that I was planning on driving into the city for this shoot and if she was going to have some time, I could come in a few days early and maybe we could spend some time together. She replied that she was leaving the country to visit her grandmother in Vienna the weekend of the shoot, but if I planned to come in early, I could stay at her home in Venice. That was really unexpected but I graciously accepted her invitation. I finally got a call from the production company saying we would be shooting the last Saturday of the month. At almost the same time I learned that the I-15 Freeway from Vegas into L.A. was being torn up in Simi Valley and that I would have to take an alternate route that would add more than an hour to my drive. I was experiencing some recurring pain in my legs and I was reconsidering my plans to drive. The production company had already sent me a ticket so instead of coming in a week early, I was to arrive the Friday before the Saturday shoot. I called Jessica and explained

A Vulcan Odyssey

the situation. She was relieved because she was in the process of getting ready for her trip and my arrival was not at a propitious time. We said that we would keep in touch, I wished her a great journey and hoped to speak with her upon her return.

A few days before I was to leave for L.A. I dropped Jessica another e-mail saying that if she had any change of plans, perhaps we could get together the coming Friday since she was not leaving until Sunday. She replied that she had cancelled her plans to visit her grandmother in Austria but would be going to New York the following week for a convention and planned to see her mother. She couldn't see me Friday night because she had a previous commitment but she would drive into town and pick me up at my hotel early Sunday morning. We could have breakfast together and she would drive me to the airport. I hated to inconvenience her but by this time I had a gnawing desire to see her. I don't know why. Perhaps curiousity, perhaps lonliness, perhaps a desire to be a part of her life. We made a date.

The flight from Vegas to Burbank was everything I thought it would be. I stood on long lines for an interminable period of time until I thought my legs would fail me. Barb Reyna picked me up at the airport and drove me to the hotel. That evening I got together with Barb and Bill, Roger and Charlotte Smith from Clark Magnet, and Cecile and Robert Wynn. We met at The Smoke House across the street from Warner Brothers. Years before I had spent many an entertaining evening at the bar after a long day on the set at WB. Barb had picked the restaurant and I found the food terribly overrated and overpriced but it was good to get together with old friends. We called it an early evening and the Reynas drove me back to my hotel. We would keep in touch.

At six thirty the following morning the van picked me up in front of the hotel. Seated in the van was Jack Treveno, one of the writers. He introduced himself.

"I'm so glad you decided to do the role. We wrote it for you, you know. My worst fear was that you wouldn't do it."

That was nice. I was very flattered that he remembered me from the original Star Trek. It was good to have someone to talk to all the way to the location. I was still worried about the lines. "They are easily manageable if obtained in their infancy." I think I shall take that line to the grave with me.

Lawrence Montaigne

STONN in *Of Gods and Men*, with Nichelle Nichols as Uhura, forty years after I created the original role 2006

A Vulcan Odyssey

Once on location, I stowed my camera and jacket in my dressing room and reported to makeup. The makeup man, Tim, looked me over. I had decided to shave off my beard a few days before my departure from Vegas. It was part of the agreement with Sky Conway when we negotiated the contract. Tim took out a black wig that looked like something Cher had been caught dead in. He fitted it on my head and began snipping away. He had to cut it back so he could apply the Vulcan ears. As I watched him at work I thought there was no way in hell I was going to appear in front of the camera looking like a drag queen in a West Hollywood saloon. When the wig was finally fitted, Tim Russ, the director, came into the makeup room and introduced himself to me.

"What do you think, Lawrence?" he asked.

"You're kidding aren't you?"

"What?"

"Hey, you're the director. You tell me. You like this wig?"

He got up and looked at me from another angle. "You're right." He turned to makeup-man-Tim. "What else have you got?"

I was hoping he would forget about the wig, just shave my head and let it go at that. No such luck. They came up with this gray job and for the next hour I had to go through the snipping all over again.

By eleven in the morning I was ready for my first shot. "They are easily manageable if obtained in their infancy. They are easily manageable if obtained..." By Jove, I had it! We reported to the set for rehearsal. There was Tim Russ directing, who was also reprising his role from another Star Trek series, Voyager, Nichelle Nichols who played Uhura in the Original Star Trek, and me along with a number of background people. Tim began the rehearsal and I waited for my cue. It never came. Something was not right.

"Whoa, whoa," I said. "Did I miss something? I didn't hear my cue."

"Right after I say..." but before he could continue I cut him off.

"You're not even in this scene," I corrected him.

"Didn't you get the new pages?" he asked. He didn't need an answer. He could tell from the look on my face that I hadn't a clue what he was talking about. He turned to his assistant. "Didn't you send Lawrence the new pages?"

"I sent them yesterday," said the assistant.

"I left Vegas yesterday and there weren't any new pages on my e-mail."

"Get him the new pages," said Tim as if this was perfectly normal.

A few moments later the assistant handed me a packet of pages. The top page was the scene on which we were working. There were six new lines for Stonn! I panicked. I walked over to Tim. "You think I could have a word with you for a moment?" and taking him by the arm I walked him out of earshot of the cast and crew. "I've been working on that one lousy line for three months and now I find it's been cut from the script. Now I've got half a dozen new lines that I've never seen before. When do you expect me to learn them?"

"Take a few minutes," he said as if that was all I needed.

I leaned in real close. "Tim, if you gave me a month I couldn't learn those six lines. I don't even know who I am half the time." I had him locked in with my look. "I'm going to need cue cards, Tim." I guess he could hear the desperation in my voice.

"No problem," he said as he turned to his assistant. "Get Lawrence some cue cards and fast. We've got to get this shot in the can…"

The disaster I had anticipated never happened. We rehearsed, I read my lines, we shot and we printed. "I like his voice," said Tim as he prepared for the next setup.

I had been on my feet for nearly fifteen hours that day. When we finally wrapped after seven that evening, I could barely walk to my dressing room. There were no "goodbyes", no "job well-done"; I just disappeared into the night. I needed to get off my feet.

The following morning at eight on the dot, Jessica pulled into the parking lot of the hotel. She got out of her car and came over to me. I held out my arms and she came to me as if it was the most natural thing in the world. We stood there for the longest time before we stepped back from each other. She looked great. I could tell that she was in great shape and there were no visible piercing or tattoos, although I knew she had them. She had sent me pictures some years back when she was competing and there, right on her ass, was a butterfly! I have always been anti-tattoo so seeing my own daughter with a tattoo on her butt raised my hackles. But standing there in the parking lot, I couldn't take my eyes off her. Finally, she turned and opened the rear of her car so I could put my bag inside. We drove over to an eatery a short distance from the hotel and took a booth. I had brought a large envelope full of family pictures that I promised I would bring for her. After all, she didn't know any of my family other than my father and on one short occasion, she had briefly met my mother. Over breakfast I introduced her to her cousins and aunts and uncles, most of whom were already deceased. And then, it was time to head for the airport. It was only a few minutes from the restaurant and I kept trying to figure out a good reason to change my plans and not return to Vegas. She dropped me curbside, we hugged and she promised that she would consider coming to Vegas for a visit in a few weeks after she got back from a trip to New York. I left Los Angeles with a light heart and the prospect that I would soon be seeing her again. Who knows? With some effort I could very well learn how to be a father. Maybe even a grandfather...once I got past the tattoos.

* * *

By the time Worldwide Translations sold, I was consumed with the prospect of finishing this book with the thought of returning to the convention world. I had appeared early in my career in Star Trek and had ended my career forty years later in Star Trek. I had run a full circle.

When I think back on it, I have had more damn fun in my life than a barrel of monkeys. I have traveled, I have taken time out to learn new things, I have made lasting friendships, I had loved and been loved, and it ain't over yet. If parts of this book are boring, that's just the way life is. One day we're bored to death and the next, we're smuggling gold into the Far East or running for our lives in some remote outpost in the Negev Desert. I wonder where I'll be tomorrow...

...and finally...

THE POWER OF STAR TREK

We arrived home at 4 PM yesterday afternoon after a tiresome but exciting trip to Sacramento. From the time we left home till the time we returned, Tisha, my lady friend, was on my case about how fast I was driving. I tried to keep my speed down to under a hundred but for some reason, the car just wanted to get up and go. Tisha kept reminding me that it was her car and that it was a virgin, having never gotten a ticket. I assured her that I could smell a patrol car five miles away but that did not diminish her anxiety and her mood tied in with the speedometer; when I hit ninety, she went into a snit.

But we managed to arrive at our destination without incident and aside from the fact that the convention that I attended was a minor disaster, we had a smashing time. On the way to Sacramento we took the southern route to Baker and then headed north through Bakersfield on into Sacramento. But we heard that the trip through Reno and then down to Vegas was the more scenic route so that is what we planned to do. On the return home, we departed Sacramento at six on Monday morning and headed east towards Reno. It was a very pretty drive and I managed to maintain a moderate speed of ninety. Then, we headed south and I began to up the ante to ninety-five and Tisha went into another snit. But traveling a two-lane highway minimized my cruising speed when I got behind an RV or a vehicle traveling the speed limit with a solid "no passing" line down the middle of the highway. Once we were out in the open, so was I.

Then we arrived at a small, non-descript village somewhere in central Nevada where I slowed down to what I thought was the speed limit. As I pulled into the town and approached the one cross-street, a black Mariah pulled out onto the highway in front of me. What the hell; he couldn't clock me from the front and I was going no faster than he was. And when he pulled over to the side of the road, I cautiously passed him, confident that I was within the legal speed limit. But I no sooner was saying goodbye to "non-descript village" than I looked into my rear view mirror only to see flashing lights beckoning me to pull over. By now, Tisha was verbally reading me the riot act as I cut the engine, rolled down the window and took out my driver's license. Through the side mirror I could see the officer get out of his vehicle and approach mine. He was very imposing-looking as he leaned into my space.

"Do you know why I pulled you over?" he asked.

"No, sir," I replied in my best innocent voice.

"Do you know how fast you were traveling, sir?"

"Well, when I looked down I realized that I was doing seventy-five in the seventy mile per hour zone so I immediately reduced my speed…"

"Sir," he interrupted, "I clocked you doing seventy-eight in a seventy mile per hour zone and then, when you got into town where the speed limit is forty, you slowed down to seventy."

"I'm sorry, officer, but I don't think that's what I did but if you say so, I don't want to argue with you."

"Well, I don't want to argue with you, either. Now let me tell you the situation, sir. This is a very small town and we have very strict laws against speeding. For every mile over the limit, the fine is ten dollars. Do you understand that?"

"Oh, yes, sir," I answered. Oh, damn, but I was in for it.

"Let me do the math for you," he offered. He began counting and finally came up with a figure. "According to my calculations, your speeding fine is three hundred dollars, plus seventy-five dollars court costs, not to mention the four points against your insurance. Do you understand me, sir?"

"Yes, sir," I answered with all the contrition I could muster. Then he reached down to his belt where he had his ticket holder and before he could manage to pull it out, I asked, "How would you like an autographed photo of me from when I was in Star Trek?"

He immediately stood upright as if I had passed gas in his direction. "You were in Star Trek?" he asked with amazement.

"Yes, sir," I replied. I turned to Tisha. "Honey, hand me my bag, will you?"

She handed me the bag and I rummaged through it coming up with a handful of trading cards. I extracted one of me in the role of Decius and handed it to the officer. He held the card in his hand as if I had passed him the Hope diamond. "Is this you?" he enquired reverently.

"Yes, sir," I said. "You have my driver's license so you can check out the name." As he was checking the name on the card against my driver's license, I extracted another card, one of Stonn. I handed it out the window."

"Hey, I know you," he said with no small amount of excitement.

"Would you like me to sign them for you?" I asked.

"Would you?"

"Sure." I took the two cards and with a shaky hand, I signed them. Then I handed them to him through the open window. He took them and stood there admiring them as I said, "That will be twenty dollars a piece."

He looked at me as if I'd just rear-ended his patrol car. "No way," he said, quite emphatically.

"Okay, I'll tell you what. How about we call it a wash," I suggested.

He stared down at me for what seemed like an eternity, then he looked down at the two trading cards in his hand. I had just bribed a member of the Nevada State Highway Patrol. I could be spending the rest of my life in this place.

Finally, a pleasant smile crossed his face. "You watch your speed, you hear?" he said as he turned and headed back to his vehicle.

I looked over to Tisha and she was doubled over with laughter and tears, all at the same time. And as the police car disappeared down the highway I couldn't wait to make up the lost time I'd been detained in that non-descript village in central Nevada…

Made in the USA